Insurance Law in Turkey

Insurance Law in Turkey

Third Edition

Meltem Deniz Güner-Özbek
Banu Bozkurt-Bozabalı
İlyas Gölcüklü
Hakan Karan
Gülfer Meri
Ural Özbek
Kemal Şenocak

This book was originally published as a monograph in the International Encyclopaedia of Laws/Insurance Law.

Founding Editor: Roger Blanpain
General Editor: Frank Hendrickx
Volume Editor: Herman Cousy

Wolters Kluwer

Published by:
Kluwer Law International B.V.
PO Box 316
2400 AH Alphen aan den Rijn
The Netherlands
E-mail: lrs-sales@wolterskluwer.com
Website: www.wolterskluwer.com/en/solutions/kluwerlawinternational

Sold and distributed by:
Wolters Kluwer Legal & Regulatory U.S.
920 Links Avenue
Landisville, PA 17538
United States of America
E-mail: customer.service@wolterskluwer.com

ISBN 978-94-035-3587-6

e-Book: ISBN 978-94-035-3597-5
web-PDF: ISBN 978-94-035-3607-1

The Author

Meltem Deniz Güner-Özbek has an LLM degree in Admiralty Law from Tulane University, USA and a Doctoral degree in Maritime Law from Hamburg University, Germany, and is a member of the Istanbul Bar Association. She is a professor of Law at Koç University Faculty of Law in Istanbul and has been teaching Maritime Law, Insurance Law, Air Law and Transport Law courses at Koç University since 2008. Previously, she was a lecturer in Maritime and Insurance Law in the Istanbul University Faculty of Law. In addition to the publication of a number of journal papers, Professor Güner-Özbek is the author of *The Carriage of Dangerous Goods by Sea* (Springer, 2008) and editor of *The United Nations Convention on Contracts for the International Carriage of Goods Wholly or Partly by Sea An Appraisal of the 'Rotterdam Rules'* (Springer, 2011). Professor Güner-Özbek would like to acknowledge Professor Dr Hakan Karan, Professor Dr Kemal Şenocak, Esq. Mr Ural Özbek, Dr Banu Bozkurt-Bozabalı, Dr Gülfer Meriç and Mr İlyas Gölcüklü for their invaluable contributions to this book and Mr Anthony Townley for editing and proofreading.

The Author

Contributing Authors

Banu Bozkurt-Bozabalı has a Bachelor of Law degree from Galatasaray University (a bilingual French/Turkish University) Faculty of Law. She obtained her LLM degree in European Union Law from the İzmir University of Economics and a Doctoral degree in Air and Maritime Law from Yeditepe University, Istanbul. She is an assistant professor of Maritime Law, Insurance Law and Air Law at the Akdeniz University Faculty of Law, Antalya.

İlyas Gölcüklü has a Bachelor of Law degree from Koç University Faculty of Law, Istanbul and two LLM degrees: one from the University of Georgia, USA and the other from Koç University. He was a research assistant at the University of Georgia during his LLM studies. Currently, he is a research assistant in International Private Law at the Istanbul Kemerburgaz University Faculty of Law while undertaking his Doctoral degree at Galatasaray University, Istanbul. He is also a member of the Istanbul Bar Association.

Hakan Karan has Bachelor of Law and LLM degrees from Ankara University and a Doctoral degree from London Metropolitan University. He is a professor of Maritime Law and Insurance Law in the Maritime Law Department of Ankara University Faculty of Law.

Gülfer Meriç has a Bachelor of Law degree from Koç University Faculty of Law. She obtained her LLM and Doctoral degrees in Private Law from Istanbul University. She is an assistant professor of Maritime and Insurance Law at Özyeğin University Faculty of Law.

Ural Özbek, *Esq.*, is a member of the Istanbul Bar Association and the managing partner of Özbek & Özbek Law Firm. His practice areas encompass all aspects of commercial law.

Kemal Şenocak has Bachelor of Law, LLM and Doctoral degrees from Ankara University. He is a professor of Insurance Law and Commercial Law in the Commercial Law Department of Ankara University Faculty of Law and the Dean of İnönü University Faculty of Law.

Contributing Authors

Table of Contents

List of Abbreviations

Art.	Article
BATİDER	Banka ve Ticaret Hukuku Dergisi
E.	Esas
EEC	European Economic Community
EU	European Union
K.	Karar
NAFTA	The North American Free Trade Agreement
No.	Number
OECD	Organization for Economic Co-Operation and Development
OG	Official Gazette
p.	page
para.	paragraph
TRY	Turkish Lira
TSB	Türkiye Sigorta Birliği
TTHK	Tüketicinin Korunması Hakkında Kanun
UK	United Kingdom
USA	United States of America
USD	United States Dollar

List of Abbreviations

1–4

General Introduction

§1. General Background Information

Ural Özbek

1. Modern Turkey, officially referred to as the Republic of Turkey (‘*Turkey*’ or the ‘*Republic*’), was founded in 1923 from the remnants of the defeated Ottoman Empire, which at the time extended from the Anatolian region of South-western Asia to Eastern Thrace and South-eastern Europe. The establishment of the new Turkish Republic is primarily attributed to the leadership of nationalist Kemal Ataturk, who was an Ottoman general initially.

2. Turkey is encircled by seas on three sides: the Mediterranean Sea lies to the south, the Aegean Sea to the west and the Black Sea to the north. The Sea of Marmara, the Bosphorus and the Dardanelles (which together form the Turkish Straits) demarcate the boundary between Thrace and Anatolia and also separate Europe and Asia. Straddling the continents of Europe and Asia, Turkey’s location makes it a country of significant geo-political importance. Turkey occupies about 785,347 square kilometres (more than double the size of Germany) and has a population of some 85.2 million people (about 98 inhabitants per square kilometre).[1]

3. Under Ataturk’s leadership, Turkey adopted wide-ranging social, legal and political reforms. After a period of one-party rule, an experiment with multi-party politics led to the election victory of the opposition party and the peaceful transfer of power. However, the democratic process in Turkey has been fractured by periods of instability and intermittent military coups (1960, 1971, 1980), which in each case eventually resulted in the return of political power to democratic civilian elections.

4. Turkey is a member of the United Nations, North Atlantic Treaty Organization, Organisation for Economic Co-operation and Development (OECD), Organization for Security and Cooperation in Europe, Organisation of Islamic Cooperation and the G-20. After becoming one of the first members of the Council of Europe in

1. At https://data.tuik.gov.tr/Bulten/Index?p=The-Results-of-Address-Based-Population-Registration-System-2022-49685&dil=2; https://www.dsi.gov.tr/Sayfa/Detay/754; https://data.tuik.gov.tr/Bulten/Index?p=Nufus-ve-Konut-Sayimi-2021-45866#:~:text=T%C3%BCrkiye%20n%C3%BCfusu%2084%20milyon%20680,680%20bin%20273%20ki%C5%9Fiye%20ula%C5%9Ft%C4%B1.

1949, Turkey became an associate member of the EEC in 1963, joined the EU Customs Union in 1995 and started full membership negotiations with the European Union (EU) in 2005. Turkey's growing economy and diplomatic initiatives have led to its recognition as a regional power. However, European Council decided to freeze negotiations with Turkey on 15 December 2021

I. Political System

5. Turkey is a unitary republic, the principal characteristics of which are defined as '*a democratic, secular, and social state governed by the rule of law* ... ' by the Constitution of 1982 (the '*Constitution*').[2] This is the third constitution of the Republic, which has so far been significantly amended several times.[3] The Constitution sets forth the separation of powers among the three branches of the State: the legislature, the executive and the judiciary. The latest constitutional amendments, which came into force on 24 June 2018, transformed the parliamentary system into a presidential one.

A. *Branches of the State*

6.

(a) The Legislature: The Parliament is composed of 600 members, all of who are elected by direct, universal suffrage every five years.[4] Powers of the Parliament were reduced by the new presidential system. The parliament makes, amends and repeals laws; however, it no longer controls the Cabinet and ministers as there is no cabinet in the new presidential system. The Parliament still accepts the budget and the final accounts; declares war but cannot approve international treaties anymore.

(b) The Executive: The executive branch has no more a dual structure. Executive power is vested in the President. The President appoints the Cabinet. The Parliament's traditional function as a check-and-balance mechanism on the executive is reduced. The President may issue decrees on political, social and economic issues that carry the force of law. The President appoints twelve out of fifteen members of the Constitutional Court, and four out of thirteen members of the Council of Judges and Prosecutors, a body responsible for appointing new judges and prosecutors as well as overseeing promotions.

Opponents believe the new system institutionalizes a version of an executive presidency – now billed as executive presidency *alla turca* – that accorded the President more powers and more independence from the check-and-balance mechanisms:

2. Article 2.
3. https://www.anayasa.gov.tr/media/7258/anayasa_eng.pdf.
4. Elections are subject to a nationwide threshold of 7%, which determines that political parties that obtain less than 7% of the total valid votes cast nationally cannot be assigned any seats in the Parliament.

12. Key sectors in Turkey are the automotive industry, shipbuilding exports, banking, construction, home appliances, electronics, textiles, tourism, oil refining, petrochemical products, food, mining, iron and steel and machine industry. Industry has always been the key sector of the Turkish economy, and it has also been dominant in this development process. Especially after the liberalization reforms, it has shown remarkable growth and level of production in reaching global standards of production. Industrial activities for defence, cement, electronics, iron and steel, automotive, glass, sugar and textiles are among the important subsectors of Turkish industry. However, Turkey's dependence on imported oil and gas (around 97% of its energy needs) and often volatile, short-term investment in finance and its relatively high current account deficit, together with its relatively low human development profile (though improving 54th in 2020, 71st in 2015 and 88th in 2003 in the World),[7] are significant disadvantages for further economic development. It is widely accepted that structural reforms are needed to avoid the *middle-income trap* by way of increasing the percentage of high-value-added products through social and education reforms.

13. Certain socio-economic reforms, hastened by Turkey's EU accession process, have already paved the way for comprehensive changes in a number of areas. These reforms have strengthened the macroeconomic fundamentals of the country, and the resulting improvements in the Turkish economy have boosted foreign trade as well as tourism revenues. However, it is widely acknowledged that more structural reforms must be implemented in order to increase the role of the private sector in the Turkish economy, enhance the efficiency and resiliency of the financial sector and place the social security system on a more solid foundation.

IV. Financial Institutions

14. Decreasing interest rates and strong economic growth have provided a positive environment for the banking sector, which has considerable importance in the financial system in Turkey. Most of the transactions and activities of money and capital markets are carried out by banks. As of the end of 2016, there were fifty-two banks consisting of deposit banks, development and investment banks and participation banks. Banking Regulation and Supervision Agency (Bankacılık Düzenleme ve Denetleme Kurulu – BDDK) is the regulatory body, and the Banks Association of Turkey (Türkiye Bankalar Birliği-TBB) is the representative body of the banking sector established for protecting and promoting the professional interest of its members.

---

7. https://www.undp.org/turkiye/news/turkey-top-human-development-category-second-time-human-development-index?utm_source=EN&utm_medium=GSR&utm_content=US_UNDP_PaidSearch_Brand_English&utm_campaign=CENTRAL&c_src=CENTRAL&c_src2=GSR&gclid=CjwKCAiA3KefBhByEiwAi2LDHP3wZZpos4mo0K1TUNVPxA99nj41WrGHpUTfRUMS1RHPneFi-ImQkxoCf8QQAvD_BwE.

15. However, despite substantial positive reforms in recent years, Turkish banking services are still undergoing a process of development in order to achieve global standards. Besides banking, insurance companies, investment-related institutions, asset management companies, leasing and factoring are among the major actors in the financial system.

V. Currency Legislation and Monetary Regulations

16. Turkey has a highly liberal exchange control regime. Laws regulating the Protection of the Value of the Turkish Currency[8] ensure the free transfer of profits, fees and royalties. The transfer of profits, dividends, proceeds of sale and liquidation, licence, know-how, technical assistance fees, and repayment of loans and interests is unrestricted. Moreover, the Turkish Lira (TRY) is fully convertible. The supply of foreign exchange is not limited, and banks may open foreign exchange deposit accounts for both residents and non-residents. Principal and interests of non-residents can be transferred through the investor's bank. Non-residents may sell and buy securities at the Istanbul Stock Exchange, without being subject to any limitation and/or approval.

VI. Insurance Business, General Organization and Special Features

17. A brief general overview of the Turkish insurance industry is given in the chapter below. Particularly worthy to mention here is the potential for growth of the insurance industry in Turkey. In developed or developing countries, economic growth and the insurance sector improve parallel to each other. In accordance with this reality, while the insurance sector grew exponentially between 2010 and 2013, this growth slowed in 2014 due to decreases in automobile sales and a general slump in the Turkish Economy. Nevertheless, in comparison with other countries, the Turkish insurance sector has not reached saturation, and it has continued to develop with considerably high potential since 2014. Statistics reveal this fact clearly. In 2013, premiums as a percentage of GDP was 1.5% (consisting of 0.2% for life business and 1.3% for non-life business) compared to OECD's 7.74% (consisting of 4.33% for life business and 3.41% for non-life business), and premiums per capita in United States Dollar (USD) were USD 166 (consisting of USD 23 for life business and USD 143 for non-life business) compared to OECD's USD 2,897.7 (consisting of USD 1,620.6 for life business and USD 1,277.1 for non-life business). Similar trend continued between 2018 and 2021, premiums as a percentage of GDP were 1.4% compared to OECD's 9.4%, and premiums per capita in USD were USD 130 compared to OECD's USD 3,600.[9] Therefore, the insurance sector

8. Act No. 1567 OG. No. 1433, Date: 25.2.1930.
9. OECD (2023), Insurance spending (indicator). doi: 10.1787/adb73055-en (Accessed on 15 Feb. 2023); OECD (2023), Gross direct insurance premiums (indicator). Doi: 10.1787/8fd6f107-en (Accessed on 15 Feb. 2023).

in Turkey is still attractive to both local and foreign investors. Competition is continuing to increase due to new players entering the market, and it is obvious that the insurance sector in Turkey is going to continue to develop

18. The insurance industry is represented by the Insurance Association of Turkey (Türkiye Sigorta Birliği (TSB) or Türkiye Sigorta, Reasürans ve Emeklilik Şirketleri Birliği), a specialist professional institution with the characteristics of a unique non-governmental institution established by law. All insurance companies operating in Turkey are members of this association.

§2. Historical Background of Insurance and Insurance Legislation

Meltem Deniz Güner-Özbek

19. Before the first and second half of the nineteenth century, the concept of insurance was almost unknown in Turkey. At that time, local syndicates were established in some villages in order to provide compensation assistance for certain damages and losses. Furthermore, merchant associations were assisting their members in cases of death or sickness. However, these examples cannot be regarded as insurance activities in the real sense. While Europe was experiencing important developments with regard to insurance, the social, religious and economic conditions of the Ottoman Empire were impeding the development of insurance in Turkey at this time.

20. Perhaps viewed as a turning point, fires that caused significant damage in the second half of the nineteenth century raised negative public opinion and resulted in the birth of insurance. In particular, the fires in Beyoğlu in the summer of 1870 (the Great Pera Fire) destroyed many places of business, houses, mosques and churches. Mostly foreigners and associated wealthy people were living in this area, and the grievances of this demographic accelerated the development process of the insurance sector. However, it should also be noted that the first insurance legislation was the Maritime Code enacted in 1864 (‘*Ticaret-i Bahriye Kanunu*’) with regard to marine insurance.[10]

21. At that time, the insurance business was mainly carried out by foreign insurance companies and the first local insurance company, *Osmanlı Umum Sigorta Şirketi*, was set up in 1893. Thereafter, the Fire Insurance Companies Syndicate and a standing auditory committee under the Syndicate were established. The name of this Syndicate was changed to ‘the Insurance Companies Operating in Turkey’ in 1914. Important steps were taken with regard to legal and institutional regulation of insurance after the proclamation of the Republic of Turkey in 1923. The Syndicate was abolished and ‘the Club of Insurers’ was established in 1924, which then took the name of ‘Central Office of Insurers’. In 1927, the *Law with regard to Inspection and Auditing of Insurance Companies* came into force. Then, the National Reinsurance

10. Rayegan Kender, *Sigorta Hukuku*, 14th ed. (XII Levha Yayınları, 2014), p. 21.

Turkish Joint Stock Company was founded in 1929 as the first insurance company in the world to have a monopoly right. Even though this monopoly was dissolved in 2001, the company still operates in Turkey today. Since 1939, insurance companies were affiliated with the Ministry of Commerce until the Insurance Auditing Act came into force in 1959. This Act was fundamentally revised in 1987 by Act No. 3379 and further revised by the decree laws in 1993 and 1994. Finally, the new era of insurance in Turkey began with the enactment of the new Insurance Activities Act No. 5684 in 2007, which repealed the former Insurance Auditing Act.

§3. Sources of Insurance Law

I. Legislation

22. Legislation is an important source of insurance law in Turkey. There are two principal laws regulating insurance: the Insurance Activities Act and the Sixth Book of the Turkish Commercial Code (‘*Türk Ticaret Kanunu*’).

23. Insurance has a vital role in both financial and social life; thus, insurance companies must be strong both financially and administratively. In order to ensure such financial and administrative strength of an insurance company, the State maintains significant regulatory control over insurance companies in Turkey. As discussed above, the Insurance Activities Act (‘*Sigortacılık Kanunu*’) No. 5684 came into force in 2007 in order to ensure the development of insurance activities, to protect the rights and interests of the parties to the insurance contract and to ensure efficient operation of the insurance sector in a safe and stable environment. Accordingly, the Act sets out rules with regard to access to insurance businesses, organizations, management, working principles, discontinuance of business, auditing and a specific arbitration system.[11]

24. Furthermore, the Sixth Book of the Turkish Commercial Code is entitled *Insurance Law*. This Book mainly regulates insurance contracts and related issues. It is to be noted that although the Insurance Activities Act should mainly deal with the establishment and operation of insurance companies, it also contains a select number of articles that regulate insurance contracts. The Turkish Commercial Code No. 6102, in general, entered into force on 1 July 2012,[12] which effectively repealed

11. Article 1 of the Insurance Activities Act.
12. There are several dates for enactment, particularly regarding the Companies and the Second Book of the Code. The reason for the Turkish Commercial Code is to regulate developments influencing the former Commercial Code directly, such as the foundation and power of the EU, European Economic Area, NAFTA; Turkey's candidacy to the full membership of the EU; technological developments and the Internet, the desire to become a part of the international markets and commercial law reforms particularly in European countries affecting the former Commercial Code.

– The President is elected by universal suffrage for five years and is eligible for re-election for a second term. The President promulgates laws or returning laws to the Parliament for reconsideration; dissolves the Parliament and calls for new elections; appoints and dismisses the deputies of the President and ministers; ratifies and promulgates international treaties. The President may issue presidential decrees on matters regarding executive power. The President, however, shall not issue presidential decrees regarding the fundamental rights, individual rights and duties and political rights and duties listed in the first, second and the fourth chapter of the Constitution. The President neither shall issue a decree on the matters which are to be regulated exclusively by Law constitutionally nor on the matters which are explicitly regulated by law.

  In case of discrepancy between provisions of the presidential decrees and laws the provisions of laws prevail. If the Grand National Assembly enacts a law on the same matter as a presidential decree, the presidential decree becomes null and void.

– There is no longer a Cabinet in the sense of a parliamentary system and a Prime Minister. A vice-President and seventeen ministers – the presidential cabinet – are appointed by the President.

(c) The Judiciary: Judges are independent in the discharge of their duties, and no authority or individual may give orders or instructions to courts or judges relating to the exercise of judicial power. Legislative and executive authorities must comply with court decisions; they cannot alter them or delay their execution. Security of tenure for judges and public prosecutors has also been recognized. Personal matters for judges and public prosecutors, such as appointments, promotions, transfers, disciplinary actions, and dismissals are within the exclusive jurisdiction of the 'Council of the Judges and Public Prosecutors', itself composed of judges.

II. Legal System

7. As is widely known, after the triumph of the movement for codification in Continental Europe during the end of the eighteenth and beginning of the nineteenth centuries, many continental countries codified much of their laws based on Roman law. During this time from 1839 (the date of proclamation of the so-called Edict of Reorganization in the Ottoman period) until the founding of the Republic (of Turkey) in 1923, the Ottoman Empire adopted only a selected number of modern western statutes from Europe, while maintaining most of the old Islamic laws and legal institutions. Following the founding of the Republic, however, Turkey experienced a period of radical legal reform. Since then, the Turkish legal system has followed the continental pattern and with the reception and codification of many Continental European laws (such as the Civil Code and Code of Obligations from Switzerland, commercial law from Germany, Criminal Code from Italy, administrative law system from France), legislation has become the most important source of law. Although some laws have been modified several times to adapt to the changing socio-economic conditions of the country, the essence and fundamental principles

of European jurisprudence have been preserved in Turkey. In recent years main acts have been fully revised. The Civil Procedural Act, the Turkish Commercial Code and the Turkish Code of Obligations are among them.

8. In addition to legislation, customary law and case law or judicial precedents[5] are sources of law to a lesser extent in Turkey. In a *civil* law case, where there isn't any applicable legislation or customary rule or any binding judicial precedents, then the Turkish judge should act as a lawmaker and lay down a new rule within the framework of the general principles of law, benefiting from any relevant judicial precedent and doctrine. Furthermore, books of authority or doctrine are also a subsidiary source of Turkish law.

9. In a basic structural sense, the courts in Turkey are divided into constitutional, civil, criminal, administrative, tax courts, etc. Except for the constitutional judiciary, these courts are further sub-divided into local courts, first-degree courts of appeal and courts of appeal.

III. Commerce and Industry

10. In the early decades of the Republic, the government had to subsidize most of the industrial projects, due to a weak private sector. However, in the period between the 1920s and the 1950s, a new generation of Turkish entrepreneurs began to establish privately owned factories, some of which evolved into the largest industrial conglomerates that dominate the Turkish economy today. During the first six decades of the Republic, Turkey generally adhered to strict government planning of the budget and government-imposed limitations over the economy. In the 1980s, however, a series of reforms designed to shift the economy from an insulated system to a more private sector, market-based model were initiated.

11. After a severe financial crisis in 2001, Turkey adopted financial and fiscal reforms that strengthened the economic fundamentals and ushered in an era of strong growth averaging more than 6% annually until 2008, which made Turkey one of the fastest-growing economies during that period. However, during the global financial crisis, growth slowed to less than 1% in 2008, and in 2009 Turkey entered a recession of around (-)5%. Following an interim period of average annual growth of 9% in 2010–2011, growth dropped to an annual average of around 3% in 2012–2016. Annual growth fluctuated from 2017 to 2022 between 0.09% and 11%.[6]

---

5. In Turkey only certain precedents are binding, such as the decision of the Constitutional Court, unifying decisions of the general assembly on the Unification of Judgements of the Supreme Court of Appeals, etc.
6. https://data.tuik.gov.tr/Bulten/Index?p=Quarterly-Gross-Domestic-Product-Quarter-III:-July---September,-2022-45551&dil=2.

the former Turkish Commercial Code No. 6762. The current Turkish Commercial Code consists of six books[13] and 1,533 articles.

25. Even though the current Turkish Commercial Code has considerably resolved operational problems and defects in the previous sections on insurance law, there remain some problems in the wording and content of certain provisions. One aspect to note is that marine insurance has been removed from the Code on the basis that marine insurance contracts operate in accordance with international laws and regulations.

26. Besides the Insurance Activities Act and the Sixth Book of the Turkish Commercial Code, the Turkish Code of Obligations also applies to insurance contracts in the absence of any other particular provision.[14] The provisions of the Turkish Commercial Code – other than the Sixth Book – also apply to the regulation of merchants, corporations and joint stock companies, among other provisions. Furthermore, the Cooperative Law[15] is also applicable on the basis that insurance companies in Turkey may be established as either a joint stock company or a cooperative. An insurance company in the form of a cooperative is a mutual insurance company. From 1997, there was not any mutual insurance company in Turkey until Koru Mutuel Sigorta was founded in the form of a cooperative in 2011. Koru Mutuel Sigorta was transformed into a joint stock company in December 2017. There are, however, other mutual insurance companies – Atlas Mütüel Sigorta and TMT ('SS Tüm Motorlu Taşıyıcılar Karşılıklı Sigorta Kooperatifi') – currently in the market. Additionally, Karayolları Trafik Kanunu ('the Highway Code'), Karayolu Taşıma Kanunu ('the Road Transport Act') and Zorunlu Deprem Sigortasına Dair Kanun Hükmünde Kararname ('Decree Law on the Compulsory Earthquake Insurance'), Tüketicinin Korunması Hakkında Kanun (TTHK) ('the Law on the Protection of the Consumer') and, as a novelty, Law on the Protection of Personal Data are among the other applicable laws in the insurance sector.

27. Turkey ratified Convention 108 of the Council of Europe,[16] and pursuant to that Convention adopted the Law on the Protection of Personal Data on 7 April 2016.[17] Before that Law, a provision on the protection of personal data was inserted in the Constitution in 2010, whereby 'protection of personal data' became a constitutional right. The Data Protection Law originates from the EU Directive 95/46/EC and is particularly important for the health and insurance sectors. The Law sets out rules, *inter alia*, for data processing, normal (non-special categories of personal data) and special categories of personal data, conditions of data processing, data security and transfer of data to third parties.

---

13. The First Book of Business Undertaking, the Second Book of Trading Corporations, the Third Book of Negotiable Instruments, the Fourth Book of Transportation Business, the Fifth Book of Maritime Commerce and the Sixth Book of Insurance Law.
14. Article 1451 of the Turkish Commercial Code.
15. Act No. 1163, Date: 24.4.1969, amended in 1988 and 2004 by the Acts No. 3476 and No. 5146, respectively.
16. Decision No. 2016/8576, OG. No. 29656, Date: 17.3.2016.
17. Act No. 6698 OG. No. 29677, Date 7.4.2016.

28. The Law applies to natural persons whose personal data is processed.[18] Personal data is any kind of information that belongs to a natural person,[19] such as a consumer, client, agency owner, company partner, or employee, whose identity is determined or may be determined. Examples of such data include name, phone number, licence plate, social security number, passport number, background, visual or audio recordings, fingerprints, and genetic information. Personal data may be processed by a natural or legal person.[20] The Law provides a general rule for processing and exceptions to the general rule. Accordingly, personal data shall only be processed with the explicit consent of the data subject.[21] 'Explicit consent' means freely given informed and specific consent.[22] In some cases, personal data can be processed without the explicit consent of the person, and such cases are related to insurance contracts as well:

- If it is expressly permitted by any law.
- If it is necessary in order to protect the life or physical integrity of the data subject or another person where the data subject is physically or legally incapable of giving consent.
- If it is necessary for, and directly related to, the execution or performance of a contract to which the data subject is a party.
- If it is necessary for compliance with a legal obligation to which the controller is subject.
- If the relevant information is revealed to the public by the data subject herself/himself.
- If it is necessary for the institution, usage or protection of a right.
- If it is necessary for the legitimate interests of the data controller, provided that the fundamental rights and freedom of the data subject are not harmed.

29. Special categories of personal data are, however, information related to race, ethnic origin, political opinions, philosophical beliefs, religion, sect or other beliefs, appearance and dressing, membership of association, foundation or trade union, health, sexual life, criminal conviction and security measures, and biometrics and genetics.[23] Processing special categories of personal data is subject to a stricter rule. Accordingly, the data controller is required to obtain the explicit consent of the data subject as well as to take adequate measures designated by the Data Protection Authority.[24] However, there is an exception to this stricter rule. Special categories of personal data, except for data concerning health and sexual life, can be processed without the explicit consent of the data subject if it is permitted by any law.[25] Data

18. Articles 2, 3.ç.
19. Article 3.d.
20. Article 2.
21. Article 5.1.
22. Article 3.a.
23. Article 6.1.
24. Article 6.2, 6.4.
25. Article 6.3.

concerning health or sexual life can only be processed for the purposes of protection of public health and for planning or sustaining healthcare services by an authorized body or persons who are under the obligation of confidentiality.[26] In these exceptional cases where the explicit consent of the data subject is not required, data controller is still required to take adequate measures designated by the Data Protection Authority. There are many insurances that use data concerning health. It may not be easy for an insurance company to obtain such data to assess whether the realized risk is covered or not as the explicit consent of the data subject is required.

30. The Law allows the transfer of personal data to third parties in Turkey or abroad by obtaining the explicit consent of the data subject.[27] Both 'normal' and special categories of personal data may be transferred to third parties in Turkey or abroad without the explicit consent of the data subject under the above-mentioned conditions where explicit consent is not required. Moreover, for personal data to be transferred abroad adequate level of protection should be provided in the foreign country where personal data is to be processed. If there is no adequate level of protection, the controllers both in Turkey and in the relevant country undertake to provide an adequate level of protection in the relevant country. Such an undertaking must be in writing. Additionally, permission from the Data Protection Board is necessary. The Data Protection Board has the authority to determine countries that have adequate protection. The Data Protection Board takes into account the following points while deciding in the country list where adequate protection is provided by granting permission:[28]

(a) international agreements to which Turkey is a party;
(b) reciprocity;
(c) nature of personal data and the purpose and period of processing with respect to each transfer;
(d) relevant legislation and its implementation in the relevant country;
(e) measures undertaken by the controller in the country where data is to be transferred;
(f) if the interests of Turkey or data subject are seriously harmed opinions of the relative state institutions and organizations will be taken into consideration. This provision was not included in the draft version of the Law and was introduced in the parliamentary discussions.

Of particular importance is the genetic information in relation to personal data. Turkey is a party to the Convention on Human Rights and Biomedicine.[29] Currently, there is no act relating to genetic diagnostics in Turkey. Article 12 of the Convention titled Predictive genetic test is as follows:

26. *Ibid.*
27. Article 8.
28. Article 9.4.
29. Decision No. 2004/7024, OG No. 25439, Date. 20.04.2004.

> Tests which are predictive of genetic diseases or which serve either to identify the subject as a carrier of a gene responsible for a disease or to detect a genetic predisposition or susceptibility to a disease may be performed only for health purposes or for scientific research linked to health purposes, and subject to appropriate genetic counselling.

Although the title is 'predictive genetic tests' it is accepted that it covers also diagnostics tests. It is set out clearly in the article which purposes genetic tests may be conducted. Accordingly, a genetic test shall not be conducted for the purpose of submitting to the insurance company even if the person consents. An insurance company shall require neither diagnostics genetic tests or predictive tests. However, if the person or insured has already such a genetic test he or she may have to, under duty, provide information to the insurer.

II. By-laws

31. According to Article 124 of the Turkish Constitution, 'The President, the ministries, and public corporate bodies may issue by-law in order to ensure the implementation of laws and presidential decrees relating to their jurisdiction, as long as they are not contrary to these laws and decrees. The law shall designate which by-law is to be published in the Official Gazette (OG)'.[30] With the new presidential system, the concept of regulation – one of the secondary sources – was removed from the Constitution. Previously promulgated regulations are still in force. Thus, secondary regulations by-laws differ from regulations which used to be issued by the Council of Ministers and indicated the implementation of laws or designated matters ordered by law, as long as they did not conflict with laws and were examined by the Council of State.[31] Regulations used to be signed by the President of the Republic and promulgated in the same manner as laws and governed the mode of the enforcement of status. In this work, we are going to use the term *by-law* for secondary regulations in accordance with the general usage in Turkish academic circles.[32]

32. Numerous by-laws have been implemented in accordance with the relevant acts and codes. Some of them are the Insurance Agencies By-law,[33] the By-law on the Distance Insurance Contracts, Insurance Contracts in favour of the Customers and Activities Considered Insurance Activities,[34] the By-law Regarding Establishment and Working Principles of Insurance and Reinsurance Companies,[35] the

30. English translation of Turkish Constitution can be found at, https://global.tbmm.gov.tr/docs/constitution_en.pdf.
31. Article 115 of the Turkish Constitution.
32. Tuğrul Ansay & Don Wallace (eds) *Introduction to Turkish Law* 8–9 (Kluwer Law 6th ed. 2011).
33. OG. No. 28980, 22.04.2014.
34. OG. No. 31513, 16.06.2021 revoked the former by-law published in OG. 25.4.2014 No. 28982.
35. OG. No. 26623, 24.8.2007.

By-law on the Working Principles and Procedures of the Turkish Insurance, Reinsurance and Pensions Companies Association,[36] the By-law on the passenger, baggage, cargo and postal items liability Insurance for the Aircrafts operating in Turkey Turkish and Foreign Civil Aircrafts Landing or Taking-off within the Borders of Republic of Turkey,[37] the By-law on the Liability Insurance Required for the Turkish and Foreign Aircrafts Flying over the Turkish Airspace,[38] the By-law on the Arbitration in Insurance Activities,[39] the By-law on the Supervision and Auditing Principles and Procedures of the Insurance Activity and Private Pension Sectors,[40] the Insurance and Reinsurance Brokers By-law[41] and the Group of Life Insurances By-law.[42]

III. General Conditions of Insurance

33. The general conditions of insurance are contractual conditions that are prepared specially for the specific type of insurance and attached to the relevant insurance policy. General conditions of insurance are prepared by the *Insurance and Private Pension Regulation and Supervision Agency* (*'Sigortacılık ve Özel Emeklilik Düzenleme ve Denetleme Kurumu'*) in accordance with the Presidential Decree No. 47.[43] Most of the general conditions of insurance are renewed or amended in accordance with new laws and recent developments.[44]

IV. Special Terms

34. Sometimes parties to the insurance contract want to agree on issues that are not regulated in either the general conditions or clauses. Consequently, parties may contractually agree to *special terms* related to a specific insurance contract. Principally, parties may agree on any issues except those that contravene the protective provisions of the Turkish Commercial Code.[45] For instance, Institute Clauses are included as special terms in marine insurance contracts.

36. OG. No. 28870, 2.1.2014.
37. O.G. No. 30136, 22.07.2017 revoveked the former by law published in OG. No. 26347, 15.11.2006.
38. OG. No. 26596, 28.07.2007.
39. OG. No. 26616, 17.08.2007.
40. OG. No. 28054, 14.09.2011.
41. OG. No. 26913, 21.06.2008.
42. OG. No. 28437, 10.10.2012.
43. Article 11(1) of the Insurance Activities Act and Art. 19 of the Presidential Decree No. 47.
44. A list of the general conditions of insurance may be found at www.tsb.org.tr.
45. The protective provisions are the protective provisions which otherwise cannot be agreed. Arts 1452, 1486, and 1520 are entitled Protective Provisions (*'Koruyucu Hükümler'*) and enumerate protective provisions in the relevant sections.

V. Private Law and Jurisdiction

35. If an insurance contract is linked to more than one country, it is necessary to use the rules of private international law, or conflict of laws, to determine under which system of law any disputes are to be resolved and to ascertain which court system has jurisdiction to hear a case and pass judgment in a third country. In Turkey, national laws determine the international jurisdiction of the Turkish Court, which is primarily governed by the Law on Private International Law and International Civil Procedure.[46] Apart from general provisions regulating jurisdiction, there is, however, recognition of a special jurisdiction with respect to insurance contracts. For disputes arising from insurance contracts, the court of the principal place of business of the insurer or of the place where the branch or agency concluding the insurance contract is situated in Turkey is deemed to have jurisdiction. However, for civil lawsuits filed against the policyholder, the insured or the beneficiary, the court of their domicile or habitual residence in Turkey is deemed to have jurisdiction.[47]

36. There are no specific provisions under the Law on Private International Law and International Civil Procedure that determine the applicable law of the international insurance contract. As a relatively new law enacted in 2007, these types of provisions for insurance contracts were considered during preparatory work for the Law on Private International Law and International Civil Procedure, but the idea was set aside for the following reasons. The first reason was that insurance transactions cover a wide variety of subjects for which there is no adequate research or capacity to address these issues in a single article. The second reason was the influence of EU Law. At the time when the Law on Private International Law and International Civil Procedure were being prepared for enactment, the Rome Convention[48] was in force, and it had implemented the discriminatory method. This meant that there were no specific legislative provisions to apply to insurance contacts, and EU Member States had the regulatory freedom to apply EU rules to insurance transactions among themselves.[49] The third reason is that laws regulating insurance transactions within Europe did not apply to non-Member States and countries like Turkey faced significant difficulty in adopting EU insurance laws into exiting Private International Law and domestic Civil Procedure Law.

37. As a result, the governing law of international insurance contracts is determined in accordance with Article 24 of the Insurance Activities Act, which states that parties to an insurance contract can choose the applicable law. Nevertheless, it

46. Article 40 of the Law on Private International Law and International Civil Procedure, Law No. 5718 Date: 27.11.2007 (OG. No. 26728, Date: 12.11.2007).
47. Article 46 of the Law on Private International Law and International Civil Procedure; Tekinalp, Nomer & Odman-Boztosun, IEL Private Law, para. 661b.
48. Convention on the Law Applicable to Contractual Obligations, EEC 80/934 (OG. L 266 Date: 9.10.1980).
49. Xandra E. Kramer, *The New European Conflict of Law Rules on Insurance Contracts in Rome I: A Complex Compromise*, VI(4) ICFAI U. J. Ins. L. 25–26 (2008); Nuray Ekşi, Türk ve Avrupa Birliği Hukukunda Yabancı Unsurlu Sigorta Sözleşmelerine Uygulanacak Hukuk, Beta, 2012, 76; Tekinalp, Nomer & Odman-Boztosun, IEL Private Law, para. 294.

must also be stated that this freedom is restricted when taking into consideration the tendency to protect the vulnerable party under Turkish law. This is evident under Article 46 of the Law on Private International Law and International Civil Procedure regarding jurisdiction, which states that the court where the principal place of business of the insurer or place of the agency or branch who executed the contract is situated has jurisdiction over the cases arising from the insurance contract. However, in case of suits against the policyholder, insured or beneficiary, the court in their domicile or habitual residence has jurisdiction.

38. If the parties have not chosen the applicable law, it is determined in accordance with Article 24(4). The fundamental operational characteristics of insurance contracts relate to the obligations of the insurer. Unless provided otherwise by the contract, the law governing the insurance contracts is the law of the country where the insurer carries out his or her business, which is defined as the place of business of the insurer.[50] Since the insurer is a legal person in Turkish law, the governing law of the insurance contract is the law of either the place of business of the headquarters or the place of business of the branch, depending on whether the contract was concluded by the headquarters or by the branches.

§4. Dispute Settlement

Meltem Deniz Güner-Özbek & İlyas Gölcüklü

I. General Principles on Dispute Settlement for Insurance Contracts

39. All issues regulated under the Turkish Commercial Code and all transactions and actions related to any business undertaking are considered as 'commercial business'.[51] Insurance companies are considered traders within the scope of the Turkish Commercial Code.[52] Civil disputes arising from issues regulated under the Turkish Commercial Code are *commercial cases* within Article 4(1) of the Turkish Commercial Code, and insurance contracts, *inter alia,* are *commercial cases* within Article 4(1) of the Turkish Commercial Code because insurance contract law is regulated under the Sixth Book of the Turkish Commercial Code (Articles 1401–1520). However, this principal rule was changed by the Consumer Protection Act.

40. Accordingly, *non-consumer* disputes arising from insurance contracts are *commercial cases* and Article 4(1) of the Turkish Commercial Code requires all such commercial suits to be brought before the Commercial Court of First Instance irrespective of total lawsuit costs. In other terms, the Commercial Court of First

50. Tekinalp, Nomer & Odman-Boztosun, IEL Private Law, para. 294.
51. Article 3 of the Turkish Commercial Code.
52. Kender, *Sigorta Hukuku*, p. 38; *see also* Art. 4(1)(a) of the Turkish Commercial Code.

Instance is authorized to have jurisdiction over commercial cases resulting from insurance contracts except consumer insurance contracts.

41. Subject to this rule, the next issue to determine is *which* Commercial Court of First Instance is authorized to hear such cases under Turkish legislation. Article 15 of the Turkish Code of Civil Procedure[53] stipulates provisions for competent commercial Courts of First Instance to hear such cases. According to Article 15(1) of the Code of Civil Procedure, all lawsuits arising from indemnity insurance contracts are heard by the Commercial Court of First Instance located in the closest proximity to the property, whether it is defined as either *movable* or *immovable* in the sense that it is fixed by its very nature or if the parties agreed so. That is to say that if a dispute arises from an insured land located in Sariyer/Istanbul, then the authorized and competent court to hear such a case will be *Caglayan Courthouse (...) Commercial Court of First Instance.*

42. If there is not any such immovable or movable property, then the commercial court located where the insured risk occurs is also competent to hear such a case. One should note that such commercial courts are optional because according to Article 6(1) of the Code of Civil Procedure, the *general competent court* for any disputes will be 'respondent's domicile court' at the date of filing such suit. So, in our above-mentioned example, *Caglayan Courthouse Commercial Court of First Instance* does not have absolute and sole jurisdiction over the case. For instance, if the respondent insurance company's registered address is Ankara then *Ankara Courthouse Commercial Court of First Instance* also becomes a competent court if the plaintiff prefers to bring the case before this court.

43. Furthermore, Article 15(2) of the Code of Civil Procedure states that all suits arising from life insurance contracts must be brought before the Commercial Court of First Instance located at the domicile of the respondent or plaintiff. These courts have absolute and sole jurisdiction over such cases to the exclusion of other courts recognized by Article 6(1) of the Code of Civil Procedure.[54]

44. As a crucial exception under Turkish law, a marine insurance contract must be settled in accordance with its own set of principles regarding the jurisdiction and competence of the courts.[55] We should emphasize here that the above-mentioned principles are the general ones, and if a marine insurance contract is subject to any special statute or provision, then the special and more detailed jurisdiction principles of this statute will apply for dispute resolution and the general provisions will not apply.

---

53. Act No. 6100 OG. Date: 4.2.2011 No. 27836.
54. Kender, *Sigorta Hukuku*, p. 340.
55. The title of the Art. 15 of the Code of Civil Procedure is 'Jurisdiction in Cases Arising from Insurance Contracts'. The Sub-paragraph (3) states that 'This provision shall not be applicable in cases arising from marine insurance contracts'.

45. According to Article 110 of the Highway Traffic Act, any *damages* resulting from motor vehicles within the scope of the Highway Traffic Act are considered a matter of criminal jurisdiction and not civil jurisdiction. Article 110 also states that any civil cases relating to the Highway Traffic Act can be brought before courts located where the accident occurs or at the insurer's principal place of business or any branches or at the place of business of the agency that executed the relevant insurance contract.[56] This example demonstrates that it is possible for the Highway Traffic Act to provide more specific options in addition to the *general principles* that govern the competent court under Article 6 of the Code of Civil Procedure for civil jurisdiction disputes.

II. Consumer Courts

46. Notwithstanding these principles recognizing the authority of commercial courts under Article 4(1) of the Turkish Commercial Code, the promulgation of the new Consumer Protection Act on 28 May 2014 has brought fundamental changes to the authority of commercial courts in Turkey.[57] Insurance transactions involving customers as *consumers* also fall within the scope of the Consumer Protection Act, and Article 83(2) states that special consumer courts are also authorized to deal with the consumer nature of disputes arising from such insurance transactions.[58] This rule clearly overrides Article 4(1) of the Turkish Commercial Code, which states that all disputes relating to insurance contracts are *commercial cases* that must be brought before commercial courts accordingly.

47. The contradiction between the acts has caused numerous subject-matter jurisdiction disputes between the courts. The 20th Circuit of Court of Appeals is authorized to review such subject matter jurisdiction disputes whereas the 11th Circuit of Court of Appeals is authorized to review insurance cases – among others. Both the 20th and 11th Circuits have considered the meaning of consumer under the Consumer Protection Act in reviewing first instances cases. The Act defines a 'consumer' as a natural or legal person who acts for non-commercial and non-professional purposes.[59] Accordingly, if the party to an insurance contract is a consumer, consumer courts have subject-matter jurisdiction, not commercial courts.[60] Life insurance, car insurance, and compulsory liability insurance for drivers were considered consumer cases when contracting parties were consumers.

56. Kender, *Sigorta Hukuku*, pp. 339–340.
57. Act No. 6502 OG. Date: 28.11.2014 No. 28835.
58. Articles 3(1) l and 83(2) of the Consumer Protection Act.
59. Article 3(1).k of the Consumer Protection Act.
60. *See* decisions of 11th Circuit of Courts of Appeals: 23.11.2015, E.2015/13163 K.2015/12363; 2.3.2016, E. 2016/1931 K.2016/2286; 28.3.2016, E.2016/1930 K.2016/3383, 7.3.2016 E.2016/1904 K. 2016/2458; 18.1.2016, E.2016/55 K. 2016/424; decisions of 20th Circuit: 24.10.2015, E.201%/12438 K.2015/9213; 16.6.2016, E.2016/5428 K.2016/7124; 4.11.2015 E.2015/8916 K.2015/10543; 19.1.2016, E.2015/15060 K.2016/580, 14.1.2016, E.2015/12678 K.2016/364 (Lexpera.com accessed 11.5.2018).

However, cases of medical malpractice insurance and aviation insurance were considered commercial cases when the third party injured seeks compensation under such insurance.[61]

III. Arbitration Committee for Consumer Transactions and Practices Towards Consumers

48. Furthermore, the Consumer Protection Act requires the Ministry of Trade to set up an *arbitration committee* for consumer *transactions and practices towards consumers* in the provincial centre and county town.[62] If the amount of the dispute is less than TRY 30,000 (approximately EUR 1,489), it must be brought before the arbitration committee for consumer problems.[63] Otherwise, disputes exceeding this amount may be brought before either the courts or special arbitration.

IV. Special Arbitration in the Turkish Insurance Law

49. Due to the heavy workload of courts in Turkey, judicial processes invariably take a long time. In order to avoid and overcome these lengthy court processes, the alternative dispute resolution system for arbitration was introduced in the field of insurance law. Although this system of arbitration resembles the process for arbitration in civil procedure in many aspects, this special arbitration system for insurance law disputes does have unique differences.[64] It is perhaps more appropriate to compare it with the ombudsman system in Germany or Switzerland, for instance, in the field of insurance and banking.

50. In accordance with Article 30 of the Insurance Activities Act, an Insurance Arbitration Commission ('The Commission') has been constituted in order to resolve disputes arising from an insurance contract. The centre of the Commission is based in Istanbul, and insurance companies are required to obtain membership in order to participate with the insured or other interested parties in such a system.[65] Insurance companies are free to participate in the system. Membership of any insurance company in the system is sufficient for bringing a dispute before this arbitration committee regardless of a special arbitration clause in the insurance contract. Insurance companies must pay membership fees whereas applicants need only pay an application fee, which is determined by the Insurance and Private Pension Regulation and Supervision Agency. The application fee is reasonably low at TRY 150

61. *See* decisions of 11th Circuit of Court of Appeals: 11.5.2016, E.2016/4948 K.2016/5303; 5.12.2016, E.2016/13640 K.2016/9304; 12.12.2016, E.2016/13942 K.2016/9470; 17.2.2016, E.2016/541 K.1621; 13.2.2017, E. 2017/270 K. 2017/76 (Lexpera.com accessed 11.5.2018).
62. Article 66 of the Consumer Protection Act.
63. Consumer Arbitration Committees By Law, O.G: No. 31960 21.09.2022.
64. A.C. Budak, Yeni Hukuk Muhakemeleri Kanunu'nun Tahkim Hükümleri (Yeni Hukuk Muhakemeleri Kanunu), (2012) Uluslararası Ticaret ve Tahkim Hukuku Dergisi, V.1. No. 1 31-60, 56.
65. Kender, *Sigorta Hukuku,* p. 337. Özdamar, M., 'Sigorta Hukukunda Uyuşmazlıkların Çözümünde Tahkim Sistemi', (2003) Gazi Üniversitesi Hukuk Fakültesi Dergisi C.XVII S.1–2, pp. 831 ff.

for disputes up to TRY 5,000, TRY 350 for disputes between TRY 5,001 and TRY 10,000, TRY 500 for disputes between TRY 10,001 and TRY 30,000 and 1.5% of the disputed amount in excess of TRY 30,001.

51. If an insured policyholder applies to the insurance company in order to resolve an insurance conflict or dispute and this application remains unanswered for fifteen days as of the date of such application, he or she may apply to the Commission to resolve such dispute.[66] The applicant may also be required to apply to the Commission where he or she should provide sufficient documents showing that his or her application has been denied partially or completely. The Commission must finalize the dispute within four months of the application if otherwise not agreed by the parties explicitly and in writing.[67] However, any pending lawsuit brought before a court cannot also be brought before the Commission.

52. On the basis that the arbitration system under the Insurance Activities Act is designed to resolve disputes brought by the insured or another interested party, it can be inferred that insurers cannot bring a claim against the insured under the arbitration system.

53. All applications are first reviewed by a rapporteur[68] to determine whether all relevant documents and information have sufficiently been provided. The rapporteur must finalize this initial review within fifteen days. A more detailed advance review is then undertaken, and if this cannot be finalized within fifteen days, a formal report must be prepared.[69]

54. After the advance review, the Commission must determine whether a commission for the specific dispute must be constituted or not. It is important to note here that a specific commission is required for all disputes valued in excess of TRY 15,000.[70] Such commissions must consist of at least one lawyer if there is a lawyer on the list of arbitrators. Decisions are made on the basis of a majority vote. If the constitution of a commission is not necessary, an arbitrator is appointed from the relevant list successively.

55. Both rapporteurs and arbitrators work in either life insurance or non-life insurance fields, and arbitration cases are classified as either *life* or *non-life* subject

66. Çeker, 78; Art. 30(13) of the Insurance Activities Act.
67. Article 16(10) of the By-law Relating to Arbitration in Insurance Activities (OG. No. 26616, Date: 17.8.2007).
68. A.C. Budak (2013) Sigortacılık Kanununda Tahkim: Sigortacılık Kanunu'nun 20. Maddesi, HMK'nun Yürürlüğe Girmesi ve 6327 Sayılı Kanun ile Değişikliğinden sonra Nasıl Yorumlanmalıdır? Sigortacılık Kanununda Tahkim, C.2 S.2 Uluslararası Tahkim ve Ticaret Hukuku Dergisi, 53–69, p. 59.
69. Article 8(3) of the By-law Relating to Arbitration in Insurance Activities (OG. No. 26616, Date: 17.8.2007).
70. Article 16(7) of the By-law Relating to Arbitration in Insurance Activities (OG. No. 26616, Date: 17.8.2007).

to the list of arbitrators. The parties are informed of the appointed arbitrator immediately, and there is also a third list of arbitrators for the denial process. Arbitrators must solely work in one of these fields. It is possible for the contracting parties to reject an arbitrator under certain conditions, in which case all arbitrators must abstain from taking duty in the specific case.[71]

56. In order to practice as an arbitrator, one must first pass an exam issued by the Insurance and Private Pension Regulation and Supervision Agency, except for associate professors or retired judges who are exempt from such an exam. Furthermore, each arbitrator is required to have a minimum of five years of experience in insurance *law* or ten years in insurance *activities*. Successful applicants are registered under the formal list of arbitrators maintained by the Commission.[72]

57. If the amount of dispute is lower than TRY 5,000, the Commission's decision regarding the case is *final* and cannot be challenged or appealed to the Commission or to the Court of Appeals.[73] If the amount of dispute is TRY 5,000 and more, a party can challenge the final decision of the Commission before the Commission itself, but only on one more occasion within ten days from the date of notification of the initial decision.[74] Otherwise, such initial decisions will be final as well. In the event of a challenge, the initial decision ceases to apply, and the dispute becomes subject to the second arbitration procedure. This second decision becomes ultimately final, and it cannot be subjected to any further challenge or appeal. Article 30 paragraph 12 of the Insurance Activities Act states that cases in excess of TRY 40,000 can also be appealed to the Court of Appeals by the relevant party due to the financial significance of the case.

58. The following grounds are sufficient for any interested party to appeal for a Commission decision before the Court of Appeals irrespective of the total amount of the dispute[75] in the event that:

- the Commission reaches a decision after the expiry of the arbitration period;
- the Commission has decided on a subject that is not claimed by the applicant;
- the appointed arbitrators decide on matters out of their authorization ('*ultra vires*'); or
- the arbitrators do not decide on the claimed issues of applicants.

59. Even though using arbitration to resolve insurance-related disputes is a relatively new initiative under Turkish Insurance Law, it is being widely applied and used by the interested parties in Turkey due to the expertise of arbitrators in the specific insurance field and time-saving characteristics of such arbitration.

---

71. Articles 17 and 18 of the By-law Relating to Arbitration in Insurance Activities (OG. No. 26616, Date: 17.8.2007); Budak (Sigortacılık Kanununda Tahkim), p. 63.
72. Article 30(8) c of the Insurance Activities Act.
73. Article 16/B of the By-law Relating to Arbitration in Insurance Activities (OG. No. 26616, Date: 17.8.2007).
74. Article 16/B.
75. *See* Art. 30(12) of the Insurance Activities Act.

60. The arbitration before the Commission is optional. Instead of applying for special arbitration before the Commission or initiating court proceedings, both parties to the dispute may apply for *domestic* arbitration under the Code of Civil Procedure or *international* arbitration. For example, the parties may agree to resort to ICC arbitration as a stipulation under a general insurance contract or under a separate written agreement. Alternatively, the parties may also agree to submit to the Istanbul Arbitration Center ('ISTAC')[76] or Istanbul Chamber of Commerce Arbitration Center[77] by applying the domestic arbitration rules of the Turkish Code of Civil Procedure.

61. However, it is doubtful if a dispute arising from a consumer insurance contract is arbitrable under the regular arbitration system of the Turkish Code of Civil Procedure. Article 17 of the Code of Civil Procedure states that only *merchants* and *public legal entities* can agree to authorize one or more courts to hear a possible dispute. It can be inferred from this wording that *consumer* contracts cannot contain arbitration provisions within the meaning of Article 17 when the rationale and purpose of the Code of Civil Procedure are taken into consideration.[78]

V. Mediation in the Turkish Insurance Law

62. The Law on Commencing Legal Proceedings for Monetary Receivables Arising from Subscription Agreements[79] introduced new provisions to the Turkish Commercial Code No 6102 ('TCC'). As of 1 January 2019, it became mandatory for claimants to apply to mediation as a prerequisite for commercial disputes before pursuing the dispute via the Turkish courts.

All issues regulated under the Turkish Commercial Code and all transactions and actions related to any business undertaking are considered 'commercial business' and insurance companies are considered merchants within the scope of the Turkish Commercial Code. Therefore, insurance contracts are commercial cases within Article 4(1) of the Turkish Commercial Code because insurance law is also regulated under the Sixth Book of the Turkish Commercial Code (Articles 1401–1520). That is to say that unless an insurance claim does not fall within the consumer transactions, it is mandatory for a prospective claimant to bring the dispute to mediation first. Otherwise, competent commercial court shall dismiss the case procedurally due to the lack of a prerequisite to file a case.

The Law Amending the Civil Procedure Law and Certain Laws[80] added 'Article 73/A' with the title of 'Mediation as a prerequisite', to the Consumer Protection Act. The amendment, as for commercial disputes, has made mediation a prerequisite for

76. *See* details at, http://istac.org.tr/en/.
77. The Istanbul Arbitration Centre was founded in Istanbul under the auspices of Istanbul Chamber of Commerce in accordance with the Istanbul Arbitration Centre Act (Act No. 6570 OG. No. 29190, Date: 29.11.2014). *See also* website of the Centre at, http://www.itotam.com/en/Default.aspx.
78. A.C. Budak, Yeni Hukuk Muhakemeleri Kanunu'nun Tahkim Hükümler, Uluslararası Ticaret ve Tahim Hukuku Dergisi, V.1. No. 1 (2012) 31-6 pp. 38–39.
79. Act No. 7155 OG. Date: 19.12.2018 No. 30630.
80. Act No. 7251 OG. Date: 28.07.2020 No. 31199.

lawsuits regarding disputes to be filed before Turkish Consumer Courts. Therefore, if a party wishes to pursue consumer claims before a Consumer Court, it must seek a solution through mediation first. If the dispute falls within the power of the Arbitration Committee for Consumer Transactions, this mandate shall not apply.

According to Article 18/A-18 of the Law on Mediation in Civil Disputes,[81] if mandatory arbitration or alternative dispute resolution methods are regulated for certain disputes under special laws or in the event of the existence of an arbitration agreement or clause between the parties, these mandatory mediation provisions shall not apply. One should note that the above-mentioned arbitration before the Commission is optional. Also, there are a few exceptions to the mandatory mediation for consumer law disputes.[82] Therefore, mandatory mediation for insurance claims is only applicable *when a claimant decides to pursue the dispute via the Turkish court system*. In other words, the claimant is not obliged to bring the case to mediation first if the claim is taken to contractual arbitration between parties, special arbitration before the Commission or Consumer Arbitration Committee. Voluntary mediation is always possible even if the insurance dispute is not subject to mandatory mediation.

§5. CONSUMER PROTECTION

Meltem Deniz Güner-Özbek

63. The law of supervision under insurance and consumer protection law are closely connected to each other.[83] The purpose of the law of supervision with respect to insurance is, in principle, to protect the rights and interests of the insured. There are provisions in the Insurance Activities Act related to consumer protection, such as the preparation of the general conditions by the Insurance and Private Pension Supervision and Regulation Agency in accordance with Article 11 and the prohibition against misleading and false advertising and advertising that perpetuates unfair competition under Article 32.

64. The new Consumer Protection Act[84] entered into force on 28 May 2014 and repealed the former act. In contrast to the former Act, the new Consumer Protection Act explicitly recognizes insurance transactions among other consumer transactions.[85] Moreover, insurance transactions are also regulated under Article 49 in relation to *distance contracts*, which are contracts finalized without any face-to-face contact, for example, via the internet or over the phone, with regard to financial services. Consequently, subject to other conditions, insurance contracts can be considered as coming within the ambit of consumer protection law. A 'consumer' is

81. Act No. 6325 OG. Date: 22.06.2012 No. 28331.
82. *See* Arts 68 and 73-A/1 of the Consumer Protection Act. For example, objections made against the Consumer Arbitration Committee's decisions are not subject to mandatory mediation.
83. Rayegan Kender, 'Sigorta Hukukunda Tüketicinin Korunması (Tüketicinin Korunması)', Erhan Adal'a Armağan Yeditepe Üniversitesi Hukuk Fakültesi Dergisi, C.8 S.2. (2011) pp. 1–27, pp. 1 ff.
84. Act No. 6502 Date: 7.11.2013 (OG. No. 28835, Date: 28.11.2013).
85. Article 3(1).l of the Consumer Protection Act.

defined as a natural or legal person who acts for non-commercial and non-professional purposes.[86] Some of the provisions of the new Act directly relate to insurance contracts whereas some have indirect applications.

65. Regarding the requisite form of contracts and statements, they must be written in an intelligible, clear, simple and readable manner and at least in twelve points font.[87] A copy of the contract, either printed or in the form of permanent data storage, should be rendered to the consumer. Absence of one or more of these conditions does not otherwise affect the validity of the contract. Similarly, Article 1425(1) of the Turkish Commercial Code states that the insurance policy must include the respective rights of the parties, provisions with regard to default, general and special conditions and must be prepared in a clear, intelligible and readable manner. It is, however, not clear whether 'intelligible' means that the contract must be understood either in the official language of the country or in the language of the relevant person.

66. Furthermore, according to the Act, any conditions of the contract must not be altered contrary to the benefit of the consumer.[88] An insurance contract may, however, contain a premium adjustment clause, and the insurer may increase the premium in accordance with the adjustment clause without altering the coverage. In such a case, the policyholder has the right to terminate the contract.[89] Additionally, the insurer may choose the option to request an additional premium in the event that he becomes aware of the facts that indicate an increase in the probability of the materialization of the risk during the contract period.[90] Although the premium adjustment clause seems to contradict Article 4(2) of the Consumer Protection Act, the latter does not because in such a case the policyholder or insured causes the alteration of the provision by failing to comply with the burden of disclosure. One of the basic principles of law is that a person must not benefit from his or her unlawful act. Accordingly, the insured consumer, who fails to comply with the burden of disclosure, must not benefit from any prohibition against the alteration of contractual terms.

67. The unfair provisions inserted in consumer contracts are null and void.[91] The invalidity of such unfair provisions does not affect the validity of the other provisions. Unfair provisions mean provisions inserted in the contract without first negotiating them with the consumer and which cause an imbalance between the rights and responsibilities of the parties to the contract contrary to the principle of good faith against the consumer.[92] Although general conditions are prepared by the Insurance and Private Pension Regulation and Supervision Agency, they may contain

86. Article 3(1).k of the Consumer Protection Act.
87. Article 4(1) of the Consumer Protection Act.
88. Article 4(2) of the Consumer Protection Act.
89. Article 1414 of Turkish Commercial Code.
90. Article 1445 of Turkish Commercial Code.
91. Article 5(2) of the Consumer Protection Act.
92. Article 5(1) of the Consumer Protection Act.

unfair provisions and are therefore subject to supervision as well.[93] Likewise, *special* provisions and clauses that are prepared in advance (such as Munich-Re Clauses) are also subject to the same supervision as for general conditions.[94]

68. In insurance practice, the insurer is not obliged to enter into a contract, except for compulsory insurance. Nevertheless, Article 6(2) of the Consumer Protection Act provides that one cannot abstain from providing insurance services unless he or she has a justifiable cause. Accordingly, the insurer must explain the reason for not concluding the contract, i.e., not providing coverage under consumer insurance contracts.

69. It was a common practice in Turkey to insert a clause to a credit contract to require the borrower to execute a life insurance policy for the benefit of the credit provider. Such an insurance contract was generally prepared by the credit provider, which in most cases was a bank acting as an agent of the insurance company. However, Articles 29 and 38 of the Consumer Protection Act have changed this practice so that an insurance contract related to consumer credit or housing finance is not to be executed without the written or explicit – via permanent data storage – request of the consumer.[95] The credit provider or housing finance institution is obliged to accept the coverage obtained from an insurance company at the discretion of the consumer. Such insurance is not only for the benefit of the credit provider but also for the consumer and his or her heirs; however, a provision for the payment of the insurance premium would be more appropriate rather than leaving the issue completely at the discretion of the consumer. In relation to prepaid housing sale contracts, insurance or any other financial security determined by the Ministry of Trade is also required.

70. However, an insurance contract for the benefit of a consumer can also be provided for particular contractual relationships. For instance, a technology store may provide insurance for customers who buy mobile phones. In such a case however, the party who is providing the insurance (in our example the technology store) is only the intermediary and must not indicate or give the policyholder the impression that the insurance coverage is being provided by him. As such, the information with regard to the insurance company and the compensation payable by the insurance company must be clearly stated in the mobile phone sale contract, which represents the main contractual relationship in this example.

71. The Consumer Protection Act requires that insurance contracts executed 'out of a business office' be in written form.[96] Although the exact meaning of a 'business office' is not clear under the Act, it should be understood that this requirement applies not only to the offices of insurance companies but also to agents' offices. However, it should be noted that these provisions for consumer insurance contracts

---

93. *See* section on interpretation of insurance contract.
94. For more discussion on this issue *see* Interpretation below.
95. Articles 29 and 38 of the Consumer Protection Act. Both articles have been recently amended.
96. Article 47.

to be in written form are not required for insurance contracts in general. Additionally, consumers have the right to cancel such contracts within fourteen days without any reason and without paying any penalty. Furthermore, Article 1489 of the Turkish Commercial Code provides such an unconditional right of cancellation for life insurance policies within fifteen days rather than fourteen days. It should also be noted that the policyholder could always cancel the contract by paying half of the agreed premium before the insurer's liability attaches.[97]

72. In the case of distance insurance contracts, the consumer must be properly informed about the content and operational meaning of the contract. Similar to the contracts concluded out of business offices, the period of cancellation is fourteen days without any requirement to provide a reason or pay any penalty.[98] However, regarding the cancellation of insurance and individual pension contracts, a more favourable period under other legislation is taken into consideration. Insurance companies or their agencies that would like to conclude distance insurance contracts must have the necessary organizational and technical infrastructure. The By-law on the Duty of Information in the Insurance Contracts[99] also applies to distant insurance contracts.[100] In relation to distance contracts executed electronically, the notification requirement is fulfilled upon the condition of confirmation in the electronic environment. For instance, such requirement is satisfied if the content of the notification has been published on the website of the insurance company or agent and the other party to the distance insurance contract has been given the opportunity to transfer this information to an electronic environment in which such party has authority.[101] The insurer is still obliged to deliver the insurance policy in distance insurance contracts in accordance with Article 1424 of the Turkish Commercial Code. However, an electronic version of the insurance policy is sufficient if such a version can be printed or transferred to any electronic environment. The signature requirement is also satisfied by electronic signature in this case. Reinsurance contracts may be executed from a distance as well.

§6. COMPULSORY INSURANCES

73. Compulsory insurance is an important subject of insurance practice and insurance law.[102] A number of insurances are compulsory in Turkey. Although most

97. Article 1430 of the Turkish Commercial Code.
98. Article 49 of the Consumer Protection Act.
99. OG. No. 26684, Date: 28.10.2007.
100. By-law on the Activities Considered Within the Insurance Activities, Insurance Contracts for the Benefit of Consumers and Distance Insurance Contracts (OG. No. 28982, Date: 25.04.2014).
101. Article 9(4) of the By-law on the Activities Considered Within the Insurance Activities, Insurance Contracts for the Benefit of Consumers and Distance Insurance Contracts (OG. No. 28982, Date: 25.4.2014).
102. 'Dünyada ve Türkiye'de Zorunlu Sigortalar, Sorunlar ve Çözüm Önerileri', Seminer, İktisadi Kalkınma Vakfı, Ankara, 2012.

such insurances are liability insurances due to the high earthquake risk in Turkey, there is also a *Compulsory Earthquake Insurance* that is not a liability insurance but relates to property insurance instead.

74. In particular, two issues must be considered while setting up compulsory insurance: there must be some legal requirement that the insurance contract be compulsory; and the insurance of a certain type of liability must also be compulsory for the execution of a liability insurance contract. According to Article 13(1) of the Insurance Activities Act, President is authorized to introduce compulsory insurance in situations that s/he considers necessary with respect to the public interest. In conformity with this requirement, insurance companies that have a licence in a particular branch of insurance are entitled to form such insurance contracts.[103]

75. The particular problem regarding compulsory insurance was that strict liability was sometimes created by a decision of the Council of Ministers even though such liability could normally only be created by an act of the Parliament. Likewise, compulsory insurance of a certain liability may also be required by a by-law rather than an act of the Parliament as well.

76. Furthermore some international conventions set out rules pertaining to compulsory insurance, such as the International Convention on Civil Liability for Oil Pollution Damage, 1992;[104] the International Convention on Civil Liability for Bunker Oil Pollution Damage, 2001;[105] and the Convention for the Unification of Certain Rules for International Carriage by Air, 1999.[106] Turkey is a party to these conventions and some others that were given effect in accordance with national procedures equivalent to the acts of the Parliament.[107] Some compulsory insurances are:

- Liability insurance by the person having *usufruct* on a property.[108]
- Liability insurance for the operation of a motor vehicle.[109]
- Compulsory liability insurance regarding a property that is the subject matter of the financial lease contract.[110]
- Liability insurance of air carriers[111] and operators.[112]
- Liability insurance for marine environment caused by shore facilities.[113]

---

103. Article 13(1) of the Insurance Activities Act. The Turkish Commercial Code sets out the same rule in Art. 1483(1).
104. Article VII. Or other financial security. In most situations, P&I Clubs provide such coverage.
105. Article VII.
106. Article 50.
107. Article 90 of Turkish Constitutional Code.
108. Article 815 of the Turkish Civil Code.
109. Article 91 of the Highway Traffic Act.
110. Article 17 of the Financial Lease Act.
111. Article 132 of the Turkish Civil Aviation Code.
112. Article 138 of the Turkish Civil Aviation Act.
113. Act on the Intervention in Emergency Cases and Compensation of Damages in Case of Pollution of Marine Environment by Oil and Other Dangerous Substances (No. 5312).

- Liability insurance of private security services.[114]
- Personal accident insurance in favour of the passengers transported on the highway.[115]
- Liability insurance for the passengers transported on the highways.[116]
- Liability insurance for dangerous substances and dangerous waste.[117]
- Professional indemnity insurance for physicians, insurance agencies and insurance brokers.
- Liability insurance of the electronic service providers.[118]
- Compulsory earthquake insurance.[119]
- Mining workers' compulsory individual accident insurance.[120]

§7. Insurance Contract Which Must Be Concluded in Turkey

77. Some insurance contracts can only be executed to be performed in Turkey. Accordingly, natural and legal persons residing in Turkey must insure their insurable interests that are located in Turkey with insurance companies operating in Turkey.[121] Exceptions to this rule are transport insurance for the import/export of goods, aircraft or vessels hull insurance when bought by foreign credit;[122] liability insurance for the operation of vessels; life insurance; personal accident, sickness, health and motor vehicle insurance when people are temporarily abroad and limited to a particular duration of stay abroad.[123] Furthermore, the insurance of vessels and yachts registered with the Turkish International Ship Registry can also be executed and performed abroad.[124] The President is authorized to broaden the types of insurance which can be executed abroad.

114. The Special Security Services Act (Act No. 5188).
115. Article 18 of the Highway Transportation Act, No. 4925, Date: 10.7.2003 (OG. No. 25173, Date: 19.7.2003); Arts 42, 47 and 48 of the Highway Transportation By-law (OG. No. 27255, Date: 11.6.2009). Not only passengers but also drivers and assistants of drivers are covered. This is a personal accident insurance.
116. Article 18 of the Highway Transportation Act. Liability insurance for damage arising from the bodily injury of passengers. This is a liability insurance and differs from the former personal accident insurance.
117. Decision of the Council of Ministers on the Liability Insurances for Dangerous Goods (Decision No. 2010/190 OG. No. 27518, Date: 11.3.2010).
118. Electronic Signature Act (No. 5070 OG. No. 25355, Date: 23.1.2004).
119. Decree on the Compulsory Earthquake Insurance (Decree No. 587).
120. Decision of the Council of Ministers (Decision No. 2015/7249 OG. No. 29259, Date: 6.2.2015).
121. Insurance Activities Act Art. 15(1).
122. Limited to the amount of credit and duration of the debt. Moreover, in the case of a financial lease contract duration of such insurance contract is limited to the duration of financial lease contract.
123. Article 15(2) of the Insurance Activities Act.
124. The Turkish International Ship Registry Act (No. 4490) Art. 13; Decision of the Council of Ministers (Decision No. 2008/143/78).

Part I. The Insurance Company

Meltem Deniz Güner-Özbek & Banu Bozkurt-Bozabalı

Chapter 1. The Insurance Company: Its Form

78. Due to their unique characteristics, including their establishment, operation and supervision, insurance companies are legislated by special provisions. The necessity for the creation of a special monetary fund due to the assurance nature of insurance may be given as an example of these special features. In most countries, insurance companies must be established as joint stock entities.[125] Correspondingly, it is forbidden for limited liability companies to perform insurance activities. The reason for this interdiction is that limited liability companies do not have enough capital and are not required to have the same transparent reporting processes as an insurance company. In other words, insurance companies must be organized as transparent joint stock companies or cooperatives that have collected enough capital from their partners.[126] The main aim of this chapter is to explain Turkish law that regulates these unique requirements of insurance companies, such as business operation and supervision. During business operations, insurance companies must fulfil certain conditions required by legislation. These conditions are examined under three subchapters: establishment, organization and restrictions. As in most countries, an insurance company must be established as Joint Stock or Cooperative, i.e., a mutual company in Turkey.[127]

79. As the concept of insurance is a legal relationship based on trust between the insurance or reinsurance company or cooperative and the policyholder or insured, the establishment and organization conditions of insurance or reinsurance companies or cooperatives are determined in detail in the Insurance Activities Act. It should be underlined here that any non-compliance with the compulsory rules on

125. For further information *see* Kender, *Sigorta Hukuku*, pp. 35–37; Ö Meriç, *Sigorta Şirketlerinin Kuruluşu ve Faaliyete Geçmesina İlişkin Esaslar* (Adalet Yayınevi 2013), 30–42.
126. E.A. Güvel & A. Güvel Öndaş, *Sigortacılık*, 6th ed. (Seçkin Yayınları 2012), pp. 221–222; Kender, *Sigorta Hukuku,* p. 34; Meriç, 31–34.
127. Article 3(1) of the Turkish Insurance Activities Act. For the unofficial translation of the Turkish Insurance Activities Act of the Association of the Insurance, Reinsurance and Pension Companies of Turkey, *see,* https://www.tsb.org.tr/laws.aspx?pageID=986 (30.10.2018).

establishment or organization will determine that the insurance or reinsurance company cannot obtain the necessary licence to start an insurance business. For any non-compliance after the establishment, the Insurance and Private Pension Regulation and Supervision Agency can require the company or cooperative to take necessary compliance measures or it may withdraw its licence.

§1. Joint Stock Companies

80. According to Article 335 of the Turkish Commercial Code, a joint stock company is established under certain stages. First, the *Articles of Association* must be prepared and signed by the partner(s).[128] The founding members must then have the capital amount[129] notarized[130] before paying for the capital, either partially or wholly.[131] The next stage is to obtain authorization for the insurance company from the Ministry of Commerce and Customs in the form of a licence to be granted by the Insurance and Private Pension Regulation and Supervision Agency pursuant to Article 5 of the Insurance Activities Act.[132] At the last stage, the company must be registered with the Trade Registry, and the registration must be published in the Trade Registry Gazette.[133]

81. Moreover, Article 3 of the Insurance Activities Act requires some qualifications for the founding members of the insurance company:

- she/he must not be bankrupt or subject to composition with creditors;
- have enough financial power and a good reputation compatible with his or her title as a founding member or shareholder;[134]

128. For further detail and the content of the article of association *see* Art. 339 of Turkish Commercial Code and Bahtiyar, *Ortaklıklar Hukuku*, 7th ed. (Beta Yayınevi, 2012), pp. 106–115; Fatih Bilgili & Ertan Demirkapı, *Şirketler Hukuku*, 9th ed. (Dora Yayınevi, 2013), pp. 226–235; Fatih Bilgili & Ertan Demirkapı, *Şirketler Hukuku (Dersleri)*, 3rd ed. (Dora Yayınevi, 2014), pp. 169–171 (Bilgili & Demirkapı (Dersler)); Reha Poroy, Ünal Tekinalp & Ersin Çamoğlu, '*Ortaklıklar Hukuku I*', 13th ed. (Vedat Kitapçılık, 2014), pp. 308–316; H. Pulaşli, '*Şirketler Hukuku Genel Esaslar*', 2nd ed. (Adalet Yayınevi, 2013), pp. 293, 297–304.
129. Bahtiyar, 115–116; Bilgili & Demirkapı, pp. 237–238; Bilgili & Demirkapı (Dersler), pp. 173–174; Pulaşlı, pp. 304–305. It should be noted that the founding members are not obliged to pay the whole capital. They may undertake to pay a part of it and go to the public for the rest of the capital after the completion of the establishment procedure. For further detail on this procedure *see* Bilgili & Demirkapı, pp. 246–249; Bilgili & Demirkapı (Dersler) pp. 177–179; Pulaşlı, 311–315.
130. Article 335 of the Turkish Commercial Code. For further detail *see* Bahtiyar, 115–116; Bilgili & Demirkapı, 235–237; Bilgili & Demirkapı (Dersler), 171–173; Pulaşlı, pp. 303–304.
131. For further detail *see* Bahtiyar, pp. 116–117; Bilgili & Demirkapı, pp. 238–241; Bilgili & Demirkapı (Dersler), pp. 174–175; Pulaşlı, pp. 305–306.
132. For further detail on the authorization *see* Bahtiyar, pp. 117–118; Bilgili & Demirkapı, pp. 241–243; Bilgili & Demirkapı (Dersler), p. 175; Pulaşlı, pp. 306–308. For further detail about the licence *see* below the subsection of License under the section Restrictions.
133. For further detail *see* Bahtiyar, pp. 118–119; Bilgili & Demirkapı, pp. 243–246; Bilgili & Demirkapı (Dersler), pp. 175–177; Pulaşlı, pp. 308–311.
134. How to determine the financial power and good reputation is explained in detail by the By-law on Establishment and Working Principles of Insurance Companies and Reinsurance Companies. For

- not hold a preferential share in the voting right or the capital which may influence the auditory board or board of directors or any other administrative or auditory body of financial institutions when subject to liquidation or the company is cited under the second and third paragraph of Article 20 of this Code;
- not be sentenced to imprisonment or convicted of any offences that may adversely affect his or her reputation;
- in the case of a legal entity, the administrative officers and auditors of this entity must also meet the same criteria prescribed for the founding members.

82. Furthermore, the shares must be issued in return for cash payment and must be registered. The amount of required capital is determined every year by the Turkish Ministry of Treasury and Finance.[135] If the company is acting '*within a holding, then the financial standing of the holding company must be sufficient to carry out insurance activities*'.[136] The founding members may draw up the Articles of Association freely. However, they must be compatible with the protective provisions of the insurance legislation. After the legal establishment of the company, a licence must be obtained by the Insurance and Private Pension Regulation and Supervision Agency.[137]

83. A joint stock company is required to have two compulsory bodies: a general assembly and a board of directors. The general assembly is not a permanent body but one in which the partners of the joint stock company are represented and exercise their rights.[138] The board of directors is the representative and administrative body of the joint stock company.[139] According to the Turkish Commercial Code, the board of directors of the joint stock company must be constituted by at least one or more persons.[140] However, the Insurance Activities Act requires that the board of directors must be constituted by at least five persons and the board of auditors by at least two persons.[141]

84. Furthermore, Article 359 of the Commercial Code requires that members of the board of directors must be natural persons or representatives of a legal entity

---

further detail *see* the second section of Art. 2. For the unofficial translation of the By-law *see*, https://www.tsb.org.tr/regulations.aspx?pageID=987 (30.10.2018).

135. According to the Circular 2022/2 the minimum capital must be TRY 325,000,000 for life insurance companies, TRY 435,000,000 for non-life insurance companies; TRY 200,000,000 for reinsurance companies. In any case, the minimum paid capital has to be not less than TRY 36,576,000.
136. Article 3(2)(c) of the Insurance Activities Act.
137. Further details on the licence application and requirements are stipulated under Part Three of the By-laws on the Establishment and Working Principles of Insurance Companies and Reinsurance Companies. For the English version of the By-law visit: http://engyeni.tsrsb.org.tr/sites/default/files/images/Kopyasi_Kurulus_ve_Calisma_Esaslari_Yonetmeligi-son.pdf (10.9.2014). For further information *see* the subsection titled License under the section titled Restrictions.
138. For further detail on general assembly and its meeting procedure *see* Bahtiyar, 126–164; Bilgili & Demirkapı, 259–361; Bilgili & Demirkapı (Dersler), 185–221; Pulaşlı, 334–392.
139. For further detail on the board of directors, its nomination, its duties, its members rights and responsibilities *see* Bahtiyar, 165–188; Bilgili & Demirkapı, 362–412; Bilgili & Demirkapı (Dersler), 222–254; Güvel & Güvel, 222–225; Pulaşlı, 393–471.
140. Article 359.
141. Article 4.

having legal capacity and do not have any nomination obstacle (such as being bankrupt), which is stipulated as a condition in the Articles of Association. In addition to these conditions, Article 4(2) of the Insurance Activities Act requires that the members of the board of directors of insurance and reinsurance companies fulfil the conditions for the founding members (except financial power) of insurance and reinsurance companies; for example, they must have at least three years of experience in certain professional areas, and the majority of members must hold an undergraduate degree.[142] The same conditions are stipulated for the members of the board of auditors as well.[143]

§2. Cooperatives (Mutual Insurance Companies)

85. According to Article 3 of the Insurance Activities Act, insurance or reinsurance companies that operate in Turkey may be established as a cooperative as well. However, the Insurance Activities Act does not stipulate any further detail on which insurance or reinsurance companies can or cannot be established as cooperatives. The Commercial Code stipulates certain obligations for mutual insurance companies. According to Article 1402 of the Turkish Commercial Code, a mutual insurance corporation must be established as a cooperative. Mutual insurance is the unification of persons (legal entities of natural persons) who undertake to compensate for the prejudice of one of them in the event of realization of risk. Even in the definition of this type of insurance, the idea of a cooperative is clear. A group of persons is unified for insuring their risks on one hand and for diminishing their expenses on the other.[144]

86. Cooperatives are classified as commercial companies according to Article 124(1) of the Turkish Commercial Code; however, the rules regulating them are not stipulated under the Turkish Commercial Code. A special Code of Cooperatives[145]

142. *See* para. 58.
143. According to Art. 400 of the Turkish Commercial Code, the members of the board of auditors must be chartered accountants, certified public accountants or companies constituted by these accountants and must not have any conflict of interest with the subject of their supervision (for instance, they must not be involved in any legal acts that they control nor the party to any agreement or must an employee of the same company). According to the old Turkish Commercial Code which was in operation until July 2012, the board of auditors was a compulsory body. The Commercial Code in operation now amends the whole structure of the board of auditors. Accordingly, the board of auditors is no longer a compulsory body for regular joint stock companies. Therefore, joint stock companies must nominate an independent auditor. That may be an independent auditor company or certified public accountant or chartered accountant. For further details on the stipulations of the Turkish Commercial Code *see* Bilgili & Demirkapı, pp. 420–438; Bahtiyar, pp. 190–207; Bilgili & Demirkapı (Dersler), pp. 255–267; Poroy, Tekinalp & Çamoğlu, pp. 450, 454–462; Pulaşlı, pp. 473–504. Therefore, as it exists some By-laws under Art. 4 of the Insurance Activities Act, the auditory board must still be classified as a compulsory body for insurance or reinsurance joint stock companies. For further detail on auditory board *see* the subsection below on cooperatives.
144. For further detail on mutual insurance *see* Mertol Can, '*Türk Özel Sigorta Hukuku*', 3rd ed., (İmaj Yayınevi, 2009), pp. 223–224; Kender, *Sigorta Hukuku,* pp. 37–38; Meriç, pp. 38–40.
145. Act No. 1163 OG. No. 13195, Date: 10.5.1969.

regulates the establishment, organization, activities and termination of cooperatives. A cooperative is established in four stages.[146] In the first stage, the Articles of Association comprehending the compulsory stipulations[147] must be prepared and signed by at least seven founding members. In the second stage, the signatures of the founding members must be notarized. According to Article 3(1) of the Code of Cooperatives, the approbation of the Ministry of Trade must be obtained in the third stage. In the fourth and final stage, the cooperative is incorporated by registration with the Turkish Trade Registry.[148]

87. Along with these provisions of the Code of Cooperatives, the Insurance Activities Act stipulates some additional conditions. In light of these conditions, it can be evaluated that there exist two types of insurance cooperatives. The first type is mutual insurance cooperatives, which may not execute an insurance contract with third parties.[149] In other words, such mutual insurance cooperatives may only execute insurance contracts with their members.[150] This type of mutual insurance cooperative may not have less than 200 partners, and managers may not be granted any privileges.[151] The second type of insurance cooperatives that have the possibility to execute insurance contracts with third parties. In other words, the legal capacity of this type of insurance cooperative is not limited to the execution of insurance contracts with their members. These cooperatives must obtain a permit from the Insurance and Supervision Regulation and Supervision Agency and stipulate this in their Articles of Association.[152] Furthermore, they must raise their capital to the amount determined by the Agency in order to start or continue with their activities.[153]

88. The Insurance Activities Act does not stipulate any provisions concerning the founding members. Therefore, by analogy, the qualifications required for the founding members of the joint stock companies in terms of reputation and performance (such as not being bankrupt or effecting a composition; having enough financial power and good reputation and not being sentenced to imprisonment or

146. Article 4 of the Code of Cooperatives.
147. According to Art. 4 of the Code of Cooperatives, the Articles of Association must include the following stipulations: the trade name and domicile address of the cooperative; its aim (purpose) and fields of activity; terms and conditions for being a partner and forfeiting the partnership; the share interests of the partners and the mode of payment of the capital, obligation to pay one-fourth of the capital in cash; the capital in kinds (the partner will or will not put capital in kinds); the legal responsibility structure of the partner from the engagement of the cooperative; the roles, competences and liabilities of its administrative and auditor bodies and the mode of election of these bodies; terms and conditions on the representation of the cooperatives; terms and conditions on the yearly calculation of incomes and expenditures; the names, surnames and business addresses of the founding members.
148. For further detail on the establishment procedure of the cooperatives *see* Bilgili & Demirkapı, pp. 785–786; Bilgili & Demirkapı (Dersler), pp. 457–458.
149. Article 3(3)(a) of the Insurance Activities Act.
150. For further detail *see* Meriç, 38.
151. For further detail on the founding members *see* Meriç, pp. 38–39.
152. Article 3(4) of the Insurance Activities Act.
153. *See* para. 58. For further details *see* Meriç, pp. 39–42.

convicted of offences that may adversely affect his or her reputation) are required for the founding members of the cooperatives as well.[154]

89. A cooperative must have three compulsory bodies: the general assembly, the board of directors and the auditor(s). The general assembly is where the partners are represented and their rights are exercised. It is not a permanent body.[155] The board of directors is the permanent, representative and administrative body of the cooperatives.[156] According to Article 55 of the Code of Cooperatives, the board of directors must have at least three members. However, Article 4 of the Insurance Activities Act, as an exception, stipulates that the board of directors must be constituted by at least five persons.

90. Furthermore, Article 56 of the Code of Cooperatives requires that members of the board of directors: must be Turkish citizens having legal capacity; should not have any other membership to the board of directors of any other cooperatives having the same field of activity; and should not have any nomination obstacles (such as being bankrupt). In addition to these conditions, according to the second paragraph of Article 4 of the Insurance Activities Act, the members of the board of directors of insurance and reinsurance companies must fulfil the conditions of the founding members (except for the financial power requirement) of insurance and reinsurance companies and cooperatives; they must have at least three years of experience in certain professional areas, and the majority of the members must hold an undergraduate degree.

91. The auditor(s) is stipulated as the compulsory body of the cooperatives according to Article 65 of the Code of Cooperatives. The duty of auditor(s) is to supervise the whole transactions, accounting and financial structure of the cooperative. A minimum number of auditors are not stipulated in the Code of Cooperatives. Therefore, according to the first paragraph of Article 4 of the Insurance Activities Act, the auditors of the insurance and reinsurance companies and cooperatives may not be less than two persons.

92. Furthermore, for the requirement of the auditors, Article 65 of the Code of Cooperatives refers to Article 56 of the same Code on the requirements of the board of directors' members. In addition to those conditions, according to paragraph 6 of Article 4 of the Insurance Activities Act, the auditors of the insurance and reinsurance companies must fulfil the conditions of the founding members (except financial power); must have at least three years of experience in some areas and must hold an undergraduate degree.

---

154. For further detail *see* Meriç, pp. 40–42.

155. For further detail on general assembly and its meeting procedure *see* Bilgili & Demirkapılı, pp. 796–799; Bilgili & Demirkapı (Dersler), pp. 469–471.

156. For further detail on the board of directors, its nomination, its duties, and its members' rights and responsibilities *see* Bilgili & Demirkapılı, pp. 799–800; Bilgili & Demirkapılı (Dersler), pp. 471–473.

§3. Foreign Insurance Companies

93. Foreign insurance companies may also operate in the Turkish market. The competence of regulating the principles and procedures for the operation of foreign insurance companies belongs to the President.[157] Decree regarding International Activities in the Field of the Insurance Sector has been put into force, to regulate international operations and activities in the insurance sector in Turkey.[158] According to the Decree, foreign insurance or reinsurance companies or cooperatives may operate in Turkey only by establishing a branch.[159] The number of branches is not limited. Where foreign insurance companies establish more than one branch, one of the branches must be designated as the primary headquarters. In such a case, a board of directors, constituted by at least three persons must be appointed as managers of this headquarter branch. According to the Decree, without prejudice to its articles, the branch activities of foreign insurance and reinsurance companies must comply with the regulations of the Insurance Activities Act and any subsequent legal provisions.

94. Regarding the establishment or organizational procedures of foreign insurance companies or cooperatives, a special Code of Direct Foreign Investment[160] regulates the principle of equality between foreign and Turkish national investors. In other words, without prejudice to any other specific provisions (such as the Insurance Activities Act or the Decree), a foreign company or cooperative is established and operated in accordance with the same rules that apply to Turkish national companies or cooperatives.[161]

§4. Restrictions in the Field of Activities of the Insurance Companies

95. Although the Turkish Commercial Code and Code of Cooperatives stipulate the possibility of having multiple fields of activity for joint stock companies and cooperatives, Article 3 of the Insurance Activities Act proscribes this possibility for insurance companies. In other words, insurance or reinsurance companies or cooperatives may not have any other field of activity other than insurance. Furthermore, Article 5(2) of the Insurance Activities Act states that an insurance company may only operate in life or non-life insurance groups. That is to say, even the groups of

157. Article 3(5) of the Insurance Activities Act.
158. OG. No. 26602, Date: 3.8.2007.
159. Article 1 of the Degree regarding International Activities in the Field of Insurance Sector.
160. Act No. 4875 OG. No. 25141, Date: 17.6.2003.
161. Furthermore, it must be noted here that for the creation of more than one branch in Turkey by a foreign investor, the appointment of a board of director can involve a different application than for a Turkish national company. Therefore, in such a case, the third section of the first article of the Decision precisely states that such board and the director and the vice directors may be classified as the general manager and vice general managers of insurance and reinsurance companies.

operation of insurance companies are limited by insurance legislation. By this restriction, the law aims to keep the financial means of insurance companies under the insurance policyholders' claims.[162]

§5. Participation Insurance ('Takaful')

96. The definition of Takaful had been included in a draft[163] legislation by using the term 'participation insurance activities'. The reason for including this explicit definition of Islamic insurance in the draft was related to the activities of Gulf States wishing to invest in the Turkish insurance sector and expecting to see such an explicit reference to Takaful in the legislation. *Participation insurance activities* when dealing with Takaful was preferred to ensuring terminological uniformity with the principle of 'participation banking'. For Islamic banking, the term 'participation banking' is employed in the Turkish banking legislation.[164] However, the reference to participation insurance activities had been withdrawn from the draft legislation – together with the draft article allowing Lloyd's to operate in Turkey.[165] Although not explicitly defined, insurance companies have been operating on participation insurance activities principles since 2015.

97. Eventually, a by-law for the participation insurance working procedures and principles was published in September 2017.[166] The by-law was adopted to ensure proper functioning, development, follow-up and trustworthiness of the system, and to protect the rights and interests of the participants. According to the by-law, participation insurance means a type of insurance where the participants participate in the risk fund to meet the claims of themselves or other participants related to the compensation and/or cash build-up. The risk fund is managed in accordance with the principle of participation finance by an insurance company that is properly licensed. This insurance is based on common risk share and solidarity. Reinsurance is also possible as participation insurance.

98. There are three models in the management of the participation insurance company: In the first model the consideration of the participation insurance company for the management of the risk fund and for other technical and legal transactions is determined in accordance with the profit share under the human (labour) capital and financial capital partnership. In the second model, the company takes a retainer fee for the management of the risk fund and other technical and legal issues in relation to insurance. The third model is a combination of the first two models. In the third model, the company takes a retainer fee for the management of the risk fund as well as for the technical and legal issues. Technical profit is fully distributed

162. For further detail *see* Can, pp. 233–234; Kender, *Sigorta Hukuku,* p. 37; Meriç, pp.47–51.
163. At http://www.tbmm.gov.tr/sirasayi/donem24/yil01/ss705.pdf.
164. Banking Act, Act No. 5411 O.J. Date: 1.11.2005 No. 25983*bi.*
165. *See* §328.
166. OG. No. 30186, Date: 20.9.2017.

among the participants; however, investment profit is shared between the participant and the company as agreed before. The insurance company may choose another management model other than these three models subject to the approval of the advisory board of the company. In that case, the management fee and its calculation method must be determined in advance. It must also be announced on the website of the company and be inserted in the insurance information form of the company. Whichever management model is applied, it must be stated in the insurance contract.

99. The company manages separately the risk fund that is composed of the participants' contribution and the shareholders' or members' contribution. The company may be in the form of a mutual company. In that case, the risk fund that is composed of the contributions of the participants and accounts of the members must be managed separately.

100. All information in relation to the participation insurance, including definition and principles of it, differences between the conventional insurance and the participation insurance, management model, must be announced on the website of the company.

101. Participation insurance companies may take out reinsurance/participation reinsurance protection to manage the risks of risk funds. In order to take out reinsurance protection, the advisory board's approval is necessary. Additionally, participants must be informed of reinsurance protection.

Chapter 2. Access to Business

§1. Authorization in Turkey

102. Due to the social and economic importance of insurance, the law has traditionally required insurance or reinsurance companies or cooperatives to obtain an establishment permit before commencing their business activities.[167] The requirement for the establishment permit was abrogated for the harmonization of the Turkish Insurance Activities Act to the *acquis communautaire.*[168] Although the establishment permit has been abrogated, Article 5 of the Insurance Activities Act stipulates that insurance or reinsurance companies or cooperatives need to obtain a licence for commencing their business activities. This licence may be classified both as an establishment permit and as a regulatory supervision tool to ensure that all insurance or reinsurance companies or cooperatives meet the legal requirements to establish an insurance business.[169] The competent authority for granting a licence is the Insurance and Private Pension Regulation and Supervision Agency.[170]

§2. Conditions for Licence

103. The conditions for assessing a licence application and granting a licence are stipulated under Articles 5 and 6 of the Insurance Activities Act. According to Article 5, an insurance company or cooperative must not commence its business activities unless and until it obtains a licence. In relation to the principle of publicity, the licence must be registered with the Trade Registry and published in the Trade Registry Gazette.

104. In relation to the licence application process, the insurance company or cooperative must first complete its establishment procedures pursuant to Article 3 of the Insurance Activities Act before applying for the licence. Furthermore, Article 5(4) of the Insurance Activities Act stipulates that the insurance company or cooperative must apply for a licence within one year of such an establishment.[171] Article 11(4) of the Regulation sets out the list of documents that must be filed to the Insurance and Private Pension Regulation and Supervision Agency for the initial licence application. Furthermore, documents that must be annexed for subsequent licence applications are detailed under Article 13. When it comes to licence applications by

167. For further detail and the situation under the repealed Insurance Audit Act No. 7397 *see* Can M, pp. 225–227; Kender, *Sigorta Hukuku,* p. 48; Meriç, 43–44.
168. For further detail *see* Kender, *Sigorta Hukuku,* pp. 48–49; Meriç, 44–47.
169. For further detail on the legal nature of the licence *see* Aral İrem, '*Hayat Dışı Sigorta Şirketlerinin Denetimi*' (XII Levha Yayınları, Şubat 2010), pp. 122–124; Kender, *Sigorta Hukuku,* p. 56; Meriç, 111–113.
170. Article 5 of the Insurance Activities Act.
171. Kender, pp. 50–54; Meriç, pp. 120–122.

foreign insurance companies, Article 15 of the Regulation stipulates a more detailed list of documents, such as formal documents relating to the establishment of the headquarters branch in Turkey.[172]

105. The assessment procedure for the licence application is regulated under Article 6 of the Insurance Activities Act. Accordingly, the licence is only granted if the founding members, managers and auditors of the insurance company meet the criteria detailed in the legislation; the business plan shows that the rights and benefits of the parties are sufficiently protected; the application gives sufficient statements or information; and the insurance or reinsurance company has the necessary infrastructure to perform the requirements of the insurance business as requested in the licence. If all such criteria stipulated under Article 6 are not met, the licence application is rejected.[173] Article 16(1) requires the Insurance and Private Pension Regulation and Supervision Agency to assess all licence applications within a maximum period of three months for an initial licence and two months for any subsequent licences. The authority to grant or reject the licence is an administrative decision based on significant discretionary powers and competencies of the Insurance and Private Pension Regulation and Supervision Agency. Therefore, in the event that the licence application is rejected, the applicant company or cooperative may bring an action for rescission to the Council of the State.[174]

106. Due to the administrative nature of the licence application and assessment process, a procedure for withdrawing a licence must also be regulated in detail. Accordingly, the Insurance and Private Pension Regulation and Supervision Agency can decide to withdraw a licence in the event that:

- there is a breach of the terms relating to the grant of the licence, and this breach is not corrected or resolved within a given time period;
- a contract has not been executed within one year after the grant of the licence or continuously within six months;
- the rights and benefits of the insurance policyholders are endangered due to practices in contravention of applicable legislation;
- there are liabilities arising from a violation of the Code and related legislation; or
- there are major derogations from the objectives of the original business plan.

107. As well as for granting a licence, any withdrawal must be registered with the Trade Registry and must be published in the Turkish Trade Registry Gazette and in two daily newspapers. In the event that a licence is withdrawn, the situation of the insurance policyholders must be protected. Article 7(2) of the Insurance Activities Act provides regulatory protection for the insurance policyholders, namely the

172. For the full text of these articles, visit: http://engyeni.tsrsb.org.tr/sites/default/files/images/Kopyasi_Kurulus_ve_Calisma_Esaslari_Yonetmeligi-son.pdf (10.9.2013); for detailed explanation *see* Aral, pp. 124–133.
173. For further detail on the criteria and licence demand rejection *see* Aral, pp. 133–135; Meriç, pp. 140–144.
174. For further detail on the action *see* Aral, pp. 135–139; Meriç, pp. 144–146.

clients of the insurance company that has had its licence withdrawn. Accordingly, this insurance company must transfer its portfolio,[175] or the transfer can be done ex officio by the authorization of the Ministry.[176]

175. For further detail on portfolio transfer *see* below the subsection Portfolio Transfer of Insurance and Reinsurance Companies and Cooperatives under the section During the Liquidation.

176. It should be stated that the Ministry responsible for regulating insurance is the Ministry of Treasury and Finance.

Chapter 3. Supervision

108. Insurance activity is based on trust. In other words, insurance companies gain the trust of the insurance policyholders by compensating for their loss in the realization of risks. As long as insurance companies preserve their financial power, insurance activity will continue to develop. Therefore, the financial power of insurance companies must be regulated and supervised.[177]

109. Throughout the world, there are three different methods for such regulation and supervision. One way relates to the *system of publicity*, whereby insurance companies must publish correct information about the financial status of the company or cooperative during the establishment and operation of its activities. Under this system, the role of the law and State is to regulate and supervise the correct and regular provision of the necessary information to insurance policyholders by the insurance companies. However, this system has been criticized for being useless as the insurance policyholders do not have enough knowledge or experience to analyse the information provided by the insurance companies.[178]

110. Under the *normative system*, specific legislation determines all of the terms and conditions that the insurance companies must adhere to and respect as the second way of supervision. In other words, the State controls the compliance and conformity of insurance companies to legal provisions. However, this system is criticized for the unlikelihood of legislators being able to anticipate all possible problems and legal solutions when drafting the applicable law.[179]

111. *Material control* system is the third and mostly used system in the world, which is based on State control of insurance companies during their establishment, operational activities and termination. The idea of protecting the interests of insurance policyholders lies at the source of State control, and the most important characteristic of this system is the power of discretion granted to administrative organizations.[180] Aiming to harmonize the Turkish insurance system with the *acquis communautaire*, the Insurance Activities Act has adopted the control system.[181]

112. In order to continue with their business activities, insurance or reinsurance companies or cooperatives must have a strong financial structure. Thus, Insurance Activities Act has special provisions for technical reserves, guarantees and a prohibition on assets reducing transactions; it also regulates the authorizations of the

---

177. Aral, 8–10; Çeker, 31; Kender, *Sigorta Hukuku,* p. 39; Meriç, p. 20.
178. For further detail and critical discussion of the system of publicity *see* Aral, pp. 10–11; Kender, *Sigorta Hukuku,* pp. 42–43; Meriç, p. 20.
179. For further details and critical discussion *see* Aral, pp. 11–12; Kender, *Sigorta Hukuku,* p. 43; Meriç, p. 21.
180. The power of discretion is granted to furnish the licence and supervise the activities of the insurance companies and cooperatives. For further details on its critical discussion *see* Aral, 12–15; Kender, *Sigorta Hukuku,* pp. 43–44; Meriç, pp. 21–22.
181. Kender, *Sigorta Hukuku,* pp. 46–47; Meriç, pp. 22–24, 26–28.

Insurance and Private Pension Regulation and Supervision Agency in relation to accounts, financial records and amendments on the partnership. Most of these regulatory provisions are included in the fourth part of the Insurance Activities Act entitled '*Financial Structure*'.

113. Similar to the regulation of the establishment and business activities of insurance companies and cooperatives, the liquidation process is also regulated to protect the rights of the policyholders and insureds. Insurance or reinsurance companies and cooperatives may terminate their activities in accordance with the provisions of the Commercial Code or Code of Cooperatives. Once the dissolution is determined, the joint stock company or cooperative enters a phase called 'winding up' or 'liquidation'.

§1. Technical Reserves

114. Article 16 of the Insurance Activities Act sets forth the obligations and principles for insurance and reinsurance companies and cooperatives with respect to the allocation of technical reserves. Technical reserves may be defined as the guarantee of the obligations of insurance and reinsurance companies and cooperatives arising from contracts that have been executed with insurance policyholders.

115. Six types of technical reserves may be determined pursuant to this article: Technical reserve of unearned premiums;[182] reserve of unexpired risks;[183] reserve of equalization;[184] mathematical reserve;[185] reserve of outstanding claims;[186] and reserves of bonus and rebate.[187] It is important to underline that for technical

182. Technical reserve of unearned premiums may be defined as follows: ' ... *for each insurance contract in effect, consists of that part of the gross premium which extends to the next fiscal period or periods on a daily basis, and in respect of annual life assurances in effect or those life assurances with periods longer than a year for which accumulation premiums are collected, it consists of that part of the gross premiums which extends to the next period or periods after the portion that has been set aside for the accumulation and the expense shares of the accumulation premiums are deducted* ... '.
183. Unexpired risks' reserve may only be allocated if *the unearned risk premiums reserve is inadequate compared to the risk undertaken by the company or cooperative and its level of expected cost.*
184. The main aim in the allocation of the equalization reserve is *to balance the claims rate fluctuations in following fiscal periods and to cover special risks that are determined by the Insurance and Private Pension Regulation and Supervision Agency.*
185. Mathematical reserve consists of the *sum of the reserves specified in the contract's technical terms and calculated using statistical and actuarial methods in order to cover the liabilities of insurance companies to policyholders and beneficiaries.*
186. The outstanding claims' reserve may be defined as *the amount of claims that has been reported but not yet paid, estimated amount of claims that has been incurred but not reported and reserves for expenses arising from such claims, and of additional reserves allocated according to the principles set by the Insurance and Private Pension Regulation and Supervision Agency for adequacy when such amounts prove to be inadequate.*
187. Bonus and rebate reserve is *the amounts of bonuses and rebates reserved for insured or beneficiaries according to the technical results of the current year if the company gives bonuses or applies rebates.*

reserves, the reinsurer share is proportional to the risk and premium. According to the last paragraph of Article 16 of the Insurance Activities Act, the assets of insurance and reinsurance companies and cooperatives must be adequate with their technical reserves.[188] Because of their importance, the technical reserves of insurance and reinsurance companies and cooperatives are supervised during the activities of the companies and cooperatives. In the event of non-allocation or inadequate allocation of technical reserves, Article 35(16) provides for a judicial fine punishment.[189]

§2. GUARANTEES

116. Article 17 of the Insurance Activities Act sets forth the principles on the allocation of guarantees by insurance and reinsurance companies and cooperatives. Guarantees may be defined as the provision of the commitments of insurance and reinsurance companies and cooperatives arising from the contracts that have been executed. The article foresees a distinction between life insurance or reinsurance companies or cooperatives and non-life insurance or reinsurance companies or cooperatives. Paragraphs 2 and 3 of the aforesaid article give a wide range of discretionary power to the Insurance and Private Pension Regulation and Supervision Agency in relation to the allocation of the guarantees of life insurance or reinsurance companies or cooperatives.

117. For non-life insurance companies or cooperatives' guarantees, Article 17(4) of the Insurance Activities Act requires the establishment of a guarantee fund in accordance with the Regulation.[190] Paragraph 5 of this Article 17 gives discretionary power to the Agency pertaining to the release of guarantees in branches in which insurance business activities have been terminated. The Agency also has a wide range of discretionary power for increasing or decreasing guarantees based on the allocation of special guarantees and on the arrangements of the financial structure and the capital requirement of insurance and reinsurance companies and the type of assets to be blocked. In the case of non-allocation or inadequate allocation of guarantees, Article 35(16) of the Insurance Activities Act[191] provides for a judicial fine punishment. Furthermore, it must also be noted that guarantees cannot be subjected to bankruptcy or liquidation and must not be exposed to an injunction or precautionary seizures until the whole payment of the receivables of the insurance policyholders is made.

---

188. For further information on the assets in which technical reserves may be invested, *see* the By-law on the Technical Reserves of the Insurance and Reinsurance Companies and Retirement Companies and the Assets in Which Technical Reserves Are to Be Invested OG. No. 26606, Date: 7.8.2007.
189. For further detail *see* Aral, 151–153.
190. For further information *see* the By-law on the Quantification and Assessment of the Capital Adequacy of the Insurance and Reinsurance Companies and Retirement Companies OG. No. 26761, Date: 19.1.2008.
191. For further detail *see* Aral, 140–145.

§3. Accountancy and Record Orders

118. According to Article 18 of the Insurance Activities Act, all the financial statements, accounts and records of insurance and reinsurance companies and cooperatives are subjected to the control of the Insurance and Private Pension Regulation and Supervision Agency. Accordingly, all financial statements must be compatible with the principles set out by the Agency to which they must be sent. Furthermore, Article 18 mandates that insurance or reinsurance companies or cooperatives publish their financial statements (balance sheets, profit and loss statements, etc.) and appoint an independent auditory firm to audit those statements.

119. Article 18 also involves authorities of the Agency checking the publication of financial statements and other ancillary financial records that companies and cooperatives are expected to keep on demand. Non-compliance with these accounting principles and the obligation to publish these financial records can result in insurance or reinsurance companies or cooperatives being punished by a judicial fine of TRY 12,000 in accordance with Article 34(2)(h) of the Insurance Activities Act.[192]

§4. Prohibition of Asset-Reducing Transactions

120. Article 19 of the Insurance Activities Act prohibits any kind of asset-reducing transactions, which are defined as the use of the company's resources directly or indirectly for personal purposes; the execution of transactions reducing the value of an asset in contravention of the rules of goodwill or the realization of disguised earning transfers by any means. In other words, these examples classified as asset-reducing transactions are not *numerus clausus*.[193]

121. For any breach of these asset-reducing transaction prohibitions, Article 35 of the Insurance Activities Act imposes a judicial fine punishment of up to 1,000 days.[194] For any breach of goodwill, Article 35(17) extends this punishment to 2,000 days. Furthermore, for any embezzlement of the company or cooperative funds or other assets, the chairman and/or the members of the board of directors and/or other employees are liable for a term of imprisonment from six months to twelve years under Article 35(3).[195]

§5. Strengthening of Financial Structure

122. According to Article 20 of the Insurance Activities Act, if the financial structure of an insurance or reinsurance company or cooperative is weakened or

192. *Ibid.*, 176–185.
193. In other words, these examples may be broadening.
194. The judicial fine is a payment done by the condemned to the State treasury.
195. For further detail *see* Aral, 170–171.

deteriorated, the Ministry may require certain measures to be taken for strengthening its financial structure. For instance, Article 20(2) authorizes the Ministry to transfer the portfolio or limit the portfolio in order to strengthen the financial structure of the insurance or reinsurance company or cooperative. If the company or cooperative fails to strengthen its financial structure, the Ministry may revoke its right to execute further contracts, withdraw its licence or block its assets in accordance with Article 20(3).

§6. Approval of Certain Transactions During the Activities

123. Insurance and reinsurance companies and cooperatives must obtain the authorization of the Insurance and Private Pension Supervision and Regulation Agency in relation to certain transactions during their activities. For instance, Article 8 of the Insurance Activities Act requires the approval of the Agency for any amendments to the Articles of Association. As such, any amendments that are not approved by the Agency may not be discussed in the general assembly of the insurance and reinsurance companies and cooperatives. If such amendments are accepted without the approval of the Agency, such amendments cannot be registered with the Trade Registry.[196]

124. Moreover, Article 9 of the Code stipulates that insurance or reinsurance companies or cooperatives must obtain the authorization of the Agency for any share transfer of more than 10% of the capital or transfer granting privileges in the nomination of the members of the executive boards. Where such transfers are made without the authorization of the Agency, the responsible persons are liable for a judicial fine of up to 300 days[197] under Article 35(12) of the Insurance Activities Act.[198]

§7. Dissolution and Liquidation

125. A joint-stock company's activities may be terminated by auto-dissolution or by dissolution. The reasons for auto-dissolution stipulated under Article 529 of the Commercial Code are:

- the scope of operation of the company becomes impossible;
- the expiration of the term of the entity (if the company does not continue its activities);
- a cause for termination specified in the Articles of Association is triggered;
- the company is declared bankrupt by a court decision; or
- the occurrence of any other auto-dissolution circumstances set forth by applicable legal provisions may be cited as reasons for auto-dissolution.

---

196. For further detail on the subject *see* Aral, pp. 171–172.
197. The judicial fine should be calculated according to the penalty of imprisonment.
198. For further detail on this subject *see* Aral, pp. 172–173.

In the event of any of these reasons, the company may enter into the phase of liquidation without taking any further decision or notification.[199]

126. There are three main reasons for dissolution, namely: (i) the voluntary dissolution of the joint-stock company by a decision of the general assembly; (ii) the non-existence of a legally required body or the general assembly is not able to convene; and (iii) dissolution with a justifiable reason. In the event of any such reasons, the competent person (or legal entity) or body must fulfil the necessary legal procedures for dissolution.[200] Except for bankruptcy, the dissolution must be registered with the Trade Registry and must be published in Trade Registry Gazette.[201]

127. After the nomination of the liquidation officers by the general assembly or according to the Articles of Association (if it contains such a stipulation), the liquidation process begins with the preparation of the first inventory and the balance sheet.[202] As the second step, the creditors must be invited to declare their receivables, and the liquidation officers must take the necessary measures to protect the receivables of the creditors who did not declare their receivables, but they can be understood by the balance sheet.[203] The liquidation officers must then liquidate all the assets of the company and pay the creditors their receivables and the return of the share value.[204] Once all the liquidation procedure is completed, the final act is to remove the company from the Trade Registry, and this removal must be published in the Trade Registry Gazette.[205]

128. In terms of cooperatives, Article 81 of the Code of Cooperatives regulates the triggers for the dissolution of cooperatives, without distinguishing dissolution from auto-dissolution. Accordingly, a cooperative may be dissolved:

- as a requirement in its Articles of Association;
- by the decision of the general assembly;
- by a declaration of bankruptcy;
- by a determination by the Ministry that the purpose of the cooperative has become impossible to achieve; or

199. The merger of the company is another reason for auto-dissolution. Therefore, in the case of a merger, the company's assets are not subjected to liquidation. Nevertheless they may be subjected to the portfolio transfer that will be explained below. Therefore, a merger is not cited nor analysed under this subsection.
For further detail on the auto-dissolution, *see* Bahtiyar, pp. 286–291; Bilgili & Demirkapı, pp. 565–568; Bilgili & Demirkapı, pp. 322–323; Pulaşlı, pp. 564–578.

200. For further detail on dissolution, *see* Bahtiyar, pp. 291–294; Bilgili & Demirkapı, pp. 568–574; Bilgili & Demirkapı (Dersler), pp. 322–323; Pulaşlı, pp. 564–578.

201. For further detail on the dissolution procedure *see* Bilgili & Demirkapı, p. 574; Bilgili & Demirkapı (Dersler), p. 323; Pulaşlı, pp. 586–587.

202. Bilgili & Demirkapı, pp. 576–579; Bilgili & Demirkapı (Dersler), pp. 325–328; Pulaşlı, pp. 587–589.

203. Bilgili & Demirkapı, p. 579; Bilgili & Demirkapı (Dersler), p. 327.

204. Bilgili & Demirkapı, pp. 580–581; Bilgili & Demirkapı (Dersler), p. 328.

205. Bilgili & Demirkapı, p. 582; Bilgili & Demirkapı, p. 329.

– the general assembly has not been able to convene for at least three years.[206]

129. The liquidation procedure is realized by the liquidation officers nominated by the general assembly or a competent court. If no officer is nominated, the members of the board of directors must act as competent liquidation officers.[207] According to Article 82 of the Code of Cooperatives, except for bankruptcy, the dissolution must be registered with the Trade Registry and must be published in the Trade Registry Gazette. After the liquidation of the assets and payment of the receivables and the share value, Article 83 of the Code of the Cooperatives states that any remaining capital is to be shared between the partners, but only if there is a special provision in the Articles of Association that so provides. If there is no such provision, the remaining capital will be allocated to the Turkish National Cooperatives Union to be used to develop other cooperatives. Finally, Article 98 of the Code of Cooperatives states that the provisions of the Commercial Code on the joint stock company will also be used for cooperatives in any case of a lacuna. In other words, the provisions of the Commercial Code pertaining to the liquidation of joint stock companies can also be applied to the liquidation of cooperatives.

130. Insurance Activities Act does not contain detailed provisions regarding liquidation. Instead, Article 10 provides legal authority to the Insurance and Private Pension Supervision and Regulation Agency to intervene and replace the liquidation officers if necessary. Therefore, Article 23 of the Insurance Activities Act only provides regulation for voluntary liquidation, which can be applied by analogy to all other kinds of liquidation. Article 23 first requires the approval of the Ministry for starting the liquidation procedure. Article 23(2) then lists the documents that must be submitted to the Agency, including a certified copy of the resolution for liquidation and a comprehensive report concerning the reasons for liquidation; the cover of the insurance policyholders' receivables during the liquidation process and the status of the revenues and expenses. In addition to these documents, the liquidation of Turkish branches of foreign insurance companies must also include a resolution of the authorized body of the headquarters company as well.

§8. Portfolio Transfer

131. As mentioned above regarding the dissolution of insurance or reinsurance companies or cooperatives, the Insurance Activities Act does not provide any special regulations. Therefore, the dissolution of insurance or reinsurance companies or cooperatives is undertaken in accordance with the provisions of the Commercial Code and Code of Cooperatives. However, the Insurance Activities Act does regulate the transfer of the portfolio in order to protect the specific rights and receivables of the policyholders.

---

206. For further detail *see* Bilgili & Demirkapı, p. 801; Bilgili & Demirkapı (Dersler), p. 474.
207. *Ibid.*

132. Portfolio transfer may be explained as the transfer of the whole or part of the insurance contract, namely all the claims and receivables of the agreements.[208] Article 7 of the Insurance Activities Act refers to the portfolio transfer when a licence is withdrawn. The portfolio transfer may be done with the authorization of the Ministry.[209] Furthermore, the transfer of the portfolio must be published at least twice in any two national newspapers in Turkey.[210] The policyholders have the possibility to terminate the transferred contracts within three months from the date of becoming aware of such transfer.[211] Details of the portfolio transfer are regulated by the By-law Regarding the Establishment and Other Working Principles of Insurance and Reinsurance Companies.[212] The By-law on Portfolio Transfer stipulates that such transfer must be done among the companies or cooperatives having the licence at the same branch, and the agreement must include the insurance and reinsurance contracts to be transferred; the reserves regarding the portfolio; investment returns and provisions on the guarantees and guarantee fund.[213]

§9. Bankruptcy

133. Due to the fact that insurance or reinsurance companies or cooperatives are at some risk of bankruptcy, their activities and financial status may be subjected to some intervention by the Insurance and Private Pension Supervision and Regulation Agency.[214] The main aim of such intervention is to strengthen the financial status of companies in order to prevent bankruptcy. Thus, in most countries, authorization from a Supervisory Board is needed before being able to declare bankruptcy. However, Turkish insurance law does not specifically require such authorization. Article 10 of the Insurance Activities Act, refers to the provisions of the Turkish Code of Enforcement and Bankruptcy.[215] According to the provisions of the Turkish Code of Enforcement and Bankruptcy, any creditor may demand that a competent court declare bankruptcy for an insurance or reinsurance company or cooperative within its own deliberation.[216] In the event of such a declaration of

208. For further detail and critical analysis of portfolio transfer *see* Aral, pp. 220–221; Kender, *Sigorta Hukuku,* pp. 74–78.
209. Article 10(1) of the Insurance Activities Act. Similar to portfolio transfer, voluntary liquidation must also be done with the authorization of the Ministry. In accordance with this provision, the By-law also regulates the authorization of the Ministry at Art. 22 with a special emphasize on the provisions of the Turkish Commercial Code and related legislations.
210. Article 10(3) of the Insurance Activities Act.
211. *Ibid.*
212. OG. No. 26623, Date: 24.8.2007.
213. Article 22 of the By-law Regarding the Establishment and Other Working Principles of Insurance and Reinsurance Companies.
214. More specifically the Insurance Controlling Board that is affiliated with the Undersecreteriat. For further detail *see* Aral, pp. 24–29.
215. Act No. 2004 OG. No. 2128, Date: 19.6.1932.
216. For further detail and critical discussion *see* Kender, *Sigorta Hukuku*, pp. 80–81.

bankruptcy, the insurance policyholders are placed in the third rank of bankruptcy, and the Agency intervenes and requires the replacement of the authorities of bankruptcy if necessary.[217]

§10. Regulatory and Supervisory Agency

134. Due to the specialized nature of certain insurance and reinsurance activities, the Insurance Activities Act sets out provisions for a special supervisory board. Before transforming into the Presidential Governmental System in 2018, Insurance Supervisory Board had been designed to execute and exercise the supervision duties of the Undersecretariat and the Ministry of Finance. With the transformation from a parliamentary regime into the Presidential Governmental System in 2018 governmental institutions were reorganized.[218] The Ministry of Finance and the Undersecretariat of Treasury were merged and became the Ministry of Treasury and Finance. The Insurance and Private Pension Regulation and Supervision Agency was established to conduct duties regarding the regulation and supervision of the insurance and private pension sectors in 2019.[219] General Directorate of Insurance and the Insurance Supervisory Board were closed down. All duties and responsibilities formerly assigned to the Ministry of Finance (current Ministry of Treasury and Finance), General Directory of Insurance and Insurance Supervisory Board are assigned to Insurance and Private Pension Regulation and Supervision Agency.[220] The Agency owns its public legal entity as well as its administrative and financial autonomy. The headquarter of the Agency is in Istanbul. The Agency is composed of the Insurance and Private Pension Regulation and Supervisory Board and the Presidential Organization.[221]

135. The structure, competencies and responsibilities of the Supervisory Board are respectively explained in the Presidential Decree. The structure of the Supervisory Board consists of five members of whom one is the main president and the

217. Article 10(4) and 10(5) of the Insurance Activities Act. According to the Turkish Code of Enforcement and Bankruptcy once the liquidation of the assets of the company starts; a list of creditors should be done. The rank of the creditor is important because the payment should be done according to the rank. More specifically, once the liquidation is terminated, the payment will start by the creditor placed in the first rank of the list. Thus, the Insurance Activity Act stipulates in detail the rank of the policyholder in the list. For further detail on the ranking of the bankruptcy under Turkish law Bilgen, *İcra ve İflas Hukukunda Sıra Cetveli,* 2nd ed. (Adalet Yayınevi, 2014), pp. 557–661; Baki Kuru, *İcra ve İflas Hukuku El Kitabı*, 2nd ed. (Adalet Yayınevi, 2013), pp. 1322–1339; B. Kuru, R. Arslan & E. Yılmaz E, *İcra ve İflas Hukuku*, 27th ed. (Yetkin Yayınları, 2013), pp. 575–578; H. Pekcanıtez, O. Atalay & M. Özekes, *İcra ve İflas Hukuku*, 11th ed. (Yetkin Yayınları, 2014), pp. 498–500; İE. Postacıoğlu, *İflas Hukuku İlkeleri, Cilt: 1, İflas* (Sulhi Garan Matbaası, 1978), pp. 73, 79–83.
218. By the Decree Law No. 703 OG.30473 (3rd repetitive), 9.7.2018.
219. Presidential Decree No. 47 OG. No. 30922 18.10.2019.
220. Presidential Decree No. 47 Art.4.
221. Presidential Decree No. 47 Art. 3.2.

other one is the secondary president appointed by the President.[222] The Board is the decision-making body of the Agency. The president of the Agency is the president of the Board.

136. The competencies for supervision that were distinguished between the Supervisory Board and the Undersecretariat in accordance with Article 28 of the Insurance Activities Act formerly now merged with the Agency.[223] The Agency must first examine and determine the financial status of the insurance or reinsurance company or cooperative.[224] In order to undertake this process of examination and inspection, the Agency may require all kinds of documents related to the financial status of the insurance or reinsurance company or cooperative. This obligation to provide necessary documents for review also concerns public institutions, such as the Association of Insurance, Reinsurance and Pension Companies of Turkey and other non-governmental organizations as well. The Agency may even demand the professional support of the auditors of these companies and cooperatives. The Agency has the authority to analyse, measure and determine the financial structure of insurance or reinsurance companies or cooperatives and monitor the risks that they may face.[225] Furthermore, the Agency can collect all necessary documentation relating to such supervision of the risk management of companies and cooperatives.[226] All necessary documents related to the financial status of the companies and cooperatives must be delivered to the Agency.[227] The Agency has the obligation of professional discretion.[228] Any person, who discloses such confidential information to third parties or misuses it for their own benefit, will be liable for two to four years imprisonment and a judicial fine of not less than 300 days[229] under Article 35(8) of the Insurance Activities Act.

§11. Other Assisting Organizations

137. In order to develop the insurance and reinsurance business and the confidence of insurance policyholders in insurance companies or cooperatives, governmental and non-governmental organizations must be created. Therefore, other organizations that assist the supervision process must be explained as components of the Supervisory Board of insurance or reinsurance companies or cooperatives.

222. Presidential Decree No. 47 Art.5.
223. Presidential Decree No. 47 Art.4.
224. Article 28(3) of the Insurance Activities Act.
225. Article 28(7) of the Insurance Activities Act.
226. Article 28(8) of the Insurance Activities Act.
227. Article 28(9) of the Insurance Activities Act. More detailed By-law on the subject is provided under the By-law on the Insurance Supervisory Board.
228. In other words, The Supervisory Board's members must not divulge any confidential information obtained during the examination and analysis process.
229. For the judicial fine *see* footnote 166.

I. Independent Auditory Firms

138. Article 18(2) of the Insurance Activities Act requires that insurance or reinsurance companies or cooperatives be audited by an independent auditing firm and publish all necessary financial documents and statements for such audit. In accordance with this article, the Insurance and Private Pension Regulation and Supervision Agency may also prepare the necessary regulation on the independent audit and the competent auditory firm of the insurance and reinsurance companies. Accordingly, two different Regulations on this subject have been prepared and published.[230]

II. Insurance Speciality Committees

139. The specialized financial nature of insurance requires specialized economic services to assist with the supervision of insurance or reinsurance companies or cooperatives. This is the rationale for the Insurance Activities Act providing the Insurance and Private Pension Regulation and Supervision Agency with the authority to create Specialty Committees comprised of people with knowledge and expertise in such business activities. The working principles and competences of these committees are regulated under the By-law on the Insurance Specialty Committees.[231]

III. The Association of Insurance, Reinsurance and Pension Companies of Turkey

140. The creation of a professional governmental organization between the insurance and reinsurance companies and cooperatives is important to develop solidarity between them and prevent unfair competition in the insurance and reinsurance business. Such an organization has been established as the Association of the Insurance, Reinsurance and Pension Companies of Turkey and is regulated under the Insurance Activities Act.

141. According to Article 24 of the Insurance Activities Act, insurance and reinsurance companies and cooperatives are obliged to become a member of the Association of the Insurance, Reinsurance and Pension Companies of Turkey within one month of obtaining the licence. The Association has a very wide regulatory competence over insurance and reinsurance companies and cooperatives, such as the preparation of general terms and conditions of insurance contracts; the creation of

---

230. Namely the By-law on the Independent Audit of Insurance, Reinsurance and Pension Companies and the By-law on the Principles of Independent Insurance Audit. For the Turkish version of these By-laws visit: http://www.tsb.org.tr/default.aspx?pageID=654&yid=65 (12.2.2014); http://www.tsb.org.tr/default.aspx?pageID=654&yid=64 (12.2.2014). For further information on this subject *see* Aral, pp. 30–35.

231. For the Turkish version of the By-law visit: http://www.resmigazete.gov.tr/eskiler/2008/06/20080622-2.htm (12.2.2014). For further detail *see* Aral, 35–37.

professional rules that must be respected by the companies and cooperatives and the supervision of the execution of arbitration clauses in relation to insurance litigation.[232] The working principles, competences and membership stipulations are enacted in detail in the Regulation on the Working Procedures and Principles of the Association of Insurance, Reinsurance and Pension Companies.

IV. Loss Adjusters' Executive Committee

142. Experts appointed as loss adjusters are insurance sector professionals working on damage assessment after the realization of the insured risk. Just like the insurance and reinsurance companies and cooperatives, loss adjusters are regulated and supervised to ensure efficacy and professionalism within the insurance sector. Article 22 of the Insurance Activities Act regulates the conditions and working principles for insurance loss adjusters and states that a natural person or legal entity can only formally be registered as a loss adjuster after obtaining the necessary licence from the Insurance and Private Pension Regulation and Supervision Agency.[233]

143. An organization for loss adjusters had also been established by the Union of Chambers and Commodity Exchanges for the Register. Therefore, in order to ensure the creation of an internal decision-making process and body, a special Loss Adjusters Executive Committee was established under Article 26 of the Insurance Activities Act. This committee has very wide competencies in relation to loss adjusters, such as defining and determining the professional rules and supervision of their activities and the withdrawal of their licence.[234]

V. Insurance Agents Executive Committee

144. Insurance agents are the representatives of insurance or reinsurance companies or cooperatives of their client, the insurance policyholder. Therefore, their role in the insurance and reinsurance sector is crucial.

145. The profession of agents is regulated in detail under the Insurance Activities Act. Article 23 regulates admission conditions and states that a natural person or legal entity can only be registered to work as an agent with the Registry of the Union of Chambers and Commodity Exchanges by first obtaining written permission from the Insurance and Private Pension Regulation and Supervision Agency.[235]

Similar to loss adjusters, a professional organization for agents was also established by the Union of Chambers and Commodity Exchanges, and Article 27 of the Code, therefore, created its own decision-making body referred to as the Insurance

232. For further detail on the Association *see* Aral, pp. 37–49.
233. For further detail on loss adjusters *see* Kender, *Sigorta Hukuku,* pp. 150–157.
234. For further detail on the Committee *see* Aral, pp. 49–54; Kender, *Sigorta Hukuku,* pp. 150–157.
235. For further detail on agents *see* Çeker, pp. 39–49; Kender, *Sigorta Hukuku,* pp. 124–134 and the By-law on the Insurance Agents. For the Turkish version of the By-law visit: http://www.tsb.org.tr/yonetmelikler.aspx?pageID=427 (12.2.2014).

Agents Executive Committee. This committee has very wide authority over agents, such as defining and determining professional rules; the registration and removal of the agents from the Registry; and the imposition of disciplinary punishment.[236] The working principles, competences and membership of agents are stipulated in detail under the Regulation on the Working Procedures and Principles of the Insurance Agents Sector Assembly and the Insurance Agents Executive Committee.[237]

146. The Turkish Insurance Activities Act and Commercial Code regulate most of the protective provisions for insurance and reinsurance companies and cooperatives. The main aim of these protective provisions is to protect the rights of insurance policyholders and to instil confidence in the insurance industry. They also enable regulatory bodies to supervise and control insurance and reinsurance business activity that maintains important links to the economy of the State. It should be noted that the Insurance Activities Act and the Turkish Commercial Code have been harmonized with the *acquis communautaire to* ensure that Turkish insurance law is predominantly up-to-date. Even though some reform is needed for certain insurance subjects, it can be concluded that the body of current legislation is generally sufficient in meeting the regulatory needs of the insurance sector in Turkey.

236. For further detail on the Committee *see* Aral, pp. 49–54; Kender, *Sigorta Hukuku,* pp. 146–150.
237. For the Turkish version of the By-law visit: http://www.tsb.org.tr/default.aspx?pageID=654&yid=9 (12.2.2014).

Part II. The Insurance Contract: General

Chapter 1. Generalities

Meltem Deniz Güner-Özbek

§1. Definition of Insurance

147. Contrary to some countries, there is a general statutory definition for insurance contracts in Turkey. Article 1401 of the Turkish Commercial Code states that:

> (1) An insurance contract means a contract under which the insurer promises, in exchange for a premium, to indemnify a loss caused by the materialisation of the danger (risk) having the consequence of harming the interest, measurable by money, of the concerned person or to effect payment or to fulfil other performances based on the lifetime or upon the occurrence of certain events in the course of the lifetime of one or several persons.[238]

This wording is the same as under the former Turkish Commercial Act, except for some changes to simplify the language. Although it is difficult to give an exact definition of an insurance contract, the purpose of drafting this provision is to assist in the determination of the 'objective fundamental elements' of such a contract. This definition of an insurance contract is criticized by some authors in terms of both its wording and the misuse of some terms.[239] There are similar discussions about the nature of an insurance contract under Swiss Law and German Law. Some analysts support *the risk of loss theory* ('*Gefahrtragung*') while others support *the payment theory* ('*Geldleistung*').[240] Furthermore, there are also specific definitions of active indemnity insurance[241] under the Property Insurance title; passive indemnity insurance[242] under the Liability Insurance title; and Life Insurance[243] in the form of contracts to pay an agreed sum when the insured event under the Life Insurance title occurs.

238. Kerim Atamer et al., *New Turkish Insurance Contract Law (Free Translation of the Provisions of the Turkish Commercial Code Regarding Insurance Contracts)* (Sigorta Hukuku Türk Derneği (AIDA Turkey), 2012), p. 12.
239. Kender, *Sigorta Hukuku,* pp. 164–170.
240. *Ibid.*, pp. 165–168; Çeker, pp. 56–57; Bozer, p. 124.
241. Article 1453 of the Turkish Commercial Code.
242. Article 1473 of the Turkish Commercial Code.
243. Article 1487 of the Turkish Commercial Code.

§2. Categories of Insurance

148. Turkish Commercial Act classifies insurance contracts as follows:

(1) Damage insurance:
   - property insurance;[244] and
   - liability insurance.[245]

(2) Life insurance:
   - life insurance;[246]
   - accident insurance;[247] and
   - sickness and health insurance.[248]

149. Although this classification is practical, the most convenient classification of the insurance contract, in conformity with modern insurance law, is done according to two different criteria.[249] These are:

- Satisfaction of the needs criterion:
  (1) Damage insurance:
    (a) Active insurance.
    (b) Passive insurance.
  (2) Fixed-sum insurance.
- The subject matter of risk:
  (1) Property insurance.
  (2) Insurance of persons.

150. Under damage insurance, the damage incurred by the person(s) is compensated in accordance with indemnity insurance policies. In relation to active damage insurance, the *active* element refers to the values of the property (such as auto, vessel, house, and receivable). However, passive damage insurance compensates for the debts that arise or increase in the property of a person. Liability insurance or reinsurance is a passive type of damage insurance. Fixed-sum insurance is a contract to pay an agreed sum and is only possible for life insurance policies. In relation to the insurance of person classification, life insurance is fixed-sum insurance. However, if life insurance covers funeral costs or if health insurance covers treatment costs, then these are regarded as damage insurance rather than fixed-sum insurance.

244. Articles 1453–1472 of the Turkish Commercial Code.
245. Articles 1473–1486 of the Turkish Commercial Code.
246. Articles 1487–1506 of the Turkish Commercial Code.
247. Articles 1507–1510 of the Turkish Commercial Code.
248. Articles 1511–1519 of the Turkish Commercial Code.
249. Kender, *Sigorta Hukuku,* pp. 207–213.

§3. RISK

151. The concept of risk is fundamental to insurance and is the most essential element of the insurance contract. In a general sense, risk is any event that may be realized in the future and if and when it does, gives rise to damage and loss or some other inconvenience to a person's needs. Due to its inherently uncertain nature, the realization of risk is possible from a range of different causes. The element of *risk* is usually associated with damage insurance such as accident, fire, robbery or liability. Risk is also associated with life insurance and death even though it is a known fact that everybody is going to die one day because the date of death is not known. Nevertheless, the fundamental difference with other insurance is that a robbery or accident may never occur.

152. In order to take out insurance, a risk must exist. Normally, risks that have already materialized cannot be insured against. Likewise, risks that cannot materialize cannot be insured either. Any insurance contract becomes invalid if the risk has materialized or the possibility of materialization has ceased and both the insurer and the policyholder are aware of this fact at the time of executing the insurance contract. This equally applies to the insured if he or she is aware of the insurance.[250] Furthermore, if this fact is known by both the policyholder and the insured but not known by the insurer, the insurer is not bound by the contract but he or she is entitled to collect the whole premium.[251] If both the insurer and the policyholder are not aware of the fact that the risk has realized, the insurance contract remains valid and enforceable.[252] This type of insurance is called retroactive insurance.

153. Under insurance contracts the risks covered and the risks excepted must be stipulated as clearly as possible in order to determine the ambit of the insurance policy. Parties to an insurance contract must mutually agree on the risks to be covered by the particular policy and the covered risks are to be shown expressly under the contract. It is also important to distinguish the nature of the risk from the subject matter of the risk. The subject matter of the risk is related to property under indemnity insurance, whereas the subject matter of the risk is related to a person under personal insurance.

154. Article 11(4) of the Insurance Activities Act provides that the insured risks as well as the excepted risks must be stipulated under insurance contracts. The risks that have not been stated under the contacts will be considered as insured risks. In other words, the 'all risks' principle has been adopted in this provision; however, it is almost impossible to apply this principle in practice.[253] The reason is that some perils are never covered under insurance contracts, and there are other perils, which

250. Article 1458 of the Turkish Commercial Code.
251. *Ibid.*
252. Kender, *Sigorta Hukuku,* p. 293; S. Çapa, *Geçmişe Etkili Sigorta* (2014) Gazi Üniversitesi Hukuk Fakültesi Dergisi, C.XVIII S. 3–4, pp. 405–426.
253. Ünan, *Some Aspects of the New Turkish Legislative Work Related to Private Insurance (Legislative Work),* in *Kompatibilitaet des türkischen und europaeischen Wirtschaftsrecth,* 134 (Y.M. Atamer & K.J. Hopt eds, 2009).

may be covered in exchange for payment of additional premiums.[254] The contracting parties must have knowledge of the risks that are covered at the time of execution of the contract and this is an essential element of contract law. On this basis, it is asserted that this specific provision has been drafted erroneously.[255] Consequently, the description and scope of the risks covered by a specific insurance contract must be precisely stated. This will enable the determination of whether or not a particular loss falls within the scope of that particular policy.

155. Some types of risk are not capable of being covered by an insurance contract generally and principally. Therefore, certain perils are generally excepted in the General Conditions and specifically included within the insurance contract when necessary. In order to provide better clarity, these risk exceptions are stipulated under insurance policies. For instance, the risks of war, hostilities, civil war, armed conflict, riot and insurrection are expressly excepted under the General Conditions for most indemnity insurances. Furthermore, loss and damage resulting from terrorism is a usual risk exception under most indemnity insurance policies. These risk exceptions must be stipulated in the insurance contract in a clear and comprehensible manner and the contracting parties must agree on them.[256] In the event that the insurer asserts that any of the risks included in the insurance contract are actually not within the ambit of a particular policy, the burden of proof lies with the insurer.[257]

156. In a fundamental sense, insurance deals with uncertainties. However, as a general rule insurance does not cover losses intentionally caused.[258] If the loss was caused by *negligence* ('*culpa*') the insurer must be able to recover the loss unless otherwise agreed.[259] For instance, the General Conditions of Electronic Device Insurance exclude damage caused by *culpa lata.*[260] This principle also applies to liability insurance. If damage is caused deliberately by the policyholder, the insurer is not obliged to compensate such liability.[261] Here there is no option for parties to exclude negligence (*culpa*) because the principal purpose of liability insurance is to indemnify against the insured's liability in the event of negligence caused to a third party.

157. Life insurance is an exception to this general principle because suicide is covered under certain conditions. If a life insurance contract providing coverage against death has been in effect for at least three years and if the insured dies as a result of suicide or attempted suicide, the insurer is obliged to pay the insurance

254. Ulaş, *Zarar Sigortaları Hukuku* (*Indemnity Insurance Law*), *Ibid.*, 48. Uluğ, pp. 316–317. Kayıhan, *Sigorta Sözleşmesinde Prim Ödeme Borcu (Obligation to Pay Premium in Insurance Contract)*, Ankara, 2004, pp. 61–62.
255. Kender, *Sigorta Hukuku,* p. 176.
256. *Ibid.*, pp. 296–299.
257. Article 1409/2 Turkish Commercial Code.
258. Article 1429(1) of Turkish Commercial Code.
259. *Ibid.*
260. Article 3.1 of the General Conditions.
261. Article 1477 of Turkish Commercial Code.

sum.[262] Furthermore, if the insured dies as a result of suicide or attempted suicide because of a mental disorder, the insurer must still pay the insured sum even if the contract has been in effect for less than three years.[263] However, the insurer is discharged from liability if the policyholder has murdered or has been involved in the murder of the insured with the intention of collecting the insurance sum.[264] This provision has been criticized as it relies on the condition that the murder is committed with the intention of collecting the insurance sum.[265] This view rather states the important element as the realization of the risk intentionally by an unlawful act of the policyholder.[266] However, the outcome is different if the beneficiary has murdered or has been involved in the murder of the insured. In such a case, no doubt, the beneficiary will not be entitled to collect the insurance sum; however, the insurer is not discharged from the liability either. The insurance sum will be paid to the inheritors of the deceased insured.[267]

§4. Characteristics of Insurance Contract Law

158. Even though many aspects of insurance contract law are regulated as a part of general contract law, it does have its own peculiarities. The principal peculiarity is that an insurance contract is a contract *uberrimae fidei.* This principle requires that both parties display utmost good faith towards each other in their dealings. The Turkish Civil Code promotes good faith as a very fundamental principle by stating that '*Every person must act in good faith in the exercise of his or her rights and in the performance of his or her obligations. The manifest abuse of a right is not protected by law*'.[268] Accordingly, both the insurer and the party wanting to be insured have a strict burden of disclosure to each other. The party seeking insurance must disclose all relevant information to the insurer to assist him/her to evaluate the risk and determine the appropriate premium. Likewise, the insurer, and its agent, must disclose all information related to the insurance contract, the insured's rights, the provisions to which the insured has to pay special attention and the duty of notification before the conclusion of the contract.[269]

§5. Interpretation

159. Sometimes there is a need for the interpretation of an insurance contract. In such a case, the parties to a contract may agree on the interpretation; if not, interpretation of the contract is brought before the court and the judge will decide on the conflict. For the interpretation of a contract, in general, the common meaning of the

262. Article 1503(1) of Turkish Commercial Code.
263. Article 1503(2) of Turkish Commercial Code.
264. Article 1504 of the Turkish Commercial Code.
265. Kender, *Sigorta Hukuku*, p. 301.
266. *Ibid.*
267. Article 1504/2 of the Turkish Commercial Code.
268. Article 2.
269. Article1423 of Turkish Commercial Code. *See* paras 226 ff. below.

parties' mutual declaration of intent is identified. While doing this, first, parties' 'real and common will' should be determined.[270] If the 'real and common will' of the parties cannot be determined, the declaration of intent of the parties may be interpreted in accordance with the *trust theory* in order to identify the *hypothetical common will* of the parties.[271] If any act has a provision for the interpretation of a matter ('interpretative legal norm'), the solution provided by this provision is applied unless the parties' common will is identified otherwise.

160. Furthermore, the rights and responsibilities of the parties to the insurance contract are contained in the general conditions of the insurance policy, and sometimes special clauses are also added to the general conditions of insurance. An insurance contract includes both legal and technical principles and sometimes also relates to liability law. Therefore, the wording of both the general conditions and special clauses has fundamental importance. In practice, the meaning or interpretation of such conditions or clauses often results in conflict. As an insurance contract is a *contract of adhesion* (i.e., the general conditions are prepared by the insurers upon approval by the Insurance and Private Pension Regulation and Supervision Agency of Treasury and the parties are required to simply accept them), the interpretation of insurance contracts is an important matter.

161. The Turkish Code of Obligations, which came into force on 1 July 2012 and repealed the former Code of Obligations, contains provisions with regard to the validity of the general conditions. According to Article 20, paragraph 1 of the Turkish Code of Obligations, the general conditions are contractual provisions that are prepared in advance by one party with the aim of using them as a template for similar contracts to be offered to other parties. As it is deciphered from the wording, such conditions are prepared in advance as a uniform way to regulate/compose the content of a particular type of contract without the option for the other party to negotiate terms and interfere with the operation of the general terms. Whether such conditions are stipulated in the text of the contract or provided in a different form in supplementary materials is irrelevant as long as the content is correct and clearly stated. 'Sole preparation' means that the other party to the contract has not participated in the preparation of such conditions. The person who prepares such conditions and the contracting party who uses them may be different persons. Even if such general conditions are prepared or approved by a governmental institution, they are still considered general conditions. Therefore, although general conditions of insurance are approved by the Insurance and Private Pension Regulation and Supervision Agency in Turkey and all insurance companies are using the same general conditions, these conditions are subject to judicial supervision.[272]

---

270. Article 19 of the Turkish Code of Obligations.
271. Kemal Oğuzman & Öz Turgut, *Borçlar Hukuku Genel Hükümler* (*Obligations Law, General Provisions*), 10th ed. (Istanbul 2009), pp. 194–196.
272. M. Yeşim Atamer, Yeni Türk Borçlar Kanunu Hükümleri Uyarınca Genel İşlem Koşulları- nın Denetlenmesi–TKHK m. 6 ve TTK m. 55, f. 1, (F) İle Karşılaştırmalı Olarak, Türk Hukukunda Genel İşlem Şartları Sempozyumu, (Ankara, 8 Nisan, 2011), Ankara 2011, p. 15.

162. Furthermore, Article 5 of the Consumer Protection Act sets out rules regulating unfair provisions, which are defined as provisions that are included in the contract without having been negotiated with the consumer and cause an imbalance against the consumer's contractual rights and obligations contrary to the *principle of good faith.* Similar wording is employed by Article 4(c) of the By-law on Unfair Provisions in Consumer Contracts.[273] It is argued that the scope of judicial supervision is broader under Article 5 of the Consumer Protection Act than Article 20 of the Turkish Code of Obligations.[274]

163. As generally accepted, there are three phases in the supervision of the general conditions. However, before any supervision of the general conditions can begin, there should first be contractual conditions that are accepted as general conditions. For instance, if a clause is negotiated by both parties, it cannot be regarded as a general condition. If contractual provisions are accepted as general conditions, the first phase is the *enforcement* phase where the contents of the contract, i.e., whether general conditions are part of the contract, are identified. If it is found that general conditions form part of the contract, then they may be *supervised* by means of interpretation. In that case, the general conditions are *interpreted* in favour of the insured customer, in other words against the insurer who relies on the general conditions in forming the contract, in order to protect customers.[275] If these two phases prove to be ineffectual, supervision of the validity of the general conditions will be necessary for the third phase.

164. The first enforcement phase is used to identify whether general conditions have been included in the contract or not. If so, such general conditions are evaluated in relation to the declaration of intent of the parties when determining the validity of the contract. In particular, the other party's construction of the declaration of intent in accordance with the *trust theory* is taken into consideration, and the contract is concluded accordingly.[276] It is to be noted that provisions of the Turkish Code of Obligations with regard to supervision of the general conditions do not differ between consumers and merchants, i.e., they apply to both consumer and merchant contracts.

165. If it is determined that the general conditions have been included in the contract, in the next stage, Article 23 of the Turkish Code of Obligations provides that any general condition provisions are interpreted against the party who prepares them and in favour of the other party if such a provision is unclear or ambiguous or have more than one meaning. Similarly, Article 6(3) of the By-law on Unfair Provisions in Consumer Contracts states that any provision in the contract that is unclear and ambiguous or has more than one meaning must be interpreted in favour

273. OG. No. 29033, Date: 17.6.2014.
274. Atamer, pp. 19–20.
275. *Ibid.*, p. 11.
276. *Ibid.*, p. 26.

of the consumer. This rule is called the 'ambiguity principle', and in the interpretation of a general condition provision, the courts will invariably favour the customer where there is ambiguity in the interpretation of the content of such provision.[277] As mentioned before, even if general conditions of insurance are prepared by an authority or institution or by the Insurance and Private Pension Regulation and Supervision Agency, they are still subject to supervision.

166. According to Article 25 of the Turkish Code of Obligations, provisions that are disadvantageous to the other party or aggravate his or her situation – contrary to the *principle of good faith* – must not be inserted in the general conditions. This supervisory focus on the *principle of good faith* under Article 25 has been criticized because of its failure to take into consideration any factors contrary to the *principle of good faith.* It is, thus, said that there is a *lacuna* here and any contradiction to the *principle of good faith* is to be assessed in the context of supervision of general conditions.[278]

167. However, Article 5 of the Consumer Protection Act, and Articles 5 and 6 of the By-law on Unfair Provisions in the Consumer Contracts (and its annex entitled Unfair Contract Provisions) provide for a more extensive review of factors related to the evaluation of general provisions inserted in consumer contracts. Furthermore, it is said that, in principle, consideration of Article 25 of the Code of Obligations is not necessary for consumer contracts on the basis that they apply transactions between merchants and not consumers. On the contrary, the detailed supervision provisions of consumer protection law do provide guidance in the application of Article 25 of the Code of Obligations.[279]

168. Furthermore, according to Article 55(1) f of the Turkish Commercial Code, using general conditions that are against the principle of good faith amounts to unfair competition. If general conditions are found to derogate from this principle, particularly when they operate deceptively against the other party – either directly in a substantive legal sense or indirectly through a process of interpretation of the applicable law – the party using such general conditions acts against the principle of good faith. Likewise, general conditions that allocate – particularly deceptively against the other party – rights and obligations that are substantially contrary to the character and intent of the contract are considered against the principle of good faith. Accordingly, it is recommended that these two criteria should be considered in filling the *lacuna,* and Article 25 of the Turkish Commercial Code should be read in conjunction with Article 55 paragraph (1) of the Turkish Commercial Code. If all these provisions are read together, the proper meaning and application of supervision can be achieved as per Article 25 of the Turkish Code of Obligations.

277. *Ibid.*, p. 35.
278. *Ibid.*, p. 42.
279. *Ibid.*, p. 42.

§6. CAUSATION

169. In order for the insurer to pay compensation and the insured to recover, it is a fundamental rule that there must be a causal link between the loss and the insured risk. In order to claim compensation, the insured is obliged to prove this causal link. Conversely, it is the duty of the insurer to prove that the loss is caused by one of the risk factors *excluded* under the contract.[280]

170. In non-marine insurance, the general principle of Turkish obligation law is that there must be an *adequate causal link* between an event or condition and the loss.[281] According to this principle, the event or condition must be sufficient enough to produce an outcome that causes the loss to be realized. In other words, not all conditions that affect the realization of the outcome *indirectly* are considered adequate. Instead, the condition must have produced the outcome in a way that is appropriate in the ordinary course of life experiences. Interpretation of this *adequate causal link* is purely objective and not dependent on whether the tortfeasor could foresee the outcome or not.

171. Regarding the damage incurred, a distinction is drawn between direct and indirect damages. Direct damage means damage that is caused directly by a particular condition or act without the intervention of any additional cause. Indirect damage involves some additional cause. This is an important consideration for the general conditions of some insurances, such as construction, fire, environmental liability and vehicle insurance, which require the existence of *direct* damage.

172. In marine insurance, *cause proxima* is applied in Turkey under the influence of Anglo-American Law, and this approach meets the needs of marine insurance better.[282] Whether there is a difference between the adequate cause principle and the proximate cause principle is not the question of our work.[283]

§7. PUBLIC POLICY

173. According to Article 1404 of the Turkish Commercial Code, insurance cannot be taken out to cover loss resulting from an act of the policyholder or the insured in breach of protective rules, moral values, public policy or rights of personality. In such a case, the insurance contract will be null and void. Recognition of this principle for insurance law is nothing more than the application of the general principle of maxim *ex turpi causa oritur actio*. Partly, this also relates to the principle that an

---

280. Article 1409 of the Turkish Commercial Code.
281. Kender, *Sigorta Hukuku,* p. 329.
282. *Ibid.*
283. B.S. Markesinis & H. Unberath, *The German Law of Torts A Comparative Treatise* 113 (Hart Publishing 4th ed. 2002).

insured party cannot recover an indemnity against the consequences of his own deliberate act as described above and as set out in Article 1429 of the Turkish Commercial Code.

174. However, there are exceptions to this general principle, which are particularly applied with respect to compulsory insurance. For instance, under compulsory motor insurance, the insured vehicle operator is liable to a third party for damage caused by him/herself. However, any *unintentional* commission of a *criminal* act will not prevent the insured from recovering from his or her insurer an indemnity against the damage. The reason for this exception is public policy that outweighs any element of criminality in awarding victims of accidents protected by compulsory insurance all compensation available to them. Nevertheless, this exception is only ensured if the negligent tortfeasors can enforce their insurance policies.

175. Furthermore, in the same insurance situation, but where the insured *intentionally* causes damage to a third party, the latter will be able to recover from the insurer. This point is clearly set out in the general conditions of some insurance policies rather than the Code. For instance, according to Article B.7 of the Highway Compulsory Financial Liability Insurance General Conditions, situations that arise from the insurance contract or legal provisions relating to the insurance contract and result in the elimination of the duty of compensation or a decrease in the amount of compensation cannot be asserted against the injured party. After the insurer has paid the compensation, he or she may have recourse against the insured to be reimbursed for the total payment of compensation or a reduction in the amount of compensation in accordance with the insurance contract and legal provisions applicable to this contract. This right of reimbursement recourse applies to any intentional act of the insured him/herself or of any persons whose acts and omissions the insured is responsible for. Other insurances that contain similar recourse provisions are: sea vehicles compulsory financial liability insurance,[284] highway passenger transport compulsory seat accident insurance,[285] shore facilities marine pollution compulsory financial liability insurance,[286] private security financial liability insurance,[287] dangerous substances compulsory financial liability insurance,[288] financial liability insurance on medical malpractice,[289] bottle gas financial liability insurance.[290] However, compulsory certificate financial liability insurance does not include any such provision.[291] Alternatively, environmental pollution financial liability insurance is not compulsory, nevertheless contains a provision for coverage up to the limits of

284. Article B.7 of the general conditions of the sea vehicles financial liability insurance.
285. Article A.7 of the general conditions of the highway passenger transport compulsory seat accident insurance.
286. Article B.7 of the general conditions of the shore facilities marine pollution compulsory financial liability insurance.
287. Article B.6 of the general conditions of the private security financial liability insurance.
288. Article B.3 of the general conditions of the dangerous substances and dangerous compulsory financial liability insurance.
289. Article B.3.6 and B.6 of the general conditions of the financial liability insurance on medical malpractice.
290. Article 4 of the general conditions of the bottle gas financial liability insurance.
291. This issue has not been considered under the Turkish law.

the shore facilities marine pollution compulsory financial liability insurance despite the intentional act of the insured.[292] This is the only exception among the optional liability insurances.

§8. Insurance as a Personal Contract

176. An important point to determine is whether insurance contracts are regarded as contracts personal to the particular person insured and whether they can be assigned by the insured. According to Article 1470 of the Turkish Commercial Code, if the contracting party who possesses an interest in the insured property is changed or substituted, unless otherwise agreed, the original insurance relationship terminates. It is to be noted that the operation of this provision is completely opposite to the former Turkish Commercial Code, under which the assignment of the contract was authorized.[293] Because most of the general conditions pertaining to insurance came into force at the time when the former Turkish Commercial Code was in force, the provisions of the general conditions regulating assignment of the insurance are still valid to transfer the insured's rights and obligations to another party. Accordingly, as the insurer and the insured have agreed on assignment terms in most of the general conditions, the insurance contract does not terminate but continues on foot with the new insured party. In some cases, the general conditions provide that the insurer must be informed of any assignment of the insurance contract within a certain number of days. If this notice is not provided, the insurer is released from all liability to pay compensation and the insurer is entitled to terminate the contract with the assignee within a certain number of days.[294]

177. Apart from the assignment of the insurance policy itself, the amount paid or payable under the insurance contract, as distinct from the contract itself, can also be assigned.[295] In other words, the insured, as with the other receivables, can freely assign the amount paid or payable under the insurance contract. According to Article 183 of the Turkish Code of Obligations, the creditor can also assign his or her receivables without the consent of the debtor, but only on providing that any act, contractual term or the nature of the particular matter does not prevent such assignment. Even though the validity of this assignment is subject to written form,[296] a promise to assign can be oral. In any case, if the debtor has not been informed of the assignment, he or she is only obligated to pay the agreed amount to the original

---

292. Article B.7 of the general conditions of the environmental pollution financial liability insurance.
293. Article 1303/1 of the former Turkish Commercial Code (Act No. 6762) provided the opposite stating that in case the owner of the insured property changes, the rights and obligations pass on to the new owner, unless parties agree otherwise. Kender asserts that the Turkish Commercial Code corrects an important mistake by removing the 'insured property' since the subject matter of an insurance contract is not the insured property but the interest on the insured property. Therefore, it is more appropriate to refer to the change of the insured interest's holder. Kender, *Sigorta Hukuku*, p. 223.
294. For instance, Art. 8 of the General Conditions of the Electronic Appliance Insurance.
295. Samim Ünan, Hayat Sigortası Sözleşmesi (Beta İstanbul 1998), p. 51.
296. Article 185 of the Turkish Code of Obligations.

policyholder.[297] Therefore, it is for the benefit of the assignee that the insurer is informed of any assignment. Such an assignment can include proceeds already recoverable, in respect of a loss that has already taken place or the proceeds of any future loss. In such a case, the assignor remains the insured, and it is only what he or she can recover that is the subject of the assignment.

297. Article 186 of the Turkish Code of Obligations.

Chapter 2. Insurable Interest

Meltem Deniz Güner-Özbek

178. Apart from the general concept of what risks can be covered by insurance, it is essential that the insured party to every contract of insurance possesses insurable interest in the insured subject matter under Turkish Law. Article 1401 of the Turkish Commercial Code provides a definition for insurance contracts, and interest is referred to as an indispensable element of any insurance contract.

§1. Insurable Interest under Life Insurance

I. Requirement

179. A life insurance contract can be taken out for both death and survival.[298] The policyholder may take out the insurance for his or her own life or for someone else's life. Insurance for someone else's life requires that the insured has an interest in the life insured.[299] For life insurance against death, if the insurance sum exceeds the regular funeral expenses, then written consent from the insured or his legal representative, if any, is required. If the insured is older than 15 years of age, his or her consent must also be obtained in addition to his or her legal representative's. If a contract has been concluded without such prior consent, it will be regarded as invalid if subsequent consent is not given.

II. The Time When Interest Is Required

180. Article 1408 of the Turkish Commercial Code is a general provision regarding the time of the insured interest. Accordingly, a contract is null and void if there is no interest at the time of execution of the contract. If the interest that exists at the time of execution ceases to exist during the contract period, the contract promptly becomes null and void at such time. A similar provision specific to life insurance under Article 1490 states that if the interest ceases after the execution of the contract, the contract becomes invalid from that time and the surrender value is paid to the policyholder. In sum, it is evident that interest is required throughout the duration of an insurance contract. However, it can be argued that these provisions are inappropriate because the policyholder may have an interest at the time of realization of the risk but not at the time of the policy. Furthermore, it is not easy to determine when interest ceases to exist during the contract period, which can then ultimately return at the time of realization of the risk. Therefore, it is asserted that the most essential matter to determine is whether the interest exists at the time the risk is realized.[300]

---

298. Article 1490(1) of the Turkish Commercial Code.
299. Article 1490(2) of the Turkish Commercial Code.
300. Kender, *Sigorta Hukuku,* pp. 215–217.

III. The Meaning of Insurable Interest under Life Insurance

181. As already mentioned, life insurance is not regarded as a contract of indemnity, which means that the prohibition against enrichment principle does not apply to life insurance policies. Therefore, the life of an individual can be insured with one or more insurers. It is asserted that the concept of *interest* is technically the subject of indemnity insurance, and there is no interest in the real sense in relation to life insurance.[301] However, some countries, such as the United States of America (USA)[302] and the United Kingdom (UK)[303] also provide for insurable interests under life insurance in the sense that the *interest* on the continuance of someone's life may be emotional or pecuniary. If the beneficiary has a pecuniary interest in someone's life, he or she can only insure to the extent of this pecuniary interest.[304] If the sum payable is higher than the pecuniary interest of the beneficiary, the excess amount is deemed payable in favour of the insured.[305] Such a case may often arise for credit life insurance purposes.[306] For instance, if a creditor has insured his or her debtor's life in order to secure credit, the limit of the interest is equal to the amount of the credit. If the insured sum exceeds the amount of the credit, namely the interest, there is over-insurance.

182. The interest in the continuance of someone's life may be either emotional or pecuniary; it is not necessary that both emotional and pecuniary interests exist at the same time. However, it is not easy to determine[307] if the condition of *moral* interest has been satisfied or not. Furthermore, it is not clear which criteria are employed to determine the intensity of the emotional interest. Merely being fond of someone, or appreciating them or feeling attracted to them is not regarded as being sufficient. Instead, there should be some element of deep loyalty for someone, whose death must traumatically affect the policyholder or the beneficiary.[308] Such an emotional interest is presumed between parents and children and between spouses.[309] It is asserted, however, that such an interest does not exist between siblings except for those living under the same roof.[310] In one case, the Court of Appeals decided that an emotional bond between blood brothers might qualify as such an interest.[311]

301. *Ibid.*, pp. 227.
302. Sharo Michael Atmeh, *Regulation Not Prohibition: The Comparative Case Against the Insurable Interest Doctrine*, 32(1) North-western Journal of International Law & Business 92–140 (2011), at 95.
303. John Birds, *Insurance Law in the United Kingdom* (Kluwer, 2010), p. 64.
304. Article 1491 of the Turkish Commercial Code.
305. Article 1491.
306. *See* credit life insurance below.
307. Ünan, *Life Insurance Contract*, p. 20.
308. *Ibid.*
309. *Ibid.*
310. *Ibid.*
311. Decision of 11th Circuit of Court of Appeals 9.6.1995 E.95/3856 K.95/4829.

§2. Insurable Interest under Indemnity Insurance

183. Problems related to insurable interest under contracts of indemnity usually arise in cases of property insurance. The other category of indemnity insurance, liability insurance, raises no real difficulties as it is clear that a party to the contract always has an unlimited interest in insuring against someone's potential liability to pay damages to a third party.

I. The Nature of Insurable Interest under Property Insurance

184. The active part of a property consists of its value, such as a house, a car, a building, a yacht, a laptop, a receivable or profit. The relationship between a person and the value of the property constitutes *interest* under insurance law, which in turn represents the subject of the insurance contract. If the value of the property has been damaged, the interest in the value will also be affected. To be able to insure a property or receivable, the insured must have a recognized right in it or a contractual right over it. A mere expectation of loss from destruction or damage to the property is not enough. Obviously, a landlord or tenant has an interest in the property, and a creditor has an interest in the receivables, such as the rent or contract of affreightment. The mere possession of the property, however, does not qualify for insurable interest unless the possessor bears some legal claim to it. A creditor has no insurable interest in the debtor's property unless he or she has a proprietary interest, such as a mortgage over it.

II. Extent of Insurable Interest under Property Insurance

185. As mentioned earlier, anyone with an interest in the property can insure it for the full value of the property or receivable. However, if there is a loss, the value of the interest becomes crucial as the insured can prima facie only recover enough to indemnify him/herself for this interest. According to Article 1455 of the Turkish Commercial Code, if a person has an insurable interest in only part of a property or a right pertaining to this property, and he or she has insured for more than this interest, the exceeding part of the insurance is deemed to be in favour of the other shareholders who have the same kind of insurable interest in other part/parts of the property or right.

III. Restrictions on the Insurable Interest

186. If a property, which has a restricted real right on, has been insured for the interest of its owner, the holder of the restricted real right has also the right on the insurance indemnity.[312] The insurer shall not pay the indemnity to the insured without the consent of the restricted real right holder. Similarly, if the insured property

312. Article 1456 of the Turkish Commercial Code.

has been seized, the insurer must pay the indemnity to the enforcement office in case the risk has realized upon the condition that the insurer has been informed of the seizure on time.[313]

IV. When Insurable Interest in Property Must Be Shown

187. In relation to life insurance discussed above, Article 1408 of the Turkish Commercial Code is a general provision concerned with the time of the interest and provides that a contract is null and void if there is no interest at the time of execution of the contract. If the interest that existed at the time of execution ceases to exist during the contract period, the contract promptly becomes null and void. In other words, insurable interest is required at all times from the execution of the contract until the realization of the risk. The criticism of this rule for life insurance discussed in the section above[314] also applies to indemnity insurance.

313. Article 1457 of the Turkish Commercial Code.
314. *See* para. 168 above.

Chapter 3. Formation of the Contract

Meltem Deniz Güner-Özbek

§1. Pre-contractual Period

188. Generally, there are two standard ways to form an insurance contract. In practice, both of these involve an offer being made by the prospective insured or the party proposing the type of insurance cover. The first way involves the completion of a proposal form, which is a standard form produced by the insurer. The second process involves the party proposing the policy (or an intermediary on his behalf) using some other contractual documents.

§2. Formalities

189. As a general rule there is no particular form required for insurance contracts. An entirely oral contract of insurance is legally binding provided that agreement on all material terms can be proven if necessary. In practice, different types of insurance policies embody certain types of insurance contracts. However, an insurance policy is not a requirement for the formation and execution of the contract, but can merely function as proof of its existence.

190. There are a number of significant disclosure requirements for the formation of an insurance contract. First, Article 11(3) of the Insurance Activities Act sets out issues that the policyholder, the beneficiary or the insured must be informed of both at the time of execution and during the contractual period as determined by by-law. In accordance with this Article, the By-law on the Duty of Information in the Insurance Contracts[315] has been promulgated, and the same principles are r also included in the Turkish Commercial Code in Article 1423.

191. According to the By-law, although these disclosure requirements can be fulfilled either orally or in writing, the written disclosure is fundamental for face-to-face interaction. For those cases where the contracting parties cannot meet physically, such as those contracts finalized over the phone, via the internet or any other similar means, disclosure may be fulfilled orally. The burden of disclosure begins before the execution of the contract and continues throughout the contract period. In accordance with the principle of good faith, the insurer must assist the policyholder with understanding the meaning of technical matters under the insurance contract, provide him/her with all relevant information about the insurance transaction (either already completed or due to be completed) and the peculiarities of the insurance procedure while abstaining from any misleading behaviour. Not only the insurer but also his agencies have these duties of disclosure. If any disclosure duty

315. New By-law that came into force 14.02.2020 repealed the former one dated 2007. OG. No. 31039, Date: 14.02.2020.

is not performed correctly, the policyholder may terminate the contract and claim compensation if he/she has suffered any damage. Moreover, a copy of the disclosure form must be given to the contracting party during the negotiation period before the contract is executed. The form and content of the disclosure form are determined by the Insurance and Private Pension Regulation and Supervision Agency.

192. Furthermore, Article 1423 paragraph (1) of the Turkish Commercial Code states that before the execution of the contract within sufficient time for due consideration, the insurer or his agent must provide the policyholder with written information regarding the insurance contract, the rights of the insured, provisions to which the insured must pay special attention and any notification duties that may arise during the contractual period depending on circumstantial developments. Additionally, the insurer must also disclose to the policyholder in writing all circumstances and developments that pertain to the contract independently from the insurance policy. In the event that the disclosure statement is not given, if the policyholder has not objected to the formation of the contract within fourteen days, the contact is deemed valid and operational in accordance with the terms written in the relevant policy. The onus of proving that the disclosure statement has been duly given lies with the insurer.

193. It is noted that the outcome of the failure to perform the duties of disclosure is not clear with respect to the period of fourteen days under the by-law. When does this fourteen-day time limit begin? What are the legal ramifications if the insurer has not performed pre-contractual disclosure duties or has performed them incompletely? What if the policyholder objects to the policy within fourteen days? With respect to the commencement of the fourteen-day time limit, two options have been advanced: One option is that the time limit begins when the insurer's offer is communicated to the policyholder. The other option is that the time limit commences with the execution of the agreement.[316] It is most likely that Article 1423 supports the second option by referring to '*objection to the execution of the contract*'. If the policyholder objects to the execution of the contract, there are three possible implications, namely: (i) that the contract has not been executed; (ii) the contract has been terminated; or (iii) that the contract provisions should be revised.[317] It is recommended that the effect of the objection should be at the discretion of the policyholder.[318] The first implication that the contract has not been executed carries some risk as it denies insurance cover for the period before the objection. Termination of the contract effective at the date of objection or revision of the contractual provisions will better serve the interest of the policyholder. Consequently, the policyholder has the option to either discontinue the contract or continue to be bound in accordance with his or her will.

316. S. Ünan, Türk Ticaret Kanunu Taslağının Sigorta Hukuku Başlıklı Altıncı Kitabı Hakkına Düşünceler (Türk Ticaret Kanunu Taslağı) (2005) Sigorta Hukuku Dergisi, Özal Sayı:1, 109–196, p. 124; M. Özdamar, Sigortacının Sözleşme Öncesi Aydınlatma Yükümlülüğü (Aydınlatma Yükümülüğü), Yetkin Yayınları, Ankara, 2009, pp. 365–366.
317. Ünan (Tasarı), p. 124.
318. Özdamar (Aydınlatma Yükümlülüğü), p. 365.

194. In addition, in line with the relevant by-law, paragraph 3 of Article 1423 of the Turkish Commercial Code states that the Insurance and Private Pension Regulation and Supervision Agency has the authority to determine the form and content of the information to be provided to the policyholder by taking into consideration the regulations of foreign countries, particularly those of the EU. In practice, the information forms prepared in accordance with the by-law remain in use, and no other new forms have been introduced by the Agency.

195. In addition, there are other disclosure requirements prescribed by the By-law on the Distance Contract in relation to Financial Services.[319] Insurance is included with the financial services regulated under the by-law, which are provided under contracts formed over distances via the internet, by phone or by post. The provider is obliged to inform the customer of the following issues in conformity with the distance communication means before the distance contract related to financial services is executed:

(a) field of activity of the provider and its representative – if any – the MERSIS[320] number, full address, e-mail address, telephone number and other means of communication, if any;
(b) if there is an intermediary between the customer and the provider of the financial services, the name of the intermediary, his or her title, full address and authority regarding the transactions;
(c) fundamental characteristics of the financial services;
(d) the total price of the financial service including all taxes. If the price cannot be calculated in advance, the way of calculating the price, associated costs and if such costs cannot be calculated in advance, information regarding the possibility of payment of such additional costs;
(e) information regarding financial matters that carry special risks due to their particular nature or transaction type or whose prices change in accordance with the fluctuation beyond the provider's control or whose past data will not be an indicator for the future value if such means are used;
(f) information regarding taxes and fees payable by the consumer, if any;
(g) if any information provided has a limited validity period, information regarding such time limit;
(h) information regarding payment and fulfilment of relevant undertakings, if any;
(i) if there are any additional costs borne by the consumer from using distance communication means, information regarding such costs;
(j) conditions, time limit, and procedures for using the right of withdrawal;
(k) full address, e-mail address, phone number and other communication means, if any, where the notification of withdrawal bill is to be sent;
(l) information regarding cases in which the customer is unable to terminate or loses the right of termination if the right of withdrawal has not been used in accordance with Article 13;

319. OG. No. 29253, Date: 31.1.2015.
320. Merkezi Sicil Sistemi (Central Registration System).

(m) the minimum contract period for financial services that are provided continuously or at regularly repeated intervals; and
(n) information about contractual provisions regarding the right of unilateral termination in cases of just cause and penalty clause, if any.

196. The customer of financial services must be informed of all the above-mentioned information, either in writing or via access to a permanent data server. The writing must be clear and readable in at least twelve-point font.[321] In addition to the information set out above, the provider of financial services must also inform the customer of the following information concerning the distance contract, either in printed form or via access to a data server: the process by which the customer can submit objections or complaints to consumer courts or arbitral organizations; the guarantee fund or other compensation schemes; other dispute resolution processes; and payment plan.[322]

§3. Formation of the Contract

197. The usual contract requirements also apply to the formation of insurance contracts. An offer including all material terms must be made by one party and accepted by the other. For insurance purposes, the offer is usually made by the party who prepares a proposal for submission as a completed insurance proposal form. Once all of the terms of the proposal are accepted by the insurer, a binding contract is formed. This is also the case for circumstances where no formal policy is issued, provided that all material terms are agreed to. If the insurer does not unequivocally accept the policyholder's proposal, for instance, if the issued policy has different provisions than what was initially proposed, this new policy constitutes a counter-offer by the insurer which must be accepted by the proposed policyholder before a binding contract is formed. Occasionally, an offer may be made by the insurer. For instance, this may occur at the time of renewal of the cover when the insurer offers a renewal or in circumstances when buying a ticket for a journey, the insurer's offer for accident insurance is accepted by payment.

198. According to Article 1405 of the Turkish Commercial Code, if the proposal form of the person seeking to execute an insurance contract with the insurer has not been rejected within thirty days from the date of the proposal, the insurance contract is deemed to have been executed. There is a similar provision under Article 11(2) of the Insurance Activities Act regarding life insurance, which states the same proposal forms issued for life insurance. These are deemed valid contracts in the event that such proposals are not rejected within thirty days after the insurer receives notice of them.

199. Nevertheless, there are fundamental differences between the two provisions. Article 1405 is a general provision applicable to all insurance contracts

321. Article 6 of the By-law on the Distance Contract in relation to Financial Services.
322. Article 7.

whereas Article 11(2) is specific to life insurance. The commencement of the thirty-day time limit is more in favour of the policyholder under Article 1405 because it takes into consideration the date of the proposal rather than the date that the insurer receives notice of it. However, in both cases, thirty days is a long time, and it does not serve the benefit of the policyholder, particularly when the insurer waits thirty days to accept the proposal.

§4. Agreement on Material Terms

200. The essential elements of offer and acceptance must include agreement on all materials terms of the contract.[323] Thus, the amount and subject matter of the insurer and the commencement and duration of the risk must be agreed upon. In most cases, these matters will be evident from the proposal form and the surrounding circumstances. For instance, the duration of risk can easily be implied because most indemnity contracts run for a year and most life contracts are valid for the entirety. The insurance premium amount is normally the first material term to be determined, as well as the extent of the obligation of the insurer to cover the type of risk.[324]

§5. Parties to the Insurance Contract

Meltem Deniz Güner-Özbek & Gülfer Meriç

I. Insurer/Insurance Company

201. One of the parties to an insurance contract is the insurer/insurance company. Only the insurance companies that fulfil the legal requirements under Turkish legislation are permitted to carry on insurance business in Turkey. The establishment and organization of insurance companies in Turkey are discussed in more detail in the 'Insurance Companies' section. An authorized agent or a company representative can negotiate and execute an insurance contract on behalf of the insurance company.[325]

II. The Policyholder

202. The other contracting party to an insurance contract is the policyholder. The policyholder is the person who is subject to contractual obligations arising from the insurance contract. Rights arising from the insurance contract – particularly the right to ask the insurer to bear the risk – also lie with the policyholder. However, in some

323. Kender, *Sigorta Hukuku,* p. 174.
324. *Ibid.*
325. *Ibid.*, p. 215; Ulaş, p. 16; Kayıhan, p. 50.

cases, rights arising from the insurance contract may be assigned to other people.[326] It is not necessary for the policyholder to act in person when executing the insurance contract, which can also be finalized through representatives or agents.[327]

203. The general principle is that anyone having the necessary insurable interest is capable of entering into a contract of insurance.[328] This general principle will be subject to certain limitations under contract law, such as the contractual capacity of the policyholder. There are also specific limitations provided under the *Insurance Law Book* of the Turkish Commercial Code. For instance, there is a limitation regarding insurable interest. Insurable interest must be present within the contract period, and in case it ceases to exist, the insurance contract immediately becomes null and void.[329] Requirements for being a policyholder under an indemnity insurance contract and a personal insurance contract also differ under the Turkish Commercial Code. In order to execute a property insurance contract, having an interest in property is required.[330] There is another limitation of life insurance contracts, which requires the beneficiary to have an interest in the survival of that person if the life of that person is insured.[331]

204. The policyholder and the insured are usually the same person. However, in the event that the policyholder takes out insurance covering not in his own interest, but in somebody else's interest, the policyholder is not referred to as the insured at the same time.[332]

III. Relevant Third Parties in Indemnity Insurance

A. *Insured*

205. Indemnity insurance contracts may be executed as third-party beneficiary contracts. In this case, the third party is named as the 'insured' person. However, it is also possible to find a liability insurance contract in favour of a third party.

206. An insurance contract in favour of a third party is a type of third-party beneficiary contract.[333] Under such an insurance contract in favour of a third party, the contracting party is the policyholder. The policyholder should pay the premium as the contracting party. However, the rights arising from the insurance contract reside with the insured person, such as the right to claim compensation. This is because

326. Kender, *Sigorta Hukuku,* p. 215; Kayıhan, p. 50.
327. Ulaş, p. 41.
328. Article 1453 of the Turkish Commercial Code.
329. Article 1408 of the Turkish Commercial Code.
330. Article 1453 of the Turkish Commercial Code.
331. Article 1490 of the Turkish Commercial Code.
332. Bozer, p. 33. Ulaş, p. 41. Kayıhan, p. 52.
333. For more information regarding third-party beneficiary insurance contracts, Mehmet Somer, *Türk Hukukunda Başkası Hesabına Sigorta* Yayınlanmamış Doçentlik Tezi (unpublished dissertation) 2000.

the insured is the party who suffers from the loss or damage. If the insurance contract is for the benefit of the third party this must be stated in the policy; otherwise, the insurance contract is valid only between the policyholder and the insurer.[334] The policyholder under an insurance contract in favour of a third party may have an interest in that particular insurance. This is possible, yet it is not necessary. The insurable interest of the insured must exist at all times, and the existence of any insurable interest of the insured is sufficient in the sense that any consideration of the type of insurable interest of the policyholder is not required.[335]

207. The policyholder is entitled to enter into a third-party beneficiary insurance contract with or without disclosing the identity of that party. Unless the parties agree otherwise, the insured is entitled to claim the insurance indemnity from the insurer or sue the insurer for the payment of the indemnity since he or she is granted the rights arising from the insurance contract. In the event that the identity of the third party is named, the policyholder will be deemed as having acted on its own behalf or in favour of the third party, rather than as a representative of the third party. The person in favour of whom the insurance contract is executed may be left undisclosed. In this case, an insurance contract 'to whom it may concern' is executable and this constitutes a third-party beneficiary contract.[336]

B. *Insurance Taken Out for 'To Whom It May Concern'*

208. In the event that the insurance is taken out for an undisclosed 'to whom it may concern', the holder of the insurable interest is entitled to claim the insurance indemnity at the time of realization of the risk.[337] The name of this person may not be included in the insurance contract. This type of insurance is most usually used for marine insurance purposes. In this way, insurance coverage is provided for the latter holder of that insurable interest; for instance, the latter owner of that good.[338]

C. *Insurance Taken Out for Common Interests*

209. Sometimes the terms of insurance contracts may cover common interests. For instance, two people may jointly own a house. In this case, one of the owners is entitled to take out insurance for the whole property in question; however, the share of the other person will be deemed to have been covered in favour of the other

334. According to the Turkish Court of Appeal decision dated 18.1.1954, in case the insurance contract does not indicate that it has been executed in favour of a third party, the contract is in effect between the policyholder and the insurer. (Decision Date: 18.1.1954, No. 3883/360) Kender asserts that this decision is effective regarding the Turkish Commercial Code. (Kender, *Sigorta Hukuku,* p. 220).
335. *Ibid.*
336. Article 1454 of the Turkish Commercial Code.
337. Article 1454(3) of the Turkish Commercial Code.
338. Kender, *Sigorta Hukuku,* p. 222; Kayıhan, pp. 53–54.

owners.[339] This is the consequence of the prohibition of enrichment principle since the owner that is taking out insurance is entitled to recover the loss that is corresponding to his own share.

D. *Change of the Insured Interest's Holder*

210. In case the holder of the insured interest changes, the insurance contract will terminate.[340] However, the contracting parties may agree otherwise.[341] For instance, the property that is the subject matter of an insurance contract may be sold during the contract period. In this case, the insurance contract is terminated if the insurer and the new owner do not agree to be bound by the original existing contract. Insurance taken out for an undisclosed 'to whom it may concern' is an exception to this rule, where the contracting parties agree otherwise.

E. *Position of the Restricted Real Right's Holder*

211. As a general rule, a charge on immovable property secures the creditor for the insurance indemnity.[342] Payment under an insurance policy may be made to the owner of the insured property only with the written consent of all of the charge creditors. Therefore, in cases where there is a charge on an immovable property, and if that property is covered by an insurance contract, the insurance indemnity is not paid to the owner. However, the law does not state who is entitled to collect the insurance indemnity. It is also noteworthy that there is an exception to this rule where the payment may be made to the owner for the purposes of restoring the property subject to the charge. In this case, the owner must provide adequate security.

212. If an insurance contract is formed in order to cover the ownership interest over an immovable property and that property is also charged with a restricted right, such as a mortgage or *usufuruct*, the extent of the restricted real right includes the insurance indemnity. However, the contracting parties are entitled to agree otherwise provided that the insurer is informed that the insured property is charged with a restricted real right.[343] However, there is no such requirement when the restricted real right is registered in the registry. If the insurer is informed of the charge or the real right is registered in the registry, the insurer must not pay the insurance indemnity to the owner of that property. In order for such a payment to be done, the approval of all of the real right holders must be given. Nevertheless, there is an exception provided for this rule; a very similar one to the exception set forth in the

339. Turkish Commercial Code Art. 1455.
340. Article 1470 of the Turkish Commercial Code.
341. *Ibid.*
342. Article 879 of the Civil Code.
343. Article 1456 of the Turkish Commercial Code.

Turkish Civil Code. The insurance indemnity can be paid to the owner of the property on the condition that it is going to be used for repair or restitution of the insured property. However, the owner must provide security before the payment of the insurance indemnity.

213. Provided that the insurer pays the insurance indemnity to the owner, even though the insurer is notified of the real right or the real right is registered in the registry, the insurer will be liable to the real right holders. The insurer may be discharged from liability by obtaining written approval.[344] The insurer must notify the real right holders in the event that the policyholder defaults in payment of the premium or the insurer requested an additional premium. The reason for this notification is that the insurer may avoid the insurance contract if the premium is not paid. Thereupon the real right holders will no longer be able to claim insurance indemnity. Therefore, the insurer must also notify the real right holders so that they may determine to pay the premium if the policyholder will not.

214. Restricted real right holders must also be notified if the contract has been avoided or cancelled by the insurer or the policyholder. After the avoidance or cancellation of the insurance contract, the contract remains in force for the real right holders for fifteen days from its termination. The restricted real right holder is entitled to uphold the contract for him/herself. In other words, the restricted real right holder becomes a party to the insurance contract. The insurer must be informed of this decision within fifteen days. If the holders of the restricted real rights do not notify the insurer of such a decision, the insurance contract is terminated for the restricted real right holders as well. If the holders of the restricted real rights uphold the insurance contract, the insurer is bound by this decision; the insurer may only reject this claim on *fair grounds*.

215. Article 1022 of the Turkish Commercial Code provides a very similar provision regarding shipping mortgages. In this respect, insurance indemnity is subject to the ship mortgage provided that the interest of the owner of the ship is covered. The insurer cannot submit that it has not been informed about the ship mortgage that is registered under the ship registry. Consequently, the ship mortgage will be attached to the insurance indemnity that is to be paid to the owner of the ship in the event of loss or damage to the ship.

F. Victim in Liability Insurance

216. Liability insurance contracts cover the invoked liability of the insured person for an amount settled in the insurance contract by the contracting parties. The right of *direct action* has been granted to the victim in liability insurance contracts with the Turkish Commercial Code. While the victim was not entitled to claim its loss directly from the insurer under the former Turkish Commercial Code, the Court of Appeals permitted the victim to claim its loss directly from the insurer, and this

344. Article 1456(2) and (3) of the Turkish Commercial Code.

right is now embodied in the Turkish Commercial Code No. 6102.[345] Accordingly, the victim is now entitled to claim its losses or damages from the insurer up to the amount stipulated under the insurance contract by the law. The right of direct action is regulated by only one condition: that the claim must be brought within the time limit applicable to the specific insurance contract in question.

IV. Relevant Third Parties in Life Insurance

A. *Insured ('Person at Risk')*

217. A person may take out life insurance on her or his own life. Likewise, a person may take out insurance on someone else's life. In this case, the person on whose life insurance is taken out is the insured. However, the concept of 'insured' only exists in the context of 'insurance in favour of a third party'. In the event that insurance is taken out on someone else's life, the policyholder is entitled to claim insurance indemnity and is granted the rights arising from the insurance contract. In this situation, the insurance is not in favour of a third party as the risk occurs on the life, health, integrity or status of a third party. In life insurance terms, the *risk* constitutes the death or survival of this person. Therefore, under the Turkish doctrine, it is claimed that the term 'insured' must not be used in life insurance and the term 'person at risk' is more appropriate in the context of life insurance.[346] Nevertheless, the term 'insured' is used in the Turkish Commercial Code as well as the former, and for this reason, we will be using the same terminology in this work.

218. Article 1490 of the Turkish Commercial Code stipulates certain conditions for taking out life insurance on the life of another person. In order to form a life insurance contract covering the death of the insured person, the beneficiary is required to have an insurable interest in the survival of that person. As already mentioned, some of the authors assert that the interest of the policyholder in the survival of the insured person must be required since the policyholder appoints the beneficiary.[347]

219. As mentioned above, insurance on somebody else's life requires the beneficiary's interest, and this interest may be either material or moral interest. Material interest is determinable; if one suffers from a material loss or damage due to the death of the insured, then that person is regarded as having a material interest in the survival of the insured. However, the situation is not the same for moral interest, and it is very difficult to establish objective criteria for the presence of moral interest. For this reason, the Court of Appeals interprets this rule restrictively. The moral interest of family members is accepted by the courts. It was held that the moral interest of friends is not an insurable interest. However, it was held that the moral

345. Turkish Court of Appeal Decision Date: 25.4.1989, No.: 1989/2606; Turkish Court of Appeal Assembly of Civil Chambers Date: 31.1.1996, No.: 1996/18; Ulaş, pp. 784–788.
346. Kender, *Sigorta Hukuku*, p. 227.
347. *Ibid.*

interest of a *blood brother* is an insurable interest since this relationship is very similar to a relationship by affinity.[348] In the event that the insurable interest ceases to exist after the conclusion of the contract, the contract becomes invalid. In this case, the insurer pays the surrender value to the policyholder.

220. With regard to life insurance contracts covering the death of a person, a written approval is needed from the insured person or its legal representative if the insurance sum exceeds the funeral expenses. The approval of both the legal representative and the insured is required in circumstances where the insured is older than 15 years of age. The insurance contract becomes invalid if such an approval is not obtained. However, the insurance contract becomes valid if the approval is given subsequently, even if the approval could not be obtained at the time of the conclusion of the contract.[349] It is also important to note that if the legal representative is the policyholder itself or appointed as the beneficiary by the policyholder, it will not represent the insured person in giving the approval.[350]

B. Beneficiary

221. Life insurance contracts may be executed in favour of a third party. In this case, the third party is called the 'beneficiary'.[351] The policyholder may take out life insurance in favour of a natural person as well as a legal person.[352] In practice, life insurances are most usually taken out in favour of natural persons. The beneficiary is entitled to claim and collect the insurance sum when the risk, which is covered by the insurance contract, is realized in the event of death or injury to the policyholder.[353]

222. The concept of beneficiary in life insurance is different to the concept of 'insured' in indemnity insurance. With regard to indemnity insurance, the risk realizes in the interest of the insured person. However, in life insurance the risk does not normally realize in the interest of the beneficiary, but it realizes only when the insured is also appointed as the beneficiary. For instance, the insured and the beneficiary may be appointed as the same person with regard to life insurance against the survival of a person.

223. As for the appointment and change of the beneficiary, the policyholder is entitled to appoint the beneficiary and must also notify the insurer about such an appointment.[354] If the policyholder does not notify the insurer about its appointment of a new beneficiary, the insurer cannot be held liable for its payment of the

348. 11th Circuit Court of Appeal, 9.6.1995, No. 95/4829.
349. Article 1490 of the Turkish Commercial Code.
350. *Ibid.*
351. Şenocak, K. Üçüncü Şahıs Lehine Hayat Sigortası Sözleşmesi, Turhan Kitabevi, Ankara 2009, pp. 41 ff.
352. Article 1493(1) of the Turkish Commercial Code.
353. Article 1493(7) of the Turkish Commercial Code.
354. Article 1493(2) of the Turkish Commercial Code.

insured sum to the former beneficiary in good faith.[355] This means that if the policyholder does not fulfil its duty of notifying the insurer of its designation, and the insurer pays the insurance sum to another person in good faith, the liability of the insurer will be ceased upon such payment.[356]

224. If the policyholder has not appointed a beneficiary, the consequences will vary according to the type of life insurance. For life insurance covering the risk of death, if the policyholder did not appoint a beneficiary, the law provides that the legitimate heirs of the policyholder will be deemed as the beneficiaries. Accordingly, the life insurance contract against the risk of death will be deemed to operate in favour of the heirs/inheritors of the policyholder. On the contrary, the situation is different for life insurance covering the risk of survival of a person. In this case, the insurance contract will be deemed to operate in favour of the insured.[357]

225. The right of changing the appointed beneficiary belongs to the policyholder. However, in certain circumstances, the appointed beneficiary will not be changed. The policyholder may waive its right to change the appointed beneficiary. If the policyholder waives its right to change the beneficiary and the insurance policy has already been delivered to the beneficiary, the policyholder can no longer change the beneficiary. However, in the event that this issue is ambiguous, it is presumed that the policyholder reserves its right to change the beneficiary.[358]

226. Above we have mentioned that if the policyholder waives its right to change the beneficiary and the insurance policy has been delivered to the beneficiary, the beneficiary cannot be changed. Nonetheless, the law aims to protect the policyholder, and there is an exception to this rule. In the event that the policyholder explicitly waives the right to change the beneficiary and delivers the insurance policy to the beneficiary, the change of beneficiary is still possible if conditions for disinheritance or avoidance of the donation are fulfilled or if the reason for the appointment of the beneficiary has ceased to exist.[359] The consent of the insurer is not required when appointing the beneficiary. This is also the same when changing the appointed beneficiary.[360]

227. The beneficiary is entitled to claim and collect the insurance sum.[361] For life insurance against the risk of death, the beneficiary can directly claim the insurance sum from the insurer. The insurance sum does not belong to the estate assets of the deceased person. Likewise, the beneficiary cannot be held liable for the debts

355. Article 1493(3) of the Turkish Commercial Code.
356. Article 1493 of the Turkish Commercial Code.
357. Article 1493/2 of the Turkish Commercial Code.
358. Article 1493(4) of the Turkish Commercial Code.
359. *Ibid.*
360. Article 1493(5) of the Turkish Commercial Code.
361. Article 1493(7) of the Turkish Commercial Code.

of the deceased person. The reason is that life insurance contracts are not testamentary dispositions.[362] Even the disclaimer or renunciation of inheritance does not affect the right of a beneficiary to claim or collect the insurance sum.

228. The beneficiary is also granted the right to claim the sum payable if the policyholder voluntarily terminates the contract. This value is payable only after one full year's premium has been paid to the insurance company.[363] Likewise, the beneficiary is entitled to claim the payable sum when the policyholder uses its right to borrow from the insurer or, unless otherwise agreed, in the event of bankruptcy of the insurer before the realization of the risk.[364] It is also important to note that this rule is applied to situations where the beneficiary cannot be changed.

C. Multiple Beneficiaries

229. In certain circumstances, there may be more than one beneficiary person stipulated in the insurance contract. In this situation, the policyholder must specify their shares of the insurance sum. For life insurance against the risk of survival of a person, not specifying the shares of the beneficiary persons will not cause problems because the policyholder will be able to settle their shares when the risk materializes. However, this is not possible for life insurance against the risk of death, since the policyholder – if it is the insured person at the same time – will not be able to determine the shares after the realization of the risk. Considering this possibility, the law provides that in these circumstances each of the beneficiaries will be able to collect the insurance sum equally. If one of the persons appointed as the beneficiary does not collect its own share of the insured sum, its share will be distributed equally to the shares of the other beneficiaries.[365]

§6. Payment of Premium and Issue of Policy

230. In principle, payment of the premium or issuance of a formal policy is not essential for the formation of a binding insurance contract. However, the existence of either action is proof that an insurance contract has been executed as there is no form requirement for insurance contracts. Usually, the insurer does not prove any separate express acceptance but instead issues the insurance policy as an agreed form of acceptance.

---

362. Kender, *Sigorta Hukuku*, p. 230; Ulaş, Işıl, *Can Sigortası Hukuku: Hayat ve Kişisel Kaza Sigortaları* (Personal Insurance Law: Life Insurance and Personal Accident Insurance), ('Can Sigortası'), p. 43 (Turhan Kitabevi, Ankara, 2002). Kayıhan, pp. 58–59.
363. This issue is regulated under Art. 1500 of Turkish Commercial Code. Pursuant to this article, the policyholder is entitled to terminate the life insurance contract in case the contract has been concluded at least one year ago and the insurance premium for one year has been paid.
364. Article 1493(6) of the Turkish Commercial Code.
365. Article 1494(1) of the Turkish Commercial Code.

231. Article 1424 of the Turkish Commercial Code requires the insurer to deliver the insurance policy to the policyholder. If the insurance contract has been executed by the insurer him/herself or his authorized agent, the insurance policy should be delivered to the policyholder within twenty-four hours from the execution of the contract. The rule also provides that *otherwise*, the insurance policy must be delivered within fifteen days. The expression 'otherwise' is used in Article 1424 but without any explanation about its scope of application. The doctrine accepts that the expression 'otherwise' stands for circumstances where the insurance contract has not been executed by the insurer or its agents authorized to execute the insurance contracts on behalf of the insurer.[366] Accordingly, in circumstances where the insurance contract has been executed by agents who are unauthorized of executing insurance contracts on behalf of the insurer or by insurance brokers, the policy must be delivered within fifteen days. Agents who are incapable of executing insurance contracts on behalf of the insurer and insurance brokers must communicate the offer to the insurance company, and then they must communicate the terms of acceptance to the prospective insured.

232. It must also be noted that the insurer will be liable for damages arising from the late delivery of the policy. It is because according to Article 1421(1) of the Turkish Commercial Code liability of the insurer to pay compensation begins upon the payment of the first instalment of the premium, if the parties agreed on the payment in instalments, or the whole premium unless otherwise[367] agreed. Thus, if the insurer does not deliver the insurance policy on time, the duty of payment of the premium of the policyholder does not become due. When the premium or the first instalment is not paid, the liability of the insurer does not begin. If the risk realizes in this period although there is a valid contract, there is no coverage as the liability of the insurer has not begun, i.e., not active, yet. Accordingly, the policyholder is entitled to claim his or her damages arising from the late delivery of the policy. This is because there is a binding insurance contract between the parties to issue a policy, yet the insurer has not fulfilled its obligation to deliver the policy. Therefore, in order to claim these damages, the policy must have been delivered later than the period determined in Article 1424 of the Turkish Commercial Code. The other condition is that the policyholder must have suffered material damage, and this damage should have been caused by the late delivery of the policy. The goods in transit insurance is an exception to the principle mentioned above. In goods in transit insurance, the liability of the insurer begins upon the execution of the contract.[368] Payment of premium is not required. Thus, even if the policy has not been delivered timely and, thus, the premium has not been paid yet, the insurer is liable if the risk realizes. However, most of the general conditions contain provisions stating that the coverage begins and/or terminates at 12.00 pm noon on the dates stipulated in the policy. Therefore, even if the premium or first instalment has been paid in exchange for the policy the liability of the insurer begins as stipulated in the policy; or in the

366. Kender, *Sigorta Hukuku*, p. 179.
367. The parties may agree that the Premium shall be paid at a later time, for instance one week or one month later. Art. 1421(1) of the Turkish Commercial Code.
368. Article 1421.

case of goods in transit insurance before the payment of the premium or first instalment, but again at the time stipulated in the policy.[369]

233. Likewise, the collection of the premium by the insurer represents evidence of the execution of the contract. According to Article 1405(2) of the Turkish Commercial Code, payments made at the time of proposal are counted as payments for the first premium once the contract has been executed. If the contract is not executed, such payments are refunded, without any deduction, together with interest.

234. Article 1425 of the Turkish Commercial Code determines the content requirements of the insurance policy. Pursuant to this rule, the insurance policy must provide the rights of the parties, provisions regarding the default of the policyholder in payment of the premium, and general and special conditions. The signing of the policy must be done by the insurer itself or by an agent who is authorized to execute an insurance contract on the insurer's behalf. In practice, the insurer usually issues three copies of the insurance policy.

235. The policy may contain terms contradictory to, or inconsistent with, the proposal form or the prior mutual agreement of the contracting parties. In this situation, the contradictory or inconsistent terms that are disadvantageous to the policyholder, the beneficiary or the insured will become invalid.[370] In practice, the insurer normally issues three copies of the insurance policy. However, in the event that there are terms that are contradictory to, or inconsistent with, the terms in other copies, the copy of the policyholder must also be taken into account.[371]

236. General conditions must be included in insurance policies.[372] The general conditions are amended from time to time. In the event of such an amendment after the policy has already been issued by the insurer, conflicts may arise. Foreseeing this possibility, legislative provisions have been made under Article 1425(3) of the Turkish Commercial Code. According to Article 1425(3), such amendments that are for the benefit of the policyholder, the insured or the beneficiary will promptly enter into force and will be enforceable immediately.

237. In certain circumstances, such enforceable amendments may require the payment of additional insurance premiums. In this case, the law grants the insurer to request the additional premium within eight days of the amendment. Should the policyholder not accept the request for additional premium, the insurance contract will continue to be in force on the basis of the prior general conditions.[373]

---

369. For instance, Art. A.8 of the General Conditions of Fire Insurance, Construction Insurance and Compulsory Liability Insurance for Motor Vehicles and Art. A.9 of Theft Insurance. Other general conditions contain similar provisions.
370. Article 1425(2) of the Turkish Commercial Code.
371. Kender, *Sigorta Hukuku*, p. 184.
372. Article 1425(1) of the Turkish Commercial Code.
373. Article 1425(3) of the Turkish Commercial Code.

§7. Cover Notes

238. It is common practice when the proposal party desires immediate cover that the insurer issues a cover note providing such temporary cover pending full consideration of the proposal form and issuance of a formal policy.[374] A properly issued cover note is a valid contract of insurance,[375] and the common features and elements of the insurance relationship apply to the cover note. Even though the repealed Turkish Commercial Code used to refer to a *temporal receipt* under Article 1265, this type of receipt differs from the cover note,[376] which is not formally regulated under Turkish law. The Turkish Commercial Code does not refer to either the cover note or such temporal receipt. Nevertheless, this does not mean that a cover note does not have a legal application under Turkish Law as it is recognized as a valid insurance contract regulated by all of the rules applicable to insurance contracts.[377]

374. Kender, *Sigorta Hukuku,* p. 188.
375. *Ibid.*, K. Şenocak, Geçici Sigorta Himayesi (Geçici Güvence), 22 BATİDER 2. ff. (2003).
376. Şeoncak (Geçici Güvence). Temporal Receipt (muvakkat sigorta ilmühaberi).
377. Şenocak (Geçici Güvence), pp. 2 ff.

Chapter 4. Burdens and Obligations of the Insured

§1. Burden of Disclosure at the Time of Execution of the Contract

Hakan Karan & Kemal Şenocak

239. According to Article 1435 of the Turkish Commercial Code, the insured is obliged to declare all the significant matters he knew or should have known during the formation of the contract: referred to as the 'Declaration procedure'. All the provisions of the Turkish Commercial Code regarding such declaration during the formation of the contract are mandated by Article 1452(III) of the Code and cannot be amended against the insured with a contract.

240. Matters which can influence the insurer's decision to conclude the contract under the same or different conditions are regarded as 'significant' in nature. 'Different conditions' refer to the 'heavier conditions' that relate to matters which would persuade the insurer to calculate the insurance premium higher or avoid insuring the risk altogether are regarded as 'significant'. The insured is obliged to declare all significant matters, which he knows or should know, during the formation of the contract. The insured must declare not only the matters he knows concretely but also those that he is expected to know.

241. The insured does not bear the burden of investigating the circumstantial facts to obtain information from third parties or enquire for any other reason. However, he or she does bear the burden of recall. The purpose behind placing the burden of declaring 'matters to know' is to increase the recall ability of the insured during the formation of the contract. The insured must declare the facts to the insurer, which he may recall through serious consideration. The insured cannot be discharged from the burden of declaration just by hiding himself or herself behind the reason that he or she forgot the matter, which he or she could be expected to recall if they properly applied their memory.

242. The insured must declare all the matters he could or should know if he or she pays enough attention expected from him/her. The degree of attention to which the insured must pay to recall is defined by considering his or her intelligence level, educational status and the experience gained in relation to the circumstances and conditions of the particular case.

243. The burden of declaration does not depend on the insured being informed of the effect of a particular matter on the risk; this kind of information may however have significance for the fault assessment. 'Significance' in terms of risk is an objective condition, and the insured does not need to have information about matters in terms of their significance. Nevertheless, even if the insured does not have information about the effect of the matter to declare the risk but does have information about the matter, there could be a breach of the burden of declaration without fault.

244. According to Article 1412 of the Turkish Commercial Code, the knowledge and behaviour of the insured being aware of the insurance, the representative acting under power and the beneficiary in life insurance are considered as the knowledge and behaviour of the policyholder by Law. The knowledge of the legal representative is taken into consideration in relation to the insurance policies taken out by the policyholder's legal representative on the basis that Article 1412 generally refers to the representative of the policyholder.

245. Article 1443 of the Turkish Commercial Code regulates provisions related to the obligation of declaration for amendments made to the insurance policy between the proposal submission and acceptance and during the execution of the contract. The burden of declaration is applied through comparison, not only at the time of execution of the insurance contract but also during the whole contractual process while the known matters are determined until the insurer notifies the insured of his or her acceptance of the declaration. Article 1406 of the Turkish Commercial Code is also significant here in stating that the insurance contract is deemed executed if the proposal submitted by the person, who wants to make a contract with the insurer, is not rejected within thirty days after the proposal date. Therefore, the insured's burden of declaration during the execution of the insurance contract continues for thirty days after the proposal date.

246. It is also important to determine for whom the matters have significance. The common view today is to make an assessment from the viewpoint of the insurer, who calculates the risk in any particular case and is nominally a party to the insurance contract. The burden of proving whether a matter is significant for him/her lies with the insurer.

247. Article 1436 of the Turkish Commercial Code regulates the declaration procedure under Article 1435 in terms of a 'list procedure'. According to the first paragraph of the article, no liability is placed on the policyholder regarding the remaining matters in the list under Article 1436 other than questions presented in a list provided by the insurer in a separate list of questions to be answered; unless the insured conceals a significant matter maliciously from questioning. If there are additional matters which have not been included in the list, but which the insurer wants to learn about, he or she can also ask the insured questions about them. The insured is obliged to answer all of these questions.

248. Even though the list procedure is adopted by the insurer, Article 1436 also provides the insurer with a 'mixed system' of procedures to choose from in the event that the insured avoids declaring a significant matter that he or she knows exists but is not included in the insurer's list. It is up to the insurer to choose which procedure to apply in any given circumstance.

249. By addressing questions to the insured, the insurer places great importance on the answers to be given to those questions when determining the formation of the insurance contract. It is possible for the insured to controvert the presumption of importance. If there are matters other than those in the list, which the insurer wants to learn about, he or she has the right to ask questions about them in an explicitly written form, and the insured must reply to them. All questions must be written in explicit form, including those that are electronically generated. The Law does not state that the insured must also answer in writing, which means that the insured can also reply verbally before the agent. The insured must answer not only the insurer's questions but also his representative insurance agent's. Pursuant to this provision, the questions of the doctor appointed by the insurer, for example, are also counted as questions of the insurer.

250. Article 1438 of the Turkish Commercial Code provides that the insurer cannot rely on the breach of the burden of declaration before execution of the contract if the real situation of a matter or a case, which was not notified at all or was misstated, is known by the insurer and he or she does not declare it, or the declared matter does not reflect the truth. The burden of proving this rests with the insured.

251. The insurer must have positive knowledge about the matter or case, which was not notified or was notified incorrectly. Knowledge by any association of the insurer or any other person with representation authority, for example, agents, is also attributed to the insurer. However, pursuant to Article 2(I)(d) of the Insurance Activities Act, any knowledge by the broker, acting as the insured's representative, cannot be attributed to the insurer.

252. Sanctions for breach of the burden of declaration are imposed by considering whether the risk had already occurred when the insurer learned about the particular breach. Article 1439(1) of the Turkish Commercial Code deals with sanctions related to the case when the breach of the burden of declaration is known before the risk had already happened. Accordingly, the insurer can terminate the contract or claim a premium difference within the period defined under Article 1440 if a matter, which is significant for the insurer, was not notified or was misstated by the policyholder. If the claimed premium difference is not accepted within ten days, the contract is deemed rescinded. According to Article 1440(2) of the Turkish Commercial Code, the rescission needs to be notified to the insured within fifteen days. This period begins on the date when the insurer learns about the breach of the burden of declaration.

253. If the right of rescission is used, the contract terminates retroactively. However, where the insurer terminates the contract pursuant to Article 1441 of the Turkish Commercial Code on the basis that the policyholder has deliberately provided misleading information at the time of contract formation, the insurer becomes entitled to the premiums from the period during which he has held the risk. The right to rescind an insurance contract is not limited to the insured's negligence in breach of the burden of declaration. Importantly, the fact that a matter was not discovered as a result of the insured's fault or the insured found it insignificant does not change the right of the insurer to rescind the contract. For initiation of the rescission period, the insurer must learn that the significant matters that were not declared, are incomplete or wrong. Estimated or implied information is not sufficient to initiate the rescission period. The insured must infer from the insurer's declaration of intent whether the contract has been rescinded or not. The decision of the insurer to rescind must be notified to the policyholder within fifteen days. The insurer's intent to terminate the contract within this period of time does not provide any conclusion by itself. The rescission must be addressed to the insured with a binding declaration, which can also be communicated to the insured's representative. The declaration of rescission is not subject to any form.

254. Circumstances that prevent the right to rescind are regulated under Article 1442 of the Turkish Commercial Code:

(a) The insurer renounces the right to rescind either explicitly or tacitly.
(b) The insurer causes the breach leading to the right to rescind.
(c) The insurer executes the insurance contract even though some of his questions were left without answers.

255. Article 1439 of the Turkish Commercial Code also sets out a rule allowing the modification of the insurance contract should the breach of the burden of declaration be learned by the insurer before the occurrence of the risk. The insurer can also claim a premium difference within ten days after learning about the breach of the burden of declaration arising from pre-contract negotiations. The premium difference refers to the difference between the premium, which the insured must pay in accordance with the real modified situation, and the premium agreed in fact. According to the provision at issue, if the insured does not accept the insurer's claim for a premium difference within ten days, the contract is automatically terminated without the need for the insurer's declaration of rescission; the termination gives a retroactive result.

256. Sanction for breach of the burden of declaration arising from pre-contractual negotiations – learned after the occurrence of the risk – is laid down in Article 1439(2) of the Turkish Commercial Code. Accordingly, when the burden of declaration is violated due to the negligence of the policyholder and this breach has the possibility to influence the amount of compensation or cost payable by the insurer or the likelihood of risk, a deduction is made from the amount of compensation payable commensurate with the degree of negligence. If the insured's negligence involves intent and there is a causal relation between the breach of the declaration obligation and the occurrence of risk, the insurer is not obliged to pay any compensation or costs; if there is no causal relation, the insurer pays the insurance compensation or cost considering the ratio between the amount of premium paid and premium due.

257. Article 1439(2) allows for different sanctions attributed to the type of breach by considering the type of fault and causal relation. In the case of an intentional breach, the degree of a sanction depends on the existence of a causal relation between the intentional breach of the burden of declaration after the risk has occurred and the actual risk. Conversely, where there is no intention of the insured in relation to negligence and breach and if this breach has the possibility to influence the amount of compensation or cost or the occurrence of risk, a deduction is made from the compensation as per the degree of negligence. If the breach has no adverse impact of influence, the full compensation is paid. For this rule, the causal relation is not enumerated as one of the sanction implementation conditions.

§2. Burdens During the Contract Period

I. Burden of Avoidance of Risk Aggravation

258. According to Article 1444 of the Turkish Commercial Code, the policy-holder cannot act in a manner or perform activities that influence an increase in the amount of compensation payable by aggravating the risk or the surrounding circumstances without the insurer's consent after the execution of the contract. With this provision, the insured is first charged with the 'burden of risk aggravation avoidance' during the contractual period.

259. *Risk aggravation* is any change in the hazard status of the risk which exists at the time of execution of the contract, increasing the possibility of risk occurrence or the amount of damage. In the event that there has been a change, and it is presumed that the insurer cannot conclude the contract under these existing conditions (such as receiving the same amount of premium), Articles 1444 and 1445 of the Turkish Commercial Code will apply, which are mandatory under Article 1452 and cannot be amended against the insured when contracting. Not only the insured's explicit actions but also his passive or tacit behaviour can aggravate the risk. It is also regarded as risk aggravation to avoid taking the necessary steps to prevent the risk aggravation or circumstances that can lead to the occurrence of a new risk situation. In order for risk aggravation to come into question, the *new risk situation* must be of a permanent nature. For example, an incident of theft resulting from a door being left open by the insured house owner when going out to empty the rubbish cannot be interpreted as risk aggravation due to the temporary nature of these circumstances.

260. Pursuant to Article 1445(1) of the Turkish Commercial Code, the insurer is entitled to terminate the contract or claim a premium difference in the case of risk aggravation. If the contract is terminated, the relationship between the parties ends prospectively. If the insurer does not use his right to terminate within one month after learning about the risk aggravation either through the policyholder's declaration or by his own means, the insurance contract continues to be binding. The one month granted to the insurer to terminate the contract is referred to as the *barring period*. The insurer can also claim the premium difference by preferring to keep the contract in operation within the one-month time bar following the date when he learns about the particular risk aggravation. If the policyholder does not accept the insurer's proposal regarding the amount of premium difference payable within ten days, the insurance contract is automatically deemed terminated.

261. The right of contract termination or claiming a premium is revoked from the insurer in some cases. If the risk increase is caused by a matter related to the insurer's interest, a case for which the insurer is responsible or the performance of a humanitarian duty and changes occurring in the insured's health status within the scope of life insurance, the insurer is not entitled to terminate the contract or claim an extra premium. The termination right is also not available when the aggravated risk situation has been eliminated, and the risk has returned to the situation as it was during the time of execution of the contract.

II. Burden of Disclosure of the Risk Aggravation

262. The policyholder is under the burden of declaration to the insurer about aggravated risk. The policyholder or, with his or her permission, someone else must immediately notify the insurer in the event he or she does anything to increase the possibility of the risk occurring or aggravating the present situation, or one of the matters, which are explicitly accepted as risk aggravation during the execution of the contract. In the event these risk-aggravation actions occur beyond the knowledge of the policyholder, a notification must be made within ten days at the latest after the policyholder (or someone else with his or her permission) learns about this matter.

263. The policyholder is subject to the burden of declaration for both subjective and objective risk aggravations. Subjective risk aggravation is an aggravation of the risk by the policyholder due to his or her own actions or behaviour or by a person appointed by the policyholder without his or her consent. By comparison, objective risk aggravation means the risk aggravation is not attributable to the insured's actions. The matters that need to be declared refer to the increase in the possibility of the risk occurring due to any reason or change in the present situation attributable to the policyholder. If the insurer knows during the conclusion of the contract that there will be such an increase or change in risk, he can agree on a higher insurance premium; if the policyholder executes the contract with such knowledge, he or she is obliged to inform the insurer about the increase or change in circumstances. Referring to the burden of declaration of the objective risk aggravation depends on its explicit acceptance during the execution of the contract. The declaration must be made within ten days from the date when the increase or change happens, or the insured becomes aware of circumstances that can lead to such an increase or change.

264. Different sanctions for the insured's breach of his or her declaration duty regarding the aggravated risk are applied depending on whether it was learned before or after the occurrence of the risk and on the existence of a causal link and the fault conditions. If the insurer learns about the policyholder's breach of the burden of declaration before the risk occurs, he or she can terminate the contract within the one-month barring period or claim a premium difference. If the premium difference claim is not accepted by the insured within ten days, the contract is deemed terminated. Even if the insurer terminates the contract upon learning prior to the risk occurrence that the insured has violated the burden of declaration intentionally, he or she becomes entitled to the premium of the insurance period, when this change happened. If it is discovered after the risk occurrence that the burden of declaration was violated due to the insured's negligence and this breach has the possibility to influence the amount of the compensation, the cost or the risk occurrence, a deduction is made from the compensation or the cost commensurate with the degree of negligence.

265. If the burden of declaration is violated intentionally, it must be determined whether there is a causal relation between the change and the risk occurrence. If a causal relation does exist, the insurer can terminate the contract in which case no insurance compensation or insurance sum is payable. If there is no causal relation, the insurer pays the insurance compensation or the amount representing the ratio between the paid premium and the premium due. Where the risk occurs in connection with any amendment within the period of declaration or termination of the contract by the insurer, the insurance compensation or insured sum is calculated considering the ratio between the paid premium and the premium due.

266. According to Article 1499 of the Turkish Commercial Code, the insurer cannot terminate a life insurance contract if five years have passed after the risk aggravation, including the renewals on the ground that the insured's burden of declaration has been violated; he can only claim a premium difference. If the insured does not accept to pay the premium difference, the insurer pays the insurance amount after the risk occurrence, considering the ratio between the paid premium and the premium due. However, the insurer can terminate the contract if the risk increase is beyond the limits defined by the technical principles due to a breach of the burden of declaration. The same right also exists when the burden of declaration is intentionally violated.

§3. Burdens after the Realization of the Risk

267. Article 1446 of the Turkish Commercial Code regulates the burden of declaration after the occurrence of the risk. This provision, which is mandatory as required by Article 1452 of the Turkish Commercial Code, cannot be amended by the insured who is a party to the contract. According to Article 1446, the insured must notify the insurer of the risk occurrence without any delay when he learns about the occurrence. The burden of declaration of the risk realization arises when the insured is aware of both the existence of the insurance contract and the occurrence of the risk. Pursuant to Article 1412 of the Turkish Commercial Code, the knowledge or the act of the insured, provided that he or she is aware of the insurance, the representative or the beneficiary is considered the same as the policyholder's knowledge or act. Accordingly, each of these persons has the burden of notifying the risk occurrence.

268. Whether the declaration was made in time is determined by paying attention, not to the receipt of the declaration by the insurer, but the date that the declaration was made. The declaration is not subject to any required form, and it is possible to do it verbally, via telephone or e-mail, etc. Where the declaration of the risk occurrence has not been made wholly or timely, and such breach causes an increase in the compensation or insured sum, a deduction is made from the compensation or the cost as per the degree of fault or negligence. If the burden of declaration has been intentionally breached, the insurer does not pay any compensation or can claim back the amount paid on the condition that a causal relation exists. The insurer must not have previously learned about the risk occurrence in order for a deduction to be made from the due insurance compensation. If the insurer previously learned about the risk occurrence, he or she cannot decrease the insurance compensation or insurance sum. If the insurer learned about the risk occurrence and an increase in the compensation or cost after the period for the performance of the burden of declaration by the insured passes, a deduction must be made from the due compensation as of the date when the insurer learned about the relevant circumstances.

I. Burden of Providing Information and Investigation

269. When the risk does occur, the insured must provide the insurer with information about the specific event so as to determine whether any compensation obligation exists and the extent of such obligation. In accordance with Article 1447(1) of the Turkish Commercial Code, the insured is obliged to provide full material information in line with the justified requirements of the insurer's information claim. This provision, which is mandatory as required by Article 1452 of the Turkish Commercial Code, cannot be amended by the insured who is a party to the contract.

270. The insured has to provide the insurer with any kind of information and documents necessary in the determination of the extent of the risk and compensation within an appropriate period of time in accordance with the contract or upon the insurer's request after the risk occurrence. Moreover, the insured is obliged to allow the insurer to inspect the place where the risk occurred or any other relevant places and to take appropriate measures expected from him/her pertaining to the received information and document quality. The insured's duty of assistance includes everything related to shedding light on the specific case of damage and risk occurrence. The extent of this assistance depends on the circumstances and properties of the particular case and a consideration of the reasonable and honest attitude of an insured with respect to his or her liability.

271. If the amount payable due to a breach of the burden of provision of information and investigation increases, a deduction is made from the compensation as per the degree of fault or negligence. Again, any causal relation between the fault, breach and the increase in the due amount is important when determining the amount of deduction from the compensation. However, it is appropriate to deny the insurer the right of benefitting from the aforementioned provision when any investigation about the matters related to the particular case is known by the insurer.

II. Burden of Taking Measures to Prevent or Mitigate the Damage and to Protect the Rights of Insurer

272. According to Article 1448 of the Turkish Commercial Code, the insured is obliged to take all possible measures to prevent or limit the amount of damage, protect the insurer's right of recourse towards third parties in cases when the risk materializes, or the possibility of its occurrence is high. This provision, which is mandatory as required by Article 1452 of the Turkish Commercial Code, cannot be amended by the insured who is a party to the contract. The burden of taking these measures is not associated just with the period following the occurrence of the risk; the insured is also bound to this burden in cases when the possibility of risk occurrence is high. The insured is only obliged to take measures which are possible and can be reasonably expected, which requires the insured to take measures and pay the same attention that would be paid by a reasonable and honest person under the same conditions. The insured cannot be obliged to take measures which are unnecessary or meaningless.

273. The insured is compelled to follow the insurer's instructions regarding the measures to be taken. If the insured notices that such instructions have been misstated or misrepresented or do not comply with the purpose explicitly or become irrelevant due to any change in the circumstances of the particular case, he or she can request the insurer to amend the instructions. Even if the measures taken by the insured in response to the instructions prove to be useless, the insurer is still liable to indemnify any expenses incurred by the insured from the insurance compensation or insurance sum. The insurer can also be obliged to pay the amount of this indemnity in advance. Furthermore, the insured cannot rely on the fact that the advance payment was not made in order to avoid taking any measures that can normally be covered by him/her in essential circumstances. If any breach of the insured's burden to prevent and decrease the amount of damage and to protect the insurer's right of recourse to third parties adversely affects the insurer, a deduction is made from the compensation commensurate with the degree of fault or negligence. Any causal relation between the fault, the breach and the increase in the amount to pay can increase the amount of deduction from the compensation.

III. Burden of Not Interfering with the Goods Damaged or the Place Where the Damage Occurred

274. Pursuant to Article 1471 of the Turkish Commercial Code, the insured must not interfere with or alter the place where the damage occurred or to the goods damaged before formal evaluation of damage, so as not to complicate or prevent identification of the damage caused and the amount of damage. This duty, which is mandated by law, covers the period after the risk occurs until the damage is surveyed and identified. After the identification process has been completed, any kind of dealing can be made in the natural flow of life. There are two exceptions to this burden of not interfering with the damaged goods or place of damage. The first one arises with the insurer's approval and the second one is applied to circumstances to decrease the amount of damage or to prevent further damage from occurring. In the event that this burden is breached due to the fault of the insured, a deduction is made from the compensation commensurate with the degree of fault level provided that there is a causal relationship between the breach and the damage. Where such a causal relationship is caused by an intentional breach by the insured, the insurer is not obligated to pay any compensation whatsoever.

IV. Other Contractual Burdens

275. According to Article 1449 of the Turkish Commercial Code, breach of any contractual burden obligation by the insured gives the insurer the right to terminate the contract, either partially or wholly, and without consequence if there is no fault on the part of the insured, but subject to the specific rules included in the Code or other laws. This provision, which is mandatory as required by Article 1452 of the Turkish Commercial Code, cannot be amended by the insured who is a party to the contract. If the breach is due to a fault, the termination right extends for one month from the identification of such fault unless the law foresees another period in particular circumstances. The insurer cannot terminate the contract in the event that the breach does not influence the risk occurring and the scope of action which must be taken by the insurer.

§4. Payment of Premium

Meltem Deniz Güner-Özbek

276. The insurance premium is the consideration given by the insured in return for the insurer's undertaking to cover the risks insured against. According to Article 1430(2) of the Turkish Commercial Code, the premium must involve the payment of money. It is common practice for the premium to be paid once at the commencement of the insurance contract, but the parties can otherwise agree to pay the premium in instalments. In such an instance, the condition is that the first instalment payment is made in cash, and subsequent instalments can be paid by bills of exchange.

277. Except for compulsory insurance, insurance companies are, in principle, free to determine the rate of premiums. In cases of compulsory insurance, the amount of insurance and rate regulations are determined by the Insurance and Private Pension Regulation and Supervision Agency.[378] However, there is an exception to this principle. If it is deemed necessary, the Insurance and Private Pension Regulation and Supervision Agency may decide to require approval of itself for the

378. Article 12 of the Insurance Activities Act.

implementation of tariffs, premiums, formulas and schemes of life assurances and personal accident, health, sickness and compulsory earthquake insurances of which duration is longer than a year.[379]

278. Payment of the premium, whether it is the full premium or the agreed first instalment, is made at the time of submission of the policy and execution of the insurance contract.[380] That is to say, payment of the premium is not due and payable as long as the policy is not submitted. The exception to this principle relates to transport insurance. Under transport insurance, the premium is to be paid at the time of execution of the contract even if the policy has not been issued. If payment of the premium has been divided into instalments, the due date and amount of each instalment and any default in payment are to be notified to the policyholder in writing or written on the policy. By agreement of the parties, payment of the full premium or any instalment may also be delayed.

§5. Fraudulent Claims

279. Any fraud involved in receiving the compensation amount or other insurance sum constitutes a crime in accordance with Article 158 of the Turkish Criminal Code.[381] The punishment for such a crime is imprisonment for a period of three to seven years and a judicial fine equivalent to up to 5,000 days: the fine must not be less than double the amount of interest derived from such a crime. Furthermore, inserting any fraudulent element in the insurance policy constitutes a documented crime that carries a punishment of one year to three years of imprisonment.[382] The person using such a fraudulent document knowingly is subject to the same punishment.

379. Article 12(2) of the Insurance Activities Act.
380. Article 1431 of the Turkish Commercial Code.
381. Code No. 5237 OG. No. 25611, Date: 12.10.2004.
382. Article 207 of the Turkish Criminal Code.

Chapter 5. Obligations of the Insurer

Meltem Deniz Güner-Özbek & Gülfer Meriç

280. The insurer is obliged to cover the loss sustained by the insurer in relation to indemnity insurance after the realization of the risk. This may be the payment of money or some form of reinstatement. Yet under life insurance, the insurer is obliged to pay the insured sum when the risk realizes. In principle, the person who is entitled to collect the compensation is indicated on the insurance policy. The burden of proving that the risk has realized after the insurance cover commences lies with the policyholder.

281. The insurer may pay the compensation or insured sum as *ex gratia* even if the loss may not legally be covered under the term of the insurance. Many insurers in Turkey had made *ex gratia* payments after the failed coup attempt on 15 July 2016.

§1. The Measurement of Loss

282. We have already mentioned several times that indemnity insurance and life insurance are governed by different principles. The measure of indemnity also differs according to the type of insurance in question. With respect to life insurance, the insured sum is paid with the realization of the risk. Under these types of policies, a fixed sum that will be paid at the time of realization of the risk is indicated. However, under indemnity insurance policies, the insured is entitled to recover strictly only for the loss sustained by him/her.[383] It is because indemnity insurance is subject to the principle of prohibition of unjust enrichment. This principle means that insurance cannot be used for the purpose of enrichment. Thus, the interest value at the time of loss is recoverable by the insured, and principally the insured cannot recover more than that.

283. In order to measure the insurance indemnity, it is crucial to distinguish between total loss and partial loss. For partial loss, the measure of indemnity is predicated upon restoring the insured to his pre-loss position. In other words, the difference in the actual value of the insured interest before and after the realization of the risk is recovered. For a total loss, the insurance indemnity is measured in accordance with the market value of the insured interest and the time and place of loss. Therefore, the insured is entitled to recover the resale value of the insured interest, unless otherwise agreed. However, this principle of indemnity is not absolute, and it is always possible for the contracting parties to agree on another principle of indemnity. Under replacement insurance, or new for old, policies, the loss or damage of the insured is recovered by providing a similar replacement. In other words, the insurer undertakes to pay a replacement value, which is the cost of

383. Article 1459 of the Turkish Commercial Code.

replacing the lost property with an equivalent new property.[384] However, it is always possible for the parties to an insurance contract to agree on the insurance value of the subject matter insured.[385] This is called valued policies, and such value is taken into consideration principally as the insured sum. If such a valuation is drastically excessive, the insurer can request a reduction of the valuation.

284. As for the insurance indemnity for liability insurance, the insurer must pay the liability of the insured, up to the amount indicated under the insurance contract.[386] The victim is granted the right of direct action from the insurer, and the victim will be compensated by the insurer for the amount specified in the policy. However, this rule is not a protective provision as the contracting parties are entitled to agree to cover fully the liability of the insured.

§2. Burden of Proof

285. The insurer's obligation to pay indemnity will only be invoked if the loss falls within the scope of the insurance cover and the loss was caused by a risk covered by the insurance contract. The burden of proving that the loss was caused by an insured risk lies with the policyholder. On the contrary, in order for the insurer to be exonerated from liability, the burden of proving that the loss does not fall within the ambit of the insurance cover lies with the insurer.[387]

§3. Procedure

286. For the determination of the loss the parties must agree on the amount of the loss sustained arising from the realization of the risk. If the parties cannot reach an agreement, general conditions usually contain rules for the procedure.[388] Accordingly, parties appoint an expert. If the parties cannot agree on the selection of a single expert each party appoints his or her own expert, and then these experts appoint an impartial third expert.[389]

---

384. Kender, *Sigorta Hukuku,* pp. 326–327. Ulaş, (*Zarar Sigortaları Hukuku*) pp. 54–55. For more information regarding repacement value insurance Huriye Kubilay, *Yeni Değer Sigortası* (Replacement Value Insurance) (Dokuz Eylül Üniversitesi Hukuk Fakültesi Döner Sermaye İşletmesi Yayınları No. 51 1994).
385. Article 1464 of the Turkish Commercial Code.
386. Article 1473 of the Turkish Commercial Code; Rayegan Kender, *Mesuliyet Sigortasının Mahiyeti ve Türleri* (*Legal Character and Types of Liability Insurance*), p. 3.
387. Article 1409(2) of the Turkish Commercial Code for more information regarding burden of proof concerning insurance contracts, Sibel Korkmaz, *Sigorta Sözleşmelerinde İspat Sorunları* (*Burden of Proof Problems under Insurance Contracts*) (Güncel Yayınevi İzmir 2004).
388. General Conditions of Theft Insurance, General Conditions of Fire Insurance, General Conditions of Construction Insurance.
389. Article B.3 of the General Conditions of the Theft Insurance; Art. B.4 of the Fire Insurance Policy, Art. B.2 of the General Conditions of the Construction Insurance.

§4. UNDER-INSURANCE

287. Under-insurance is in question where the sum insured is less than the value of the property insured under an insurance contract. The value of the property insured matters only in relation to indemnity insurance, particularly for active insurance. Therefore, under-insurance is also only possible for active insurance.[390] Under-insurance can occur when the policyholder wilfully under-insures the property, for instance, to pay a lower premium.[391] On the contrary, the property may also become under-insured over time due to inflation or other increases in the value of the property. For instance, insured real estate may increase in value over time, and the real estate then becomes under-insured.

288. In the event of under-insurance, the scope of the obligation to pay indemnity is determined proportionally. The insured is entitled to collect not the loss sustained by him/her, but the sum insured for the total loss. However, if a partial loss is sustained, the insured is entitled to collect the part of the loss calculated according to the proportion between the insured sum and the value of the insured.[392] However, the contracting parties are entitled to agree otherwise, as this provision is not a protective one.[393] Where the parties agree that the total loss is payable, the compensation is not determined pro rata. The insured will recover the loss sustained by him/her up to the amount of the insured sum. Certainly, such a policy will require a higher premium since the risk is aggravated. If there is no such agreement, the insurance policy will be subject to the principle of pro rata.[394]

§5. OVER-INSURANCE

289. In the event that the sum insured exceeds the value of the insured property, there is over-insurance, and the exceeding part of the sum insured becomes invalid. The insurer must return the part of the insurance premium that represents the exceeding part of the sum insured.[395] Over-insurance is drawn into question for indemnity insurance, particularly active insurance.[396] The policyholder may either deliberately form an over-insurance contract, or in some circumstances, the value of the insured property may decrease due to factors such as age or deflation.[397] The

390. In other words under-insurance is not possible for liability insurances or personal insurances. (Samim Ünan, *İsteğe Bağlı Genel Sorumluluk Sigortasında Riziko)* (Risk in Voluntary Liability Insurance) (İstanbul: Beta, 1998), p. 17.
391. Kender, *Sigorta Hukuk*, p. 311; Bozer, p. 75. Can, *Birden Çok Sigorta* (Multiple Insurance), pp. 27–28.
392. Article 1462 of the Turkish Commercial Code.
393. Article 1486 of the Turkish Commercial Code.
394. Kender, *Sigorta Hukuku*, p. 312; Bozer, p. 76. Can, (*Birden Çok Sigorta*) p. 29.
395. Article 1463 of the Turkish Commercial Code.
396. Kender, (*Mesuliyet Sigortasının Mahiyeti ve Türleri*), p. 11. Ünan, (*steğe Bağlı Genel Sorumluluk Sigortasında Riziko*), p. 17.
397. Kender, *Sigorta Hukuku*, 313; Bozer, 73; Can, (*Birden Çok Sigorta*), p. 30.

insured is entitled to collect part of the insurance premium that corresponds to the exceeding part of the sum insured. This rule has been adopted under Article 1463 of the Turkish Commercial Code. One may interpret this rule in a way that the insured is entitled to recover surplus premiums that correspond to the exceeding part of the sum insured from the commencement of the contract. However, this means that the insurer assumes the whole risk until it has been discovered that the property has been over-insured. Therefore, any surplus premiums that correspond to the exceeding part of the sum insured for the period after it has been discovered that the property has been over-insured may be recovered by the insured. Although this legal application is not clear under the relevant provision of the Turkish Commercial Code, it can be observed that this principle has already been adopted under most insurance policies.[398]

290. In certain cases the policyholder may deliberately and intentionally over-insure the property to gain unlawful profit. In this case, the over-insurance contract that is formed in bad faith becomes null and void. If the insurer does not know that the property has been over-insured, the insurer will be entitled to collect the entire premium that corresponds to the coverage period.[399] In order to be entitled to the premium, the insurer must prove that the property has been over-insured and that the policyholder intentionally over-insured the property in bad faith in order to gain unlawful profit.

§6. Multiple Insurance

291. The general rule is that a person may execute as many insurance contracts as he or she wishes against the same risks and at the same time. Indemnity insurance is subject to the prohibition of unjust enrichment. Thus multiple insurance policies for indemnity insurance are specifically regulated under the Turkish Commercial Code. However, one may conclude as many life insurance contracts as he or she wishes as this is not subject to the principle of unjust enrichment. Co-insurance, double insurance and partial insurance will be discussed below.

I. Co-insurance

292. In practice, major ('gross') risks are covered by more than one insurer. Thereby the major risk is shared between several insurance companies. Co-insurance is commonly used in the insurance of giant industrial companies, airlines, and energy companies. The most fundamental principle of co-insurance is that the insurers assume the risk altogether.[400] Therefore, it is possible for an interest to

398. Kender, *Sigorta Hukuku*, p. 314.
399. Article 1463(2) of the Turkish Commercial Code.
400. Kender, *Sigorta Hukuku*, p. 317. For detailed information regarding co-insurance; Can (*Birden Çok Sigorta*), pp. 39–83.

be covered by several insurers on the same date, for the same period and against the same risks. These insurance contracts are only valid for sums up to the value of the insured property. If the total sum exceeds the damaged value, every insurer is liable for the proportion between its insured sums and the total of the insurance sums.[401]

293. In principle, co-insurers are not jointly and severally liable; the risk is shared between the insurers. Yet the contracting parties are entitled to agree that the insurers will be jointly liable. In this case, each insurer will be liable for the loss up to the proportionate sum that they are insured.[402] In other words, the insured is entitled to claim his/her loss from any one of the co-insurers up to the agreed amount in his policy. Because the insurance contract is still subject to the principle of the prohibition of enrichment the insured can only recover the loss sustained by him/her. If parties agree on the joint liability of insurers and the insured claimed his/her loss from one of the co-insurers, the co-insurer who indemnified the insured is granted the right of recourse to the other insurers. The right of recourse will be used according to the proportion that the insurers have to pay pursuant to their insurance policy.[403]

294. The total sum insured under the co-insurance contract is, in principle, equal to the value of the property or the interest. The reason is that co-insurance policies are designed to share the risk between several insurers. Under co-insurance contracts, each insurer is liable for the risk it covers. If the property is over-insured, the exceeding part of the sum insured will become invalid. The insurers assume the risk together under co-insurance, and for this reason, they may choose to issue a collective insurance policy together, or each insurer may issue separate policies. If a collective policy is issued, it must be signed by every co-insurer.[404]

II. Double Insurance

295. In principle, policies for the same property or the same interest covered against the same risk and for the same period of time will be deemed valid only under certain conditions.[405] In order for the following rules to apply the insurance must be taken out to cover the interest for its full value. Insurance contracts with a different scope do not constitute double insurance policies. Double insurance is valid under three conditions:

401. Article 1466(1) of the Turkish Commercial Code.
402. Bozer, p. 79. Kender, *Sigorta Hukuku*, p. 319.
403. Article 1466(2) of the Turkish Commercial Code.
404. Kender, *Sigorta Hukuku*, p. 319.
405. Double insurance may be possible for liability insurances and rules regarding double insurance are also applicable for liability insurances. In this respect, the insurers will be liable up to the amount limit determined under their insurance contract. Double insurance for liability insurance is controversial in the doctrine. Ünan, *İsteğe Bağlı Genel Sorumluluk Sigortasında Riziko*, p. 18. For detailed information regarding double insurance, *see* Can, *Birden Çok Sigorta*, pp. 85–135.

(1) If the latter and former insurers give approval for double insurance, it will constitute a co-insurance, and the contract will be subject to the rules of co-insurance.[406] Hence every insurer will be liable according to the proportion between its insured sum and the total of the insurance sums.
(2) The policyholder may assign the rights arising from the former insurance contract to the latter insurer. In this case, double insurance will be deemed valid provided that the assignment is indicated under the latter insurance contract. Otherwise, the latter insurance contract becomes null and void.[407]
(3) The contracting parties for the latter insurance contract may agree that the latter insurer is liable to recover only for the amount of loss that the former insurer did not recover. In this case, double insurance is valid provided that the existence of the former insurance contract is referred to under the latter contract. If there is no such reference, the latter insurance contract becomes null and void.[408]

296. Therefore the validity of double insurance is ensured by co-insurance, although they represent two different types of multiple insurances. The above-mentioned conditions are stipulated under the Turkish Commercial Code, yet one could reach the same solution even if the law did not provide specific regulations for double insurance. The reason is that double insurance can be inferred from the general principles governing indemnity insurance.

III. Partial Insurance

297. It is also possible for a person to take out several insurance policies to cover the interest for less than its full value. In this case, the insurance in question does not constitute a co-insurance because the insurers do not share the intention of assuming the risk altogether. However, each insurer will be liable pursuant to the specific insurance contract that it is party to. In conclusion, if one takes out insurance to cover an interest for less than its full value, he or she may take out several other insurances covering the remaining part of the full value.[409] In such circumstances, the latter insurers will be liable from the date of execution of the insurance contract. If the insurance contracts are executed on the same date, the contracts will be deemed to have been executed at the same time.[410] Such insurance will be subject to the principles governing under-insurance, and the insurers will not be held jointly and severally liable.[411]

406. Article 1467/(1) a of the Turkish Commercial Code.
407. Article 1467/(1) b of the Turkish Commercial Code.
408. Article 1467/(1) c of the Turkish Commercial Code.
409. For detailed information regarding co-insurance, *see* Can, (*Birden Çok Sigorta*), pp. 137–142.
410. Article 1468 of the Turkish Commercial Code.
411. Bozer, p. 80.

§7. Partial Loss

298. In case of partial loss the insured is indemnified only for the amount of the loss sustained. The amount of indemnity paid in such a circumstance is reduced from the original insurance sum; however, the parties may agree otherwise.[412] This principle, reducing the paid amount from the original sum, does not apply to liability insurance. The concept of partial loss is not relevant to life insurances; hence, it does not apply to them. The parties to the insurance contract have the right to terminate the contract in case of partial loss.[413] Yet, the insurer's right to terminate the insurance contract may only be used after indemnification of partial loss.

§8. Subrogation of the Insurer

Hakan Karan & Kemal Şenocak

299. Under Article 1472(1) of the Turkish Commercial Code, the insurer is granted the insured's rights following payment of the insurance compensation, and an action can be directly filed against third parties who are responsible for the damage incurred. This subrogated right of recourse has two basic reasons. First, the damage suffered by the insured can only be compensated once due to the prohibition against unjust enrichment under damage insurance rules. Second, the principle of subrogation enables the insurer to consult the person who is really responsible for the damage, and this person is made to bear liability for the damage that he or she has caused.

300. First, there must be an insurance contract between the compensated person and the insurer, which covers the damage. The damage must then be brought about by a third party within the scope of this contract so that the insurer can have the right of recourse. For payments based on an invalid insurance contract, the insurer cannot have recourse to third parties, who are responsible for the damage, by relying on the subrogation principle. In such a case, the insurer can claim the amount that is paid to the insured from the third party, who is responsible for the damage, only if the insured assigns his claims against the third party who is responsible for the damage. Furthermore, the insurer must have already made a payment to the insured for the damage included in the insurance coverage. Likewise, the subrogation right is limited to the amount of the payment made to the insured without exceeding the insurance amount; if he pays more than this amount, he cannot be compensated for damage to parts of the good(s) that exceed the insurance amount. The insurer cannot gain the right of recourse without paying the compensation.

301. Pursuant to Article 1421 of the Turkish Commercial Code, the insurer's obligation to pay insurance compensation begins with the payment of the first premium by the insured. Therefore, the insurer's subrogation is only recognized after

412. Article 1428(1) of the Turkish Commercial Code.
413. Article 1428(2) of the Turkish Commercial Code.

the first premium payment. If the risk occurs between the dates when the contract was executed and the first premium was paid, the insurer will not be able to subrogate the insured's rights as he has not been formally required to compensate for the damage incurred. If the insurer pays the insured for damage that has been incurred within this period, the insurer will only be able to claim this amount when the insured's compensation claim against the liable third party is assigned to the insurer.

302. The insurer must make insurance compensation payment to the legitimate rights holder. For example, the insurer cannot gain the right of subrogation for sales conducted through the retention of title if he makes a payment to the seller whose property is undamaged. If the insured goes bankrupt, the insurance compensation must be paid to the bankrupt's estate for the insurer to be granted the right of subrogation.

303. No legal subrogation arises for the insurer due to payments (*ex gratia payment*), which he made to the legitimate rights holder for damages outside the scope of the insurance coverage. The insured's right to claim compensation from the third party who is responsible for the damage extends to damage to parts of the goods not compensated by the insurer. Even if the insurer has paid more compensation to the insured, he is only entitled to claim the real damage payment for the loss that the insured actually suffered. This compensation amount that is paid for the real damage constitutes the upper limit of the insurer's recourse rights and no more than this compensation amount is submitted to the insurer.

304. The other necessary condition for the insurer to have the right of recourse is that the insured must have the right to claim compensation from the particular third party who caused the damage. If the insured does not have such a right, the insurer does not have the right to obtain compensation from such a third party either. The cause of action of the insured is not significant in terms of the insured's right of recourse. In order for the insurer to have the right of recourse, the insured's right of litigation against the third party who is responsible for the damage must continue until compensation payment is made to the insured. If the insured violates the right of litigation against the third party, for example, by consulting with the insurer for the damage compensation while acquitting the third party, no litigation right can be subrogated by the insurer. However, if the insured's acquittal of the third party is invalid and does not lead to any legal consequence after he or she receives the insurance compensation, the insurer will be able to subrogate the right of litigation following the time of payment because the insured does not have the power of disposition over this right anymore.

305. As a rule, the insurer's right of recourse is used against the person who caused the subject matter risk to occur. However, in some circumstances, it may not be possible to assert this right of recourse against the people responsible for the damage. For example, if the circumstances leading to the incident of damage were caused or contributed by the insured or the policyholder, the insurer cannot use the right of recourse against those third parties. The insured's right of recourse has validity according to the compensation paid by him/her and to the extent that it does not exceed the actual damage amount. By making a payment to the insured, the insurer becomes entitled to claim interest from the payment date thereafter. However, notice must first be given before becoming entitled to claim an interest in step with the recourse action filed by the insurer of the relevant damage; otherwise, the interest will begin to accrue following the date initiating legal action as the insurer of the damage will have defaulted on this date.

306. According to the Court of Appeals Decision of Joint Chambers dated 17 January 1972 and number 2/1, the insurer can submit all pleas of the insured against the third party responsible for the damage relying on the principle of subrogation. The same consequence is also valid for all recourse actions filed by the insurer of the party who has suffered a loss against the insurer of the parties responsible for such loss and damage. For example, a driver's insurer can submit exemptions under Article 86 of the Highway Traffic Act, which discharges or decreases the liability of the driver in response to an action for damages that have been filed against him due to a traffic accident. The action filed by the insurer is subject to the same limits as the action, which can be filed by the insured against the same person.

307. The insured has the burden of protecting the insurer's subrogation-based rights by avoiding any breach of them. However, the insured must also take the necessary measures so that these rights can be used by the insurer. The burden of taking the protective measures regulated under Article 1448 of the Turkish Commercial Code constitutes both negative and positive actions in this way. In turn, the insured must protect and pay attention to the accessory rights together with the compensation credit.

Examples that can be given for breach of this burden of the insured include:

- any failure to issue a notice of a claim protecting compensation entitlements resulting from damage to the item carried under the cargo insurance; the insured's acquisition of compensation also from the third party responsible for the damage or his liability insurer after obtaining the insurance compensation;
- the insured's acquittal of the third party;
- conveying the compensation owed against the third party to someone else before payment is made by the insurer.

308. If the insured violates any right to be subrogated and prevents the insured from filing a recourse action against the person(s) responsible for the damage, the insurer cannot claim the compensation, which will be paid to the insured notwithstanding the fact that they are at fault. If the insured prevents the insurer from subrogating a right due to his or her actions after the payment of compensation, he or she does not have the power of disposition over the right of legal action as this right will be transferred to the insurer following the time of payment. However, the person(s) liable for the damage, and who make compensation payment to the insured in good faith without knowing the situation, must also be protected. Pursuant to

Article 186 of the Obligations Law, the debtor, who makes a payment to the previous creditor in good faith without knowing about the transfer of the credit, is discharged from liability. This provision must also be deemed valid for insurance law activities, and compensation payments made by third parties to the insured without knowing the legal insurance relation of the insured must be considered valid as well. In this case, it is possible for the insurer to claim compensation from the insured for the damage he or she has incurred due to the breach of his recourse right.

309. The rule of subrogation only exists in property and liability insurances, and the insurer does not have the right of recourse in life insurance according to Article 1491 of the Turkish Commercial Code. Moreover, the insured and his or her heirs who collect the agreed insurance amount from the insurer, and the heirs of the people who deal with the risk, cannot transfer to the insurer any compensation claim that they are entitled to against the third party causing the risk to occur in accordance with a life insurance contract and the explicit provisions of the Code. However, the rule of subrogation has partial application in the area of liability insurance. According to Article 1481 of the Turkish Commercial Code, the insured has the right of legal action against the person(s) responsible for the damage incurred, which in turn belongs to the insurer to the amount of the compensated cost. Under this provision, the insurer's legal subrogation under liability insurance acquires currency if the other people together with the insured are responsible jointly and severally for the same and single damage. If the insurer of one of the people, who is responsible jointly and severally for the damage, covers liability for the victim's damage wholly, the insurer may recourse to other responsible parties by subrogating the rights of his insured to recover the amount that he has paid more.

310. By law, the spouse, mother, father and children of the insured and the people with whom he or she lives are also subject to the insurer's right of legal subrogation. Therefore, the insurer can file a recourse action against these people relying on the legal subrogation principle, unless otherwise agreed under the insurance.

Chapter 6. Termination of the Insurance Contract

Meltem Deniz Güner-Özbek & lyas Gölcüklü

311. Termination of an insurance contract may arise from various situations.[414] Some of these situations will result in the termination of the insurance contract without even requiring notice to be sent for such termination. Termination occurs as soon as a particular condition is met. Some other circumstances may give rise to a right for one contracting party to terminate a contract due to a material breach. In such cases, the terminating party is required to send notice of termination to the breaching party.

§1. Invalidity of the Insurance Contract

312. If an insurance contract is in breach of protective provisions, moral values, public order or rights of personality then such a contract is null and void.[415] In such a case, the notice of termination is not required. In other words, such a contract does not need to be terminated separately by one of the contracting parties. Where there is a *lack of the insurable* interest at the time of execution, such a contract will be null and void. Such invalidity arises due to the lack of subject matter in the insurance contract.[416] If the insured interest ceases to exist within the contract period, then the valid insurance contract becomes promptly null and void at such time too.

§2. Grounds for Termination

313. In cases such as when the *insurer* declares composition of debts or its licence in the relevant insurance branch is revoked, or its power to execute the insurance contract is abrogated, the policyholder is entitled to terminate the insurance contract *within one month* of the date that he or she becomes aware of such facts.[417] Use of the term 'in cases *such as*' means that these grounds are not limited and the policyholder can rely on similar other grounds for the termination as long as it fulfils the burden of proving such grounds for termination.

314. When the insurer becomes bankrupt, the insurance contract terminates immediately without any notice from the policyholder required.[418] This is one of the exceptional grounds to terminate an insurance contract. Article 1417 of the Turkish Commercial Code regulates 'insolvency of the parties' and 'enforcement without outcome' situations. In such cases, the policyholder is entitled to request security

414. Kender, *Sigorta Hukuku*, p. 340; Çeker, Mustafa, 'Sigorta Hukuku' (Insurance Law), Karahan Basımevi (Adana 2008), p. 84; Can, (Sigorta Hukuku), p. 276; Kubilay, Huriye, 'Uygulamalı Özel Sigorta Hukuku' (Applied Private Insurance Law), Barış Publication (İzmir 2003), p. 171.
415. *See* Art. 1404 of the Turkish Commercial Code.
416. Çeker (Sigorta Hukuku), p. 51; also *see* Art. 1408 of the Turkish Commercial Code.
417. Kender, *Sigorta Hukuku*, p. 342; also *see* Art. 1413(1) of the Turkish Commercial Code.
418. Article 1418(1) of the Turkish Commercial Code.

from the insurer to ensure that the insurer will fulfil its obligations regarding insured interests. If such security is not provided within one week of the request, the policyholder is entitled to terminate the insurance contract. The second paragraph of this Article 1417 gives the same right to the insurer as well. According to this provision in the same circumstances, the insurer may request security for the premium, and if such security is not given, the insurer may terminate the insurance contract without sending a notice. The Turkish Commercial Code provides the same termination rights in favour of the *insurer* by stating that if the policyholder declares a moratorium before paying the whole premium, the insurer may terminate such insurance contract within one month from the date of becoming aware of such moratorium.[419]

315. In practice, insurers usually insert an adjustment clause under the contract for increasing the premium without changing the scope of the contract. In such cases, the policyholder has the right to terminate the contract within one month from the date of receiving notification from the insurer of such an increase.[420]

316. Turkish law gives both parties the right to terminate the insurance contract partially. According to the Turkish Commercial Code, if the insurer cancels or terminates certain terms of the contract on valid and justified grounds, and if it appears from the situation that the insurer would not have executed the contract on the same conditions with the remaining terms, he or she may terminate or cancel the contract entirely.[421] In such a case, there is no time limit for termination or cancellation, but the insurer should use this legal right in a reasonable period of time. If the insurer has cancelled or partially terminated the contract, the policyholder may cancel or terminate the contract entirely as well.[422]

317. Apart from these conditions, both parties may agree on termination mutually at any time during the term of the contract.[423] Furthermore, the insurance contract automatically terminates if the insured risk materializes and *total loss* occurs.[424] However, where only *partial loss* occurs, the insurance contract remains effective and operational for the remaining amount of insurance.[425] Therefore, the insurance contract will only terminate if *complete loss* is suffered by the insured.

419. Article 1413(2) of the Turkish Commercial Code.
420. Article 1414 of the Turkish Commercial Code.
421. Çeker, p. 84; Kender, *Sigorta Hukuku*, p. 341; Art. 1415(1) of the Turkish Commercial Code.
422. *See* Art. 1415(2) of the Turkish Commercial Code.
423. Kender, *Sigorta Hukuku*, p. 342; Çeker, *Sigorta Hukuku*, p. 84.
424. Çeker, *Sigorta Hukuku*, p. 85.
425. Kender, *Sigorta Hukuku*, pp. 304 ff.

Part III. Property and Liability Insurance

Chapter 1. Fire Insurance

Meltem Deniz Güner-Özbek & Banu Bozkurt-Bozabalı

318. Fire as a risk has threatened people's lives and properties for centuries. With technological developments, the types of fire risks have changed, and with it, the need for different preventative measures against fire has also increased. As such, fire was one of the original subjects to be covered by the insurance concept, and the type of coverage has also had to be developed over the years.

319. In principle, fire insurance is classified as active property insurance because the main aim of fire insurance is to cover the possible material damage to property or goods caused by fire. However, fire may give rise to liability. Thus liability insurance for fire is also possible.

§1. The Meaning of Fire

320. In relation to the definition of fire, a distinction between *hostile* and *friendly flame* (fire) should be made. Accordingly, a fire is defined as friendly when its source, such as a chimney, or kiln, can be controlled. In contrast, fire is hostile when it becomes dangerous and threatening by spreading out of the controlled place.[426] According to this distinction, a fire for insurance purposes may be defined as a flame burning outside the controlled place that may spread by its own power. In a determinant sense a fire should have three essential characteristics: (i) it must be a flame; (ii) it must be uncontrolled or uncontrollable; and (iii) it must have the power or capacity to spread.[427] Conversely, if there isn't any flame or the fire is under control or doesn't have enough power to spread, it will not be defined as a fire for insurance purposes.

---

426. For further detail on the definition *see* Ali Bozer, '*Sigorta Hukuku*', 2nd ed. (Banka ve Ticaret Enstitüsü, 2007), pp. 99–101; Can (Sigorta Hukuku), pp. 175–176; Çeker (Sigorta Hukuku) pp. 184–185 Tekin Memiş, '*Yangın Sigortasında Riziko*', (Seçkin Yayınları, 2001), pp. 25–27.
427. For further details on these characteristics *see* Memiş, pp. 26–42.

§2. Standard Policy Cover and Exceptions

321. Fire insurance is designed to cover the material damage to property or goods caused by fire. Similar to the definition of fire above, the cover of fire insurance should also be explained in relation to the concepts of *covered* (standard cover) and *uncovered* risks (exceptions). The fire insurance policy covers the risk of burning movable goods and immovable property (or real estate) of the policyholder or insured. If there is not a special, additional coverage clause, the policy only covers the *direct* damage caused by the fire.[428] According to the general terms of the fire insurance policy, the insurer must indemnify the damage of the insured goods and real estate if such damage has been caused by fire or a stroke of lightning or explosion, or by smoke, vapour or heat caused by the fire.[429] In other words, if the damage is caused by the inherent defect of the insured goods or real estate or by inherent heat or fermentation or transformation, fire insurance cover will not apply.[430]

322. Furthermore, according to the general terms of the fire insurance policy, if the fire is caused by an explosion, any damage arising after the explosion is not covered by the fire insurance policy. The exception to this rule is that if the explosion is caused by the fire, any damage arising from that explosion is covered by the insurance.[431] Thus, in the event of an explosion, the source of the explosion should be determined clearly. Additionally, the fire does not have to start on the insurance property. In other words, fire insurance also covers the damage caused by a fire that starts in another place and spreads to the insured property or estate.[432]

323. Paragraph A4 of the general terms of fire insurance policy sets out the risks that are not covered by fire insurance:[433]

- any damage arising from any kind of military and disciplinary activities, any kind of war incident, occupation, hostile foreigner activities, combat activities (even without a war), civil war, revolution, riot, rebellion;
- any damage caused by the necessary military and disciplinary actions and precautions for preventing the radiation and radioactivity contaminations of nuclear fuel or nuclear waste resulting from the burning of nuclear fuel or any other reason arising from such events;

---

428. For further detail *see* Çeker (Sigorta Hukuku), p. 185–186; F. Kaya, *Sigortacılı k*, 3. Bası, (Beta Yayınevi, 2014), pp. 363–364; Memiş, pp. 25–47.
429. For further detail *see* Can (Sigorta Hukuku), p. 177; Çeker (Sigorta Hukuku), pp. 186–187; Kaya, p. 363. For the Turkish version of the general conditions of the insurance policy *see,* http://www.tsb.org.tr/Default.aspx?pageID=524&srch=yangınsigortasıgenelşartları (26.9.2014).
430. Çeker, (Sigorta Hukuku), p. 186.
431. *Ibid.*; Memiş, pp. 70–72.
432. 11th Circuit of the Court of Appeals discusses this issue in one of its cases 2.11.2000, No. 2000/7077. For the Turkish full text of the case *see,* http://www.kazanci.com/kho2/ibb/giris.htm (26.5.2014, online search); Çeker (Sigorta Hukuku) pp. 188–189.
433. For the Turkish version of the general conditions of the insurance policy *see* http://www.tsb.org.tr/Default.aspx?pageID=524&srch=yangınsigortasıgenelşartları (26.9.2014). For further detail *see* Memiş, pp. 94–108.

- any kind of damage caused by the intervention of administrative authorities on the insured goods or real estate;
- any kind of damage resulting from the own default or fermentation or burning or any other deformation of the insured goods without the presence of the fire;
- any kind of damage caused by the exposure of the insured movable good to fire or to heat for work or for any other useful purpose; by the drop of these goods to the chimney or any other fire place; by the combustion or burning of clothes without fire or by the touch of heating, lightening or ironing installations along with lights, candles or cigarettes;
- any kind of damage arising from the induction and heating caused by short circuits, grounding?? or changes in the voltage of any kind of motors operated by electric or electronic equipment, device, installation and cables;
- any kind of damage arising from the collapse, deformation and wear and tear of the vessels caused by low pressure along with damage in the insured devices and motors resulting from mechanical incidents and centrifugal force would not be indemnified by the fire insurance.

324. Furthermore, according to paragraph B7(2) of the general terms,[434] if the fire is started because of the intentional or reckless acts of the policyholder, any damage caused by such fire is not covered by the insurance. Therefore, the policyholder should first prove that the fire is not caused by his or her intentional or reckless acts.[435]

There exists a second list of incidents that are not normally covered by general fire insurance policy but can be included under additional cover.[436]

§3. Subject Matter of the Insurance

325. Any kind of moveable good or immoveable property (real estate) may be the subject of the fire insurance policy. Accordingly, fire insurance for real estate covers damage caused to the main building or property and the component parts or annexes such as the garage, water tank and coal house. It also covers damage to the complementary accessories of the building such as the systems, installations, elevators or television antenna. The building foundations and retaining walls are also covered.[437] Any other things such as walls other than the retaining walls (for

434. For the Turkish version of the general conditions of the insurance policy *see* http://www.tsb.org.tr/Default.aspx?pageID=524&srch=yangınsigortasıgenelşartları (26.9.2014).
435. For further detail *see* Çeker (Sigorta Hukuku), p. 188; Memiş, pp. 146–150.
436. These incidents will be explained in details below in the Additional Insurable Risk section.
437. Bozer, p. 104; Kaya, p. 364. For the Turkish version of the general conditions of the insurance policy *see,* http://www.tsb.org.tr/Default.aspx?pageID=524&srch=yangınsigortasıgenelşartları (26.9.2014).

instance, garden walls), terraces, ports or landing stages, sculptures, pools or cisterns outside of the building may only be covered by the insurance if it is cited specifically under the policy.[438] The coverage for goods is determined by articles or categories, whereby any good identified under these articles or categories is covered by the fire insurance policy. Therefore, any fire damage caused to these goods must be indemnified by the insurer.[439]

§4. Premium

326. The insurance premium is the cash remuneration of the risk coverage of the insurer. Accordingly, the premium should be determined in a balanced way. If it is determined too high, the policyholder may avoid or hesitate to execute the insurance contract. On the contrary, if the premium is determined too low, then the insurer may hesitate to provide the insurance coverage.[440] Accordingly, for determining the premium under the fire insurance policy for real estate, the construction material and style of the property is significant in determining the amount of the insurance policy. Regarding the construction material, real estate property can be distinguished as either stone or brick, frame building or timbered building, and this distinction affects the total amount of the premium.[441] The possibility of the realization of the risk is another important factor in the determination of the premium. Therefore, the intended use of the property is also important and civil, commercial and industrial risks are distinguished from each other.[442]

§5. Types of Fire Insurance Policies

327. Under the fire insurance policy, along with other conditions, the emplacement, the construction material and style and the intended use of the building should be specified.[443] Furthermore, in practice, some special types of insurance policies

438. Subparagraph 1.2 of the Art. A.2 of the general conditions of the fire insurance. According to subpara. 1.3, the value of the land should not be taken into consideration for the determination of the insured value. For the Turkish version of the general conditions of the insurance policy *see,* http://www.tsb.org.tr/Default.aspx?pageID=524&srch=yangınsigortasıgenelşartları (26.9.2014).
439. For further detail *see* Bozer, p. 105; subpara. 2.2 of the Art. A2 of the general conditions of the insurance policy. For the Turkish version of the general conditions of the insurance policy *see,* http://www.tsb.org.tr/Default.aspx?pageID=524&srch=yangınsigortasıgenelşartları (26.9.2014).
440. For further detail on the premium in insurance contracts *see* Bozer, pp. 37–40; Çeker, pp. 68–70; Kender, (*Sigorta Hukuku*), pp. 235–252.
441. For further detail *see* Bozer, pp. 104–105; Can, p. 177.
442. Therefore the premium of fire insurance of property used at home is less than property used for commercial or industrial purpose. The premium also differs for different types of commercial or industrial property. For further detail *see* Çeker, p. 191.
443. Bozer, p. 106; Çeker, p. 191.

are used to cover some special risks that may not be covered under general insurance policies. The most commonly known special fire insurance policies are as follows.[444]

328. In circumstances where there are quick changes in the value of stocks, it is difficult to effectively determine the insured value,[445] and a floating fire insurance policy is created in practice. Accordingly, the maximum amount of the stock in the insurance term is taken into consideration, and the policyholder pays a premium of 40% of the first insured value (namely the maximum amount of the stock). Subsequently, the policyholder should inform the insurer periodically about any changes in the stock, and supplementary policies will be issued in accordance with these changes.[446] Where the existence of more than one good cannot be separated from each other because of the emplacement and insured value, an interpenetrated fire insurance policy is executed for goods having different values situated in the same property or different types of goods distributed to more than one property.[447]

329. The value of the insured goods may change during the policy term. Therefore, the insured value may fall below that of the changed, real value of the insured goods during the term of the policy, which may lead to under-insurance. In order to prevent such a case, in practice, the value of the insured goods may be index-linked to foreign currency or some other coefficient for change.[448] Normally, if the insured good or real estate is damaged totally or partially by fire, the possible maximum compensation will be the insured value of the goods. In *first fire* insurance policies, the parties agree on the payment of a certain amount determined in the policy. Policies with *value as new clause* allow for ordinary wear and tear. In such policies, the insured value is determined according to the value as the new one of the insured good instead of its actual value.[449] In other words under such policies, the insured value is determined as the insured good would be replaced by a new one.

§6. Additional Insurable Risk

330. Under the fire insurance policy, the main covered risk is the damage that is caused by fire. Therefore in practice, some insurance cover in addition to the risk of fire may be added to the policy, which is explained briefly in this section. Natural disasters, earthquakes and volcanic eruptions have traditionally not been covered

444. For other examples *see* Can, pp. 177–178; Kaya, pp. 372–374.
445. It should be underlined here that for insurance of properties, the insured value should be equal to the policy value. For further detail *see* Bozer, pp. 36–37, 70–82; Kender, *Sigorta Hukuku,* pp. 307–311.
446. Çeker, pp. 192–193; Kaya, p. 372.
447. For instance, in the production of automobile accessories, different accessories having different values are produced in one property or in case of the distribution of these accessories to different properties for dyeing; the interpenetrated fire insurance policy gives the possibility to execute one insurance contract for all of these accessories. For further detail and the premium *see* Çeker, p. 193.
448. For further detail *see* Çeker, pp. 193–194.
449. For further detail *see* Çeker, p. 194; Kaya, p. 372.

under insurance policies. However, with the improvement of technologies for sharing the possible damage with policyholders, earthquake and eruption insurance is now available under insurance contracts. Yet, as the possible damage from such natural disasters cannot be calculated precisely, such insurance contracts serve only to create an insurance fund and cannot be qualified as insurance within the legal meaning of the concept.[450] Furthermore, the consequential fire of an earthquake or eruption cannot be covered by a fire insurance policy unless an additional cover is provided for these disasters. In other words, the fire insurance policy may be executed in a way that also covers the fire resulting from an earthquake or eruption.[451]

331. Floodwater is caused by the overflow of rivers, streams, runs or water canals as well as by broken domestic water systems and overflowing water tanks. The damage that arises from floodwater may not be covered by the fire insurance policy. However, by adding floodwater under the coverage of the insurance contract, damage can be indemnified with fire insurance.[452] Storms, either directly or indirectly (with the scattered articles), can cause damage. This damage can be additionally covered with fire insurance if such additional cover is specified under the policy. According to the additional storm clause, only the direct damage (including the damage caused by scattered articles) is indemnified if the storm (more specifically the wind speed) exceeds the foreseen limits.[453]

332. In society, mass actions such as strikes, lockouts or civil commotions sometimes occur. During such actions, damage to properties may arise, which can be covered under a fire insurance policy as additional cover. In such cases, the policy would cover direct damage that arises from the strike, lockout or civil commotion and damage that arises during the intervention of law-enforcement in relation to such strike, lockout or civil commotion.[454] In addition to strikes, lockouts and civil commotions, any other hostile activities caused by third persons[455] may be also covered under the fire insurance policy by additional cover.[456] For example, terrorist activities that aim to weaken, destruct, amend or endanger the authority of the State should be specified under the fire insurance policy as additional cover for indemnifying damage arising from such activities.[457]

333. Possible damage arising from landslips can also be added to the fire insurance policy. In such cases, the damage that may arise from the landslip in or around

---

450. *See* paras 414 ff. below. For further detail on the subject *see* Bozer, pp. 31–40; Kender, *Sigorta Hukuku*, pp. 163–171.
451. For further detail on the earthquake and eruption additional covers *see* Çeker, pp. 195–196; Kaya, p. 326; Memiş, p. 114. It should be noted here that such an additional cover cannot reinstate the compulsory earthquake insurance.
452. For further detail *see* Çeker, p. 196; Kaya, pp. 369–370; Memiş, pp. 115–116.
453. For further detail *see* Çeker, p. 196; Kaya, p. 368; Memiş, pp. 117–118.
454. For further detail *see* Çeker, pp. 196–197; Kaya, pp. 366–368; Memiş, pp. 109–112.
455. The 'third person' is referred to persons other than the ascendants and descendants of the policyholder. Kaya, p. 367; Memiş, p. 121.
456. Çeker, p. 197; Kaya, p. 367; Memiş, p. 121.
457. For further detail *see* Kaya, pp. 366–367; Memiş, pp. 112–113.

the insured property is covered by the insurance. It is important to note here the distinction that insurance only covers landslips that arise from natural causes but not landslips that are caused by a human fault.[458] The damage that is caused by the collision of vehicles to the building or the collision of planes to multi-storey buildings may be covered by a fire insurance policy if such collisions are specified as additional covers under the agreement.[459] The premiums of these additional covers are determined in accordance with the emplacement of the building.[460] Smoke caused by fire also normally comes under the cover of the insurance policy. However, when smoke arises without a fire,[461] the damage caused by this smoke will only be indemnified by the fire insurance if it is specified under the policy as an additional cover.[462] In the event of heavy snow, the weight of the snow may cause the collapse of the roof and such damage to the insured property (including damage to goods inside of the property) can be covered by the insurer additionally.[463]

---

458. The fault of the contractor in the excavation of the foundation may be given as an example of such human made fault. For further detail *see* Çeker, p. 197; Kaya, p. 369; Memiş, pp. 116–117.
459. For further detail *see* Çeker, pp. 197–198; Kaya, p. 370; Memiş, pp. 120–121.
460. For instance, if the multi-storey building is situated in a 5-kilometre radius of an airport, the premium would be higher than a multi-storey building in downtown. For further detail *see* Çeker, p. 198.
461. The smoke from a chimney that does not work properly may be given as an example.
462. For further detail *see* Çeker, p. 198; Kaya, p. 370; Memiş, p. 120.
463. Çeker, p. 198; Kaya, p. 368; Memiş, p. 115.

Chapter 2. Loss of Benefits Insurance

Meltem Deniz Güner-Özbek

334. Loss of benefits insurance is normally referred to as consequential loss or business interruption insurance. Ordinary indemnity insurance of property does not cover profits lost or incurred because of the loss of the property. For this reason, interruption insurance, which can cover any type of consequential loss may be helpful for businesses. Such a loss of profit insurance is a separate cover but is dependent on fire regulated by the General Conditions of Loss of Profit Dependent on Fire. The cover is normally subject to material damage which requires a policy in force and a claim paid or admitted under it for material damage caused by fire before the loss of profit insurance is effective.[464]

335. Unless otherwise agreed, due to peculiarities of the insured's business and a definition been provided, compensation is calculated by deducting expenditures not paid or saved due to damage that must be paid from a gross profit during the interruption period, from a gross loss of profit resulting in a decrease in revenue and increase in the business cost.[465] The insured is under a duty to take all reasonable steps to minimize his loss.[466]

464. Article A.1 of the General Conditions of Loss of Profit Dependent on Fire.
465. Article B.6.
466. Article B.1–B.2.

Chapter 3. Transport Insurance

Meltem Deniz Güner-Özbek

336. The description 'transport insurance' is not one that is conventionally used in Turkey, but it refers to insurance of goods in transit whether by sea, road, air or rail. In Turkey the types of insurance concerned are recognized as goods in transit insurance (or cargo insurance), insurance of the liability of the carrier and hull insurance.

§1. Goods in Transit Insurance

I. Description

337. The type of goods in transport insurance effected will depend upon the legal relationship between the carrier and the owner of the goods if they are different, and also whether the goods are being imported, exported or transported domestically. If goods are being imported they may be insured by a marine or an airfreight policy until the time they reach their destination in Turkey. Likewise, goods being exported may be covered by a marine or an airfreight policy; or they may be insured separately if they are sold under an FOB contract. If the goods are transported domestically they will be insured for domestic transport.

338. Fourth Book of the Turkish Commercial Code entitled '*Transport Business*' and contractual terms covering the transport of goods domestically impose some duty on the carrier in the event of loss due to the carrier's fault, and thus, the carrier normally takes out *liability* insurance to cover this. The well-advised owner of the goods probably will not be content with this and is likely to insure the goods under some other form as well. There may be difficulty in the meaning of the words 'in transit'. Normally, transit begins when the goods are received by the carrier and ends when the goods have been unloaded off the vehicle and given into the custody of the recipients.[467]

II. Warranties, Conditions and Exceptions

339. The General Conditions of Goods in Transit Insurance have been in force since 1953. Its language is heavy, and provisions are – in general – based mostly on the carriage by sea. A draft entitled 'Cargo Insurance' with modern and plain language in conformity with the latest form of general conditions and the Turkish Commercial Code has been prepared by the Insurance Association of Turkey and submitted to the General Directorate of Insurance. According to Article A.3, transport vehicle means vehicles that can move on the sea, road, on rail or in the air

467. Zehra Şeker, Deniz Yoluyla Yük Taşınmasında Sigorta Himayesinin Kapsamı (Beta, 2001), pp. 108, 112–113.

depending on the type of transport. Accordingly, any vehicle falls under the general conditions. Article 15 of the General Conditions obliges the insured and authorizes the insurer to take all protective measures or impel to or request to take such measures; to supervise or to undertake actively rescue of insured goods in order to save them. The standard conditions of goods in transit policies cover such matters as average,[468] contribution and subrogation,[469] cancellation[470] and the claims procedure.[471]

468. Articles 5, 16–20, 22–24 of the General Conditions.
469. Article 26.
470. Article 9.
471. Articles 21–25.

Chapter 4. Marine Insurance

Meltem Deniz Güner-Özbek

340. In Turkey there is no specific marine insurance act. The former Turkish Commercial Code had made a distinction between non-marine and marine insurances; however, the current Turkish Commercial Code that entered into force on 1 July 2012 removed this distinction. Accordingly, all general provisions are applicable to marine insurance, as well as indemnity insurance provisions on the basis that marine insurance is mainly a contract of indemnity.

§1. Marine Insurance Business in Turkey

341. Despite the fact that Turkey is surrounded by three seas (the Aegean, the Mediterranean and the Black Sea) and has the interior Marmara Sea, the shipping and marine insurance business is not at an advanced level to date. In terms of overall insurance premium revenue, the share of marine insurance is low around 2.5%–3%.[472] In order to provide marine hull, goods or liability coverage, an insurance company must hold a licence in each of these branches.[473] It is to be noted that transportation insurance is provided for goods which are subject to export and import. Hull insurance is designed to protect ships (as well as aircraft) which are purchased with foreign loans, exclusively limited to the loan amount and applicable for the term until the foreign debt is paid up, or limited to the period of financial leasing if the same is brought home by financial leasing obtained abroad. Liability insurance arising from the operation of ships,[474] and ships registered with the Turkish International Ship Registry can be insured abroad. Besides this exception, people residing in Turkey must insure their interests located in Turkey with insurance companies established in Turkey.

342. Over thirty insurance companies have the requisite licences to cover marine risks.[475] There is also Turkish P&I, the first P&I insurance company in Turkey, which was founded on 31 December 2013.[476] Furthermore, the British insurance giant Lloyds announced its decision to enter the Turkish market in 2011[477] and is still in discussion with the Turkish government to enable it to become licensed in

472. http://www.tsb.org.tr/official-statistics.aspx?pageID=1003.
473. Article 5 of the Insurance Activities Act; Communique in relation to the branches of insurance No. 2007/1 OG. No. 26579, Date: 11.7.2007.
474. Article 15 of the Insurance Activities Act and Art. 13 of the Turkish International Ship Registry Act No. 4490.
475. At https://www.seddk.gov.tr/upload/doc/hayat-disi-grubu-sigorta-branslarinda-faaliyet-gosteren-sirketler-2.pdf.
476. At http://turkpandi.com/home-en-US. Turkish P&I is not a mutual insurance company it is rather a joint stock company: Türk P ve I Sigorta A.Ş.
477. At http://www.invest.gov.tr/en-US/infocenter/news/Pages/070711-lloyds-entering-turkey-insurance-market.aspx.

Turkey.[478] In a Draft Omnibus Act on the revision of some acts and decree-laws, there was a provision revising the Insurance Activities Act and allowing the structure of Lloyds to obtain a licence in Turkey.[479] However, this provision has been retracted from the draft law.

§2. Institute Clauses

343. As already expressed earlier in this book, the content of an insurance contract is executed in accordance with the General Conditions specific for each type of insurance contract that is approved by the Insurance and Private Pension Regulation and Supervision Agency.[480] Additionally, parties may agree on special terms that are specific to a contract. The General conditions of insurance generally contain a provision stating that special terms, that are not contrary to general conditions, may be inserted in the insurance contracts.[481] It is common knowledge that the UK is the centre of the world for marine insurance as English rules and clauses are applied worldwide. In Turkey as well, Institute Clauses are inserted into marine insurance contracts in addition to the General Conditions. Institute Clauses are special terms which are inserted in a marine insurance contract to complete, explain or change any general or abstract insurance contract.[482]

344. The scope of these special terms is broad, and they are designed to regulate the rights and obligations of the parties not under regulation by the General Conditions. Similar to the general and abstract nature of the General Conditions, these special terms are prepared by the insurer in advance to be inserted in the insurance contract without any negotiation with the policyholder. Even though Institute Clauses are considered general terms prepared in advance for use in more than one contract and subject to supervision, they become specific to the contract if they are negotiated between the parties and accepted afterwards. Which relevant Institute Clause will be inserted in the contract depends on the choice of the policyholder. When special terms are inserted in the insurance contract, such special term takes precedents over the general conditions.[483]

345. Act No. 805 states that companies having Turkish nationality must conclude all their contracts in Turkish language in Turkey. The Act also allows Turkish companies to conclude contracts in foreign languages, but a Turkish version of the contract is necessary along with the foreign language. In addition, in case of any conflict between the two languages, the Turkish version of the contract prevails.

---

478. Lloyd's November 2014.
479. Legislation Period: 24 Date: 9.3.2015 No. 2/2736; http://www.tbmm.gov.tr/sirasayi/donem24/yil01/ss705.pdf www.tbmm.gov.tr.
480. Article 11 of the Insurance Activities Act. *See* para. 28 above.
481. *See*, for instance, Art. C.7 of the General Conditions of Hull Policy, Art. 28 of the General Conditions of Goods in Transport Insurance.
482. Yazıcıoğlu, (Tekne Sigortası Sözleşmesi), pp. 48–52.
483. Article C.7 of the General Conditions of Hull Policy, Art. 28 of the General Conditions of Goods in Transport Insurance.

This is an overriding provision which otherwise cannot be agreed. Foreign companies concluding contracts in Turkey are exempt from this requirement except for the documents they present to public bodies. Accordingly, companies having Turkish nationality must conclude insurance contracts in the Turkish language in Turkey as well.

346. Additionally, Insurance Activities Act specifically regulates the usage of the Turkish language in the insurance contracts in Article 11(5). Insurance contracts must be in Turkish; foreign languages shall not be used in insurance contracts or policies. In terms of Institute Clauses, Turkish translation of the Clauses may be used to meet this requirement in addition to the English version.[484]

§3. Insurable Interest

347. As noted above, there are no special provisions for marine insurance under Turkish law. Marine insurance contracts, of the hull, cargo and freight, are regarded as contracts of indemnity, and the general provisions of the Turkish Commercial Code are therefore applied. According to Article 1408 of the Turkish Commercial Code, an insurable interest is required at all times from the execution of the contract until the realization of the risk. If the interest is not available at all times, the contract becomes null and void. Certainly, an owner of a vessel or goods or the recipient of freight has an insurable interest in these subjects. Insurance of any liability in relation to marine navigation is also possible.

348. Furthermore, Article 1126 of the Turkish Commercial Code contains a special provision with regard to bareboat charters. Accordingly, the lessee is obliged to insure the vessel for marine and liability risk until the re-delivery of the vessel. The lessor must be named both in the contract and in the policy, and the contract must be *insurance for whom it may concern*. This Article 1126 operates in conformity with Article 13 of the BARECON 2001. Additionally, a restricted real right owner has a right to insurance where the owner's property right has been insured. The same right is regulated by Article 879 of the Turkish Civil Code and Article 1022 of the Turkish Commercial Code with respect to *hypothecs* in vessels. Article 1456 of the Turkish Commercial Code now regulates the issue generally. Accordingly, a holder of a restricted right has the right to insurance compensation where the owner's property interest has been insured under such an insurance contract. It is, however, worth noting that insurance compensation is not included within the scope of *maritime liens*. This principle is clearly stated in Article 1321(2) of the Turkish Commercial Code. Thus, the holder of a maritime lien has no right to insurance compensation.

484. At http://www.tsb.org.tr/nakliyat-klozlari.aspx?pageID=498.

§4. BURDEN OF DISCLOSURE

349. As stated earlier, the policyholder, the insured (if he or she has the knowledge of the insurance) and the agency (in cases where an agent executes the insurance contract) have the burden of disclosure at the time of execution of the contract, during the contract period and when the risk is realized.[485] These general principles are applicable to marine insurance contracts as well.

§5. THE POLICY

I. General Rules

350. In line with the general principle for all insurance contracts, the marine insurance contract is not subject to any prescribed form. However, some form of written evidence is required in order to prove the existence of an insurance contract, and it is customary in insurance law and a duty of the insurer to provide a policy.[486] The content of the policy is generally regulated by the Turkish Commercial Code, which invariably consists of the rights of the parties, the default provisions and the General Conditions and special terms, if there are any.[487] Nevertheless, some content terms must be stated in the policy, such as the duration of cover, the insured sum, the names of the policyholder and insured and their trade names and addresses and the date of issue.[488]

II. Classification of Policies

351. In principle, marine insurance can be classified into three groups: hull insurance, cargo insurance and liability insurance. However, it should also be noted that the insurable interest is not limited to the above-mentioned categories. Freight, carriage charges, loss of profit, collision liability, general average contribution and a similar interest in relation to the safety of both hull and cargo can also be insured.

A. Voyage and Time Policies

352. Hull insurance can be executed for one voyage or more voyages or for a certain time. Accordingly, hull insurance can be defined as either voyage or hull insurance. In line with the technical developments in shipping, the navigational areas of vessels have been extended. Vessels can now navigate without calling at the port of registry for months. For this reason, time policies are the preferred type

485. *See* paras 226 ff. above.
486. Article 1421(1) of the Turkish Commercial Code.
487. Article 1425(1) of the Turkish Commercial Code.
488. Kender, *Sigorta Hukuku*, p. 180.

of marine insurance policy because voyage insurance is both expensive and disadvantageous for vessels that are constantly navigating. Time policies are usually for one year. Both the commencement and termination dates are determined in the contract and stated in the policy. Likewise in voyage policies, both the commencement and the termination of voyages are important as the voyage policy covers the period between the commencement and termination of the voyage.

B. Valued and Unvalued Policies

353. Parties to an insurance contract may agree on the insurance value of the subject matter insured.[489] When such valuation has been agreed, in principle, this amount is taken into consideration. Such an agreed valuation can be made either at the time of execution of the insurance contract or after execution. Such a valuation is binding on the parties to the insurance contract. In cases where the agreed valuation includes anticipated profit, the insurer can request its reduction if such an agreed valuation exceeds possible earnings that are commercially anticipated at the time of execution of the contract. Additionally, the insurer can also request a reduction if the valuation is exorbitant.[490] The advantage of valued policies is that they avoid disputes when a claim is made.

354. If the parties have not agreed on a specific value for the subject matter insured, the insurance sum determined in the contract is the maximum amount payable in the event of the realization of risk. However, the determination of the insurance sum differs from the agreed valuation. Compensation is therefore calculated in accordance with the value of the subject matter at the time of realization of risk up to the limit stated in the policy.[491]

C. Floating Policies

355. Despite their common use in practice, neither the former Turkish Commercial Code nor the current Turkish Commercial Code has regulated floating policies. Such a policy states the general nature of the insured subject matter but leaves the exact amount and kind of the subject matter of insurance to be fixed at a later stage. Floating policies are particularly suitable for export, import and storage businesses. Because the floating policy is not regulated by legislation, the theory behind the floating policy is based on the freedom of contract principle.[492] However, there is some dispute as to whether floating insurance is a contract of insurance in itself or

---

489. Article 1464 of the Turkish Commercial Code.
490. *Ibid.*
491. Articles 1460 and 1461 of the Turkish Commercial Code.
492. Serap Amasya, 'Abonman Sigortaları', Yeni Türk Ticaret Kanununda Deniz Sigortaları, Deniz Hukuku Derneği & Sigorta Hukuku Derneği, 2012, pp. 132–133; Kender, *Sigorta Hukuku*, p. 189.

whether it is merely a contractual framework. In practice, floating insurance operates in a master policy that defines an insurance sum. Each time there is a shipment, the overall value of the specific policy is reduced from the sum defined in the master policy.

§6. Open Cover

356. In Turkish legal practice, floating policy and open cover are used interchangeably on the basis that the details of subsequent shipments are unknown at the time of execution for both types of insurance contracts. There are, however, slight differences between the two covers and open cover represents an alternative to floating policy. The main difference is that open cover does not have any limit regarding the insurance sum, and the contract terminates upon the expiry of the period.

§7. Blanket Cover

357. Blanket cover is a comprehensive coverage. It is distinguished from open cover and floating policy by not requiring declarations for each shipment.

§8. Subject Matter of Insurance

358. Under a marine policy, ships, goods and freight can be insured. Additionally, insurance of profits, wages and liability is also possible.

§9. Attachment and Duration of Risk

I. Time Policies

359. Insurance coverage is limited to a certain time period, and the commencement and termination of coverage are important matters of insurance law. Article 1421 of the Turkish Commercial Code states that unless *otherwise* agreed, the liability of the insurer begins with the payment of the premium, or the first instalment if the parties have agreed on instalment payments.[493] Accordingly, the parties can agree, for instance, that coverage is to commence before payment of the premium or its first instalment. This is a unilaterally protective provision, which cannot be amended contrary to the benefit of the insured.[494] In other words, the parties cannot agree that coverage begins sometime after payment of the premium. Moreover, Article A.6 of the General Conditions of Hull Policy states that unless otherwise agreed, insurance coverage both commences and terminates at 12.00 pm on the

493. *See* para. 219 above.
494. Article 1452 of the Turkish Commercial Code.

respective dates specified in the policy.[495] In both instances, the applicable time is the time of the location of the vessel or any other water or inland waterways craft. Consequently, the coverage, i.e., liability of the insurer, commences at 12.00 pm stated in the policy upon the condition that the premium has been paid, or payment of the premium has been delayed upon the agreement of the parties.

II. Voyage Policies

A. *Hulls*

360. In Turkey, there are no specific general conditions for hull insurance for voyage charter; thus, the General Conditions of Hull Policy are applicable to voyage charter policies. As explained above, the liability of the insurer begins with payment of the premium or the first instalment unless otherwise agreed, and Article A.6 of the General Conditions of Hull Policy states that, unless otherwise agreed, insurance commences at 12.00 pm on the date stipulated in the policy and terminates at 12.00 pm on the date stipulated in the policy as well.[496]

361. In comparison, the Institute Voyage Clauses (Hulls), which are often included as special terms under insurance contracts in Turkey, only state that 'The vessel is covered subject to the provisions of this insurance *at all times* …'[497] Neither this provision nor any other provision in the Clauses sheds light on the actual commencement of coverage and attachment of risk. Regarding the continuation of coverage, sections 45 and 49 of the Marine Insurance Act (UK) enumerate circumstances where the insurer is discharged from liability unless otherwise agreed. Similarly, Article 2 of the Institute Voyage Clauses Hulls provides for the possibility of the continuance of coverage. This is a held covered provision in case of deviation or change in the voyage or any breach of warranty as to towage or salvage services, provided that notice is given to the Underwriters and any amended terms of cover and any additional premium required by them are agreed.

362. On the contrary, in German jurisdiction, which has significantly influenced the Turkish legal system, Article 2 of the German DTV-Casco Clauses 1978/2004 states that insurance commences and terminates on the dates stipulated in the policy. Article 9 of the DTV[498] German Standard Terms and Conditions of Insurance for Ocean-going Vessels 2009 (DTV-ADS[499] 2009) contains similar wording, but it also specifies the exact time on these dates as 00.00 and 24.00. This provision is in line with regulation in the General Conditions of Hull Policy in Turkey. In conclusion, it can be summarized that coverage for voyage policies in Turkey also commences

495. This is the term that is included in most general provisions.
496. This is a general provision. Almost all general conditions consist a similar clause.
497. Article 1.1 of the Institute Voyage Clauses Hull (1995).
498. Deutsche Transport-Versicherungs-Verband.
499. Allgemeine Deutsche Seeschiffsversicherungsbedingungen.

and terminates on dates stated in the relevant policy at 12.00 pm pursuant to Article A.6 of the General Conditions of Hull Policy.

B. Cargo

363. The exception to the above-mentioned general principle for the commencement of coverage is the transport of goods insurance. Paragraph 2 of Article 1421(1) of the Turkish Commercial Code states that for insurance of transport by road and by sea,[500] the liability of the insurer commences with the execution of the contract. Even though payment of the premium is therefore not necessary for the commencement of coverage, the premium invariably also becomes due with the execution of the contract. On the contrary, Article 8 of the General Conditions of Goods in Transit Insurance states that coverage commences when the goods are delivered by the ship owner or the disponent owner for transport or temporary storage in the event that transport does not start immediately. If the goods are delivered to the port or similar authority for the purpose of delivery of goods it is deemed that such authority is the representative of the owner or the disponent owner. Accordingly, coverage commences with the commencement of the voyage.[501] The goods are also covered during loading and unloading if the goods are on-board of the port vessels for this purpose. The coverage terminates when the goods are delivered by the consignee, or when the goods are stored in a warehouse or sold due to some obstacle to delivery. In any case, the coverage is deemed terminated within fifteen days at the latest following unloading. When taken into consideration, both Article 1421 and Article 8 of the General Conditions provide that coverage does not commence if the goods are not delivered to the ship owner or the disponent owner at the time of execution of the contract. However, Article 1421 does apply if the goods have already been delivered at the time of execution of the contract.

364. If any of the Institute Cargo Clauses have been inserted in the policy as a special term, it takes precedent over the General Conditions of the Goods in Transit Insurance.[502] The duration of insurance in Article 8 is identical in the Institute Cargo Clauses A, B and C. Accordingly, the risk attaches from the time the goods are moved into the warehouse named in the policy. This commencement of coverage continues *during the ordinary course of transit*. In order to avoid delay, Article 18 of the Institute Cargo Clauses states that the insured must *act with reasonable dispatch in all circumstances within his control.* Article 8(3) then provides that *the insurance remains in force during delay beyond the control of the Assured, or any deviation, forced discharge, reshipment or trans-shipment and during any variation of the voyage arising from the exercise of a liberty granted to ship owners or charterers under the contract of affreightment.* If the discharged cargo starts on a new

500. Although this article only states road and sea transport of cargo, this provision is equally applicable to other insurance of goods transported by other modes.
501. Article 8 of the General Conditions of Goods in Transit Insurance.
502. Article C.7 of the General Conditions of Goods in Transit Insurance.

transit route, the insurance terminates on the commencement of the new transit.[503] Finally, insurance terminates in either of the following circumstances:

- on completion of unloading from the transport vehicle or other conveyance in or at the final warehouse or place of storage at the destination named in the contract of insurance; or
- on completion of unloading from the transport vehicle or other conveyance in or at any other warehouse or place of storage, whether prior to or at the destination named in the contract of insurance, which the Assured or their employees elect to use either for storage other than in the ordinary course of transit or for allocation or distribution; or
- when the Assured or their employees elect to use any transport vehicle or other conveyance or any container for storage other than in the ordinary course of transit; or
- on the expiry of sixty days after completion of discharge overside of the subject matter insured from the oversea vessel at the final port of discharge.[504]

§10. Risks

I. Risks Included in a Marine Policy

365. The General Conditions of Hull Policy do not contain any provisions regarding risks. Instead, Article A.3 states that the content of coverage in terms of risks is, *inter alia,* ascertained pursuant to clauses inserted in the policy. Thus, the Institute Hull Clauses inserted in the policy in accordance with the agreement of the parties determine the content of the policy.

366. Risks recognized by the Institute Hull Clauses include perils of the sea; fire and explosion; violent theft by persons from outside of the vessel; jettison; piracy; contact with land conveyance, dock or harbour equipment or installation; earthquake, volcanic eruption or lightning; accidents in loading, discharging or shifting cargo or fuel; contact with satellites, aircraft, helicopters or similar objects, or objects falling therefrom. Additionally, this insurance covers the bursting of boilers, breakage of shafts or any latent defect in the machinery or hull, but except for repairing, replacing or correcting such item; the negligence of the Master Officers Crew or Pilots; the negligence of repairers or charterers provided such repairers or charterers are not an Assured barratry of the Master Officers or Crew, provided that such loss or damage has not resulted from want of due diligence by the assured, or the owners or managers; and pollution hazard.[505] The Institute Time Hull Clauses 1995 are very similar to these terms, but *breakdowns or accidents within nuclear installations or reactors* covered by the International Hull Clauses 2003 and *latent defects* covered by the Institute Time Clauses Hulls 1983 are excluded.

503. Article 8.2 of the Institute Cargo Clauses.
504. Article 8.1.1–8.1.3 of the Institute Cargo Clauses (2009).
505. Articles 2 and 5 of the International Hull Clauses (2003).

367. Contrary to the General Conditions of Hull Policy, the General Conditions of Goods in Transit Insurance contain provisions regarding the content of the insurance in terms of risks. Accordingly, the risks covered include storm, ice damage, stranding of the vessel, breaking of the vessel, collision or allusion; jettison; fire, explosion, lighting; barratry of the pilot or crew.[506] If any of the Institute Cargo Clauses have been inserted as a special term in the policy, it will take precedent over the provisions of the General Conditions of Goods in Transit Insurance.[507] Institute Cargo Clauses A covers all risks except for risks specified in Articles 4–7, which will be discussed below. Institute Cargo Clauses B and C cover fire or explosion; stranding, grounding, sinking or capsizing of the vessel; overturning or derailment of land conveyance; collision or allision; discharge of cargo at a port of distress;[508] general average sacrifice and jettison. In addition to these risks, B clauses also cover earthquake, volcanic eruption or lightning;[509] washing overboard; entry of water into the vessel; total loss of any package lost overboard or dropped whilst loading onto or unloading from the vessel.

II. Risks Excluded in a Marine Policy

368. The International Hull Clauses (2003) exclude war and strikes; terrorist, politically motivated and malicious acts; and radioactive contamination, chemical, biological, bio-chemical and electromagnetic weapons.[510] The Institute Time Clauses 1983 have similar exclusions, but they are comparatively narrower.[511] Regarding cargo insurance, the General Conditions of Goods in Transit Insurance exclude inherent vice and defect; shortage; rusting and moulding; leakage, usual breakage; self-heating; insufficient packaging; vapour; damage caused by mice; the negligence of the policyholder or the insured; loading of insured goods with dangerous goods; damage arising from delay; war and similar risks; seizure; strikes; and piracy.[512]

369. Under the Institute Cargo Clauses, the following damages are excluded when caused by the wilful misconduct of the Assured: ordinary leakage, ordinary loss in weight or volume, or ordinary wear and tear; the insufficiency or unsuitability of packing or preparation; inherent vice or nature; insolvency or financial default of the owners, managers, charterers or operators; weapons or devices employing atomic or nuclear fission and/or fusion or other like reaction or radioactive force or matter; un-seaworthiness or unfitness; unfitness of container or conveyance; war, civil war, revolution, rebellion, insurrection or civil strife or any hostile act; capture, seizure, arrest, restraint or detainment; and derelict mines, torpedoes, bombs or other derelict weapons of war; strikes, locked-out workmen or persons taking part

506. Article 1 of the General Conditions of Goods in Transit Insurance.
507. Article C.7 of the General Conditions of Goods in Transit Insurance.
508. Article 1.1.1–1.1.5 and 1.2.1–1.2.2 of the Institute Cargo Clauses B and C (2009).
509. Article 1.1.6, 1.2.2, 1.2.3, and 1.3 of the Institute Cargo Clauses B (2009).
510. Articles 29–31.
511. Articles 23–26.
512. Articles 2–6 of the General Conditions of Goods in Transit Insurance.

in labour disturbances, riots or civil commotions; strikes, lockouts, labour disturbances, riots or civil commotions; or any act of terrorism or acts that have a political, ideological or religious motive.[513]

§11. Excluded Loss

I. Doctrine of Proximate Cause

370. As explained before, the Turkish Law doctrine of the *adequate causal link* is applicable to insurance claims.[514] For marine insurance, however, it is not always easy to establish a causal link between the damage and risks, particularly if more than one risk, covered or uncovered or insured by different insurers, is realized concurrently or affects each other. Accordingly, the approach for marine insurance is that the *adequate causal link* is first applied. And if this theory is inefficient, the causal link is then determined in accordance with the doctrine of *proximate cause*.[515]

II. The Burden of Proof

371. The burden of proving that the loss comes within the ambit of the policy lies with the insured. Once this is established, the onus then shifts to the insurer to prove that the risk is excluded.[516]

§12. Particular and General Average Losses

372. Where the vessel, goods and freight are involved in a marine voyage that is threatened by an extraordinary common danger, and one of them bears the loss for the safety of the common voyage, the person suffering that loss is entitled to a contribution from its beneficiaries, which are referred to as the *general average*. The loss suffered for this purpose and the liability to contribute to it are both types of general average loss. The *particular average*, however, relates to the loss caused by a non-common danger. Such losses can also be the subject matter of insurance.[517] In relation to the general average, rather than claiming from each other, the parties claim in accordance with their own insurance policy. This avoids the complications of average adjustment.

513. Clauses 4–7 of the Institute Cargo Clauses A, B and C 2009.
514. *See* para. 157 above.
515. Yazıcıoğlu (Tekne Sigortası), p. 200; Ülgener, p. 181; Şeker (Deniz Yoluyla Yük Taşınmasında Sigorta Himayesinin Kapsamı), p. 214.
516. Article 1409(2) of the Turkish Commercial Code.
517. Clause 8 of the International Hull Clauses; Arts 17 and 19 of the General Conditions of Goods in Transit Insurance; Clause 1.2.1 of the Institute Cargo Clauses A, B and C (2009).

§13. Partial Loss and Total Loss

373. Damage or loss occurs when any risk covered by the insurance is realized. Loss can be *total* or *partial*. Furthermore, the total loss is sub-divided into an *actual* total loss or a *constructive* total loss. However, there is no provision in the Turkish Commercial Code regulating constructive total loss. Instead, there are clauses in the Institute Clauses that are inserted as special terms in the contract to regulate constructive total loss. Clause 21 of the International Hull Clauses 2003 also provides that:

> in ascertaining whether the vessel is a constructive total loss, 80% of the insured value of the vessel shall be taken as the repaired value and nothing in respect of the damaged or break-up value of the vessel or wreck shall be taken into account, and no claim for the constructive total loss of the vessel based upon the cost of recovery and/or repair of the vessel shall be recoverable hereunder unless such cost would exceed 80% of the insured value of the vessel. In making this determination, only the cost relating to a single accident or sequence of damages arising from the same accident shall be taken into account.

Furthermore, Clause 13 of the Institute Cargo Clauses A, B, C (2009) sets out that:

> no claim for constructive total loss shall be recoverable hereunder unless the subject-matter insured is reasonably abandoned either on account of its actual total loss on appearing to be unavoidable or because the cost of recovering, reconditioning, and forwarding the subject-matter insured to the destination to which its insured would exceed its value on arrival.

§14. Premiums

374. The full insurance premium or the first instalment, if the parties agreed on the payment in instalments, must be paid immediately upon execution of the contract in exchange for the delivery of the insurance policy.[518] The General Conditions of Hull Policy has similar wording in Article C.2. However, Article 27 of the General Conditions of Goods in Transport Insurance sets out that the insurance premium is due upon delivery of the policy. However, this is adjusted to the time of execution of the contract in cases where the immediate delivery of the policy is not common practice. As expressed throughout this section, the Institute Clauses are inserted as special terms in marine insurance contracts, which also include clauses

518. Article 1431 of the Turkish Commercial Code.

related to the payment of the premium. Such Clauses take precedent over the General Conditions of Hull Policy[519] and Goods in Transit Insurance[520] in accordance with the parties' agreement.

§15. Duty to Prevent and Mitigate the Loss

375. When the risk has been realized, or the possibility of realization is high, the policyholder must take measures, within the bounds of possibility, to avert the loss or any increase in the loss, to mitigate the loss and to protect the insurer's right of recourse against third parties.[521] If any breach of this duty creates a detrimental situation for the insurer, the insurance indemnity is reduced proportionally to the degree of negligence by the policyholder. There are similar provisions for this in the International Hull Clauses (2003)[522] and Institute Cargo Clauses A, B and C (2009).[523]

§16. Assignment

376. In principle, any change in ownership of the insured interest results in the automatic termination of the insurance contract, unless parties agree otherwise.[524] In marine insurance, any change in the ownership of a vessel is a sensitive issue because it may affect the risk. In contrast, cargo policies are usually assignable as cargo changes hands frequently. However, under Turkish Law, an insurable interest is required at all times for the duration of the insurance contract.[525] Thus, in case of assignment, the assignee must have an interest at the time of assignment.

§17. Subrogation

377. The insurer can subrogate the litigious claim rights of the insured to any liable persons in proportion to the amount of the indemnity paid.[526] It must be stressed that the subrogation rights of the insurer are restricted to the amount of the insurance indemnity paid by the insurer. Thus, if the rights of the insured towards liable third persons exceed the amount of the indemnity paid by the insurer, the insured has the right to such exceeding amount.

---

519. Article C.7.
520. Article 28.
521. Article 1448 of the Turkish Commercial Code.
522. Clause 9.
523. Clause 16.
524. Article 1470 of the Turkish Commercial Code.
525. Article 1408 of the Turkish Commercial Code.
526. Article 1472 of the Turkish Commercial Code.

Chapter 5. Liability Insurance

Meltem Deniz Güner-Özbek & Banu Bozkurt-Bozabalı

§1. General

378. As discussed throughout this book, one of the main aims of insurance is to ensure that all people feel secure with the different types of insurance that have been created. In social life, persons or legal entities may cause damage to third persons, and this is called *legal liability*. This damage may result from either professional or personal activity, and liability is therefore an important part of the social lives of people and legal entities. The development of the concept of liability has an important link with the level of development of society. A society without the recognition of the liability of persons or legal entities does not exist. The development and extension of the concept of liability in societies are directly related to the occurrence of damage and the need to protect and secure the rights of third persons. At this juncture, the legal concept of liability insurance is created in order to financially cover the liability of the person or legal entity.

379. One of the main principles of the law of obligations is *freedom of contract*. This principle covers the freedom of entering into a contract or not; of having the liberty to choose the other party to the contract and negotiating the content of the contract without any prejudice of statutory legislation and moral rules.[527] However, in practice, there are significant restrictions on this broad principle of the freedom of contract in certain legislation.[528]

380. Under liability insurance, the freedom of contract is sometimes limited for social reasons.[529] For instance, Article 1483 of the Turkish Commercial Code states that the insurer may not amend the clauses of the insurance contract to the detriment of the policyholder on the condition that the policyholder executes the insurance contract with the insurer. The main aim behind this intervention of the law on the freedom of contract principle is to protect people who are exposed to risk.[530] It

527. For further detail on the freedom of contract *see* G. Antalya, *Borçlar Hukuku Genel Hükümler*, Beta Yayınevi (İstanbul, 2012) C: 1, pp. 261–285; Hatemi & Gökyayla, *Borçlar Hukuku Genel Bölüm*, Vedat Kitapçılık (İstanbul, 2011), pp. 58–61; A. Kılıçoğlu, *Borçlar Hukuku Genel Hükümler*, Turhan Kitabevi, 16. Baskı, Ankara, 2012, pp. 73–78; Kemal Oğuzman & Öz Turgut, *Borçlar Hukuku Genel Hükümler*, Vedat Kitapçılık, İstanbul, 2011, c: 1, pp.24–29; S. Repisoğlu, *Türk Borçlar Hukuku Genel Hükümler*, Beta Yayınevi, 23. Baskı (İstanbul 2012) pp. 133–141.

528. For further detail on the restriction on the freedom of contract *see* Antalya, pp. 261–267; Oğuzman & Öz, pp. 194–201.

529. Bozer, pp. 132–133; M. Can, '*Mesleki Sorumluluk Sigortası Genel Şartlarına Genel Bir Bakış*' (Mesleki Sorumluluk), Banka ve Ticaret Hukuku Araştırma Enstitüsü, Yayın No. 431, p. 11; Güvel & Güvel, p. 182; Kaya, p. 274.

530. In other words, the main aim of the lawmaker is to strengthen social security through the realization of social benefit. M.K. Omağ, '*Türk Hukukunda Mecburi Sigortalara ve Sorunlarına Genel Bakış*' Zorunlu Sigortalar Paneli, Sigorta Hukuku Türk Derneği, 19.11.1993 (Paper presented during the panel organized by the Association of Turkish Insurance Law) (Omağ, Paper). It should be

should be underlined here that as compulsory liability insurance restricts the freedom of contract for social reasons; this obligation should be formally legislated. However, according to Article 13 of the Insurance Activities Act, compulsory liability insurance may be created with the decision of the President. Furthermore, in practice, there also exists some compulsory liability insurance established by by-laws.[531]

381. There are different kinds of compulsory liability insurances established for professional liability[532] or for the liability of professionals operating or involved in high damage risk.[533] In either situation, compulsory liability insurance is created for the public interest.[534] In the event that a person or legal entity fails to execute a compulsory liability insurance contract, the obliged person or legal entity will have personal liability, and he or she will be punished in accordance with the legislation in the jurisdiction where compulsory liability insurance is regulated.[535] However, as a reflection of the principle of freedom of contract, the execution of a liability insurance contract should be voluntary based on the free will of the policyholder. In other words, the person or legal entity that will benefit from the voluntary insurance cover will decide freely whether or not he or she will execute this contract. However, it should be underlined here that even though voluntary liability insurance is the reflection of the freedom of contract, the parties are not free to determine the terms and conditions of the contract.[536] Furthermore, if the obligation to execute a liability insurance contract arises from a contractual relation, this does not impact its voluntary character.[537]

---

underlined here that the aim of the compulsory liability insurance cannot result in the creation of a fund. The idea of creation of a fund contradicts with the aim of the insurance, that is, to divide the risk between the persons (or legal entities) that are exposed to it. Therefore, compulsory insurance on earthquakes, which is sometimes cited as an example of existing essential compulsory liability insurance, may not be classified as insurance because of its main aim to create a fund to compensate the possible victims of an earthquake. For further detail *see* Rayegan Kender, '*Mesuliyet Sigortasının Mahiyeti ve Türleri*' ('Mesuliyet Sigortası') Zorunlu Sigortalar Paneli, Sigorta Hukuku Türk Derneği, 19.11.1993 (Paper presented during the panel organized by the Association of Turkish Insurance Law).

531. *See* section 'Compulsory Insurances'.
532. For instance, the compulsory liability insurance for the legal liability of doctors in the case of malpractice.
533. For instance, the compulsory liability insurance on the transport of passenger by sea; the compulsory liability insurance on the transport by road may be cited as examples.
534. The public interest exists if the number of possible victims of the compulsory liability insurance covered risk is importantly high or if the covered activity concerns an important threat that may possibly harm third persons. For further detail *see* Can (Mesleki Sorumluluk), p. 12; Kender, *Mesuliyet Sigortası*.
535. The fine or penalty may be the withdrawal of the licence or other activity permission or the payment of an administrative fine or the termination of the activity.
536. According to the Insurance Activities Act, the general conditions should be determined or approved by the Insurance and Private Pension Regulation and Supervision Agency; the amendments on the general conditions may be valid if they are not in contradiction with the benefit of the policyholder. For further detail *see* Çeker, pp. 72–74.
537. In other words, as long as the obligation of concluding the liability insurance contract does not arise from legislation; the contract continues to keep its voluntary nature. For further detail *see* Can (Mesleki Sorumluluk) pp. 10–11.

382. In many instances, the policyholder of the compulsory liability insurance chooses to enter into a voluntary liability insurance contract as well. The main aim of the policyholder to enter into a voluntary liability insurance contract in addition to the compulsory one is to extend the degree of insurance security. It is because the voluntary liability insurance coverage is usually broader than the compulsory liability insurances; thus, the policyholder of the compulsory liability insurance prefers also to execute the voluntary liability insurance contract in order to cover his/her liability exceeding the cover under the compulsory insurance.

§2. Subject and the Content of the Liability Insurance

383. In Turkish Law, principally, liability insurance covers the liability of the insured arising from the insured event occurring *during the contract* period even if *damage arises after the contract* period.[538] Obviously, this reflects the *occurrence-based* system. This provision is not protective;[539] thus, parties to an insurance contract may agree otherwise, i.e., claims based or both claims-based and occurrence-based systems.[540]

384. The main risk that is covered by the liability insurance is the possible decrease of the assets of the policyholder. In other words, where the policyholder has liability towards a third (damaged) person, the liability insurer will try to minimize the possible decrease of the assets of that person by indemnifying the possible damage.[541] However, the liability insurance may not cover any illegal or immoral activities damage.[542] Another question may rise about pecuniary penalties and whether they are subject to the liability insurance. Pecuniary penalties are the type of penalties aiming to prevent particular tortuous acts or crimes. Therefore, there exists a principle of *individuality* for such penalties. On the basis that this principle of individuality would be broken if such penalties were covered by liability insurance, any pecuniary penalty even for minor offences cannot be covered by liability insurance.[543]

538. Article 1473 of the Turkish Commercial Code.

539. Article 1486 of the Turkish Commercial Code.

540. *See*, for instance, Art. A.1 of the General Conditions of the Professional Indemnity Insurance.

541. For further detail on the definition of liability insurance *see* Bozer, p. 132; Çeker pp. 257–258; Güvel & Güvel, p. 180; Kender, *Sigorta Hukuku*, p. 208; Kaya, pp. 272–273; Z. Metezade & N. Güleli, *Türk Ticaret Kanunu, Altıncı Kitap, Sigorta Hukuku*, Gürer Yayınlar (İstanbul, 2011), pp. 176–177. Accordingly, liability insurance may be classified as a passive loss insurance contract. For further detail *see* Can (Mesleki Sorumluluk), pp. 7–9.

542. For further detail *see* Can (Sigorta Hukuku), pp. 169–170. For instance, the liability insurer may not be liable for the indemnity in relation to the legal responsibility of a gynaecologist for a proscribed abortion.

543. For further detail *see* Can, (Sigorta Hukuku), pp. 170–171. That is to say, liability insurance covers only damage such as punitive or exemplary.

385. The liability insurance covers both the risk of damage to property (such as a car crash) as well as to persons (such as bodily injury or moral injury). The liability of the insurer is limited to the amount stipulated in the policy.[544] According to Article 1473(2), if the liability insurance contract has been executed for the liability of a business enterprise, such insurance covers both the liability of the representatives as well as the liability of the persons who are in the management or supervision of the business enterprise or are employed by the business. The parties may agree otherwise.[545] Such coverage should be stipulated under the general conditions of the insurance contract.[546] When a claim is asserted against the insured reasonable legal expenses are also covered by the liability insurance. Parties may also agree on the payment of legal expenses exceeding the sum insured.[547]

§3. Admission of Liability and the Conduct of Proceedings

386. The insured is obliged to notify the insurer in the event that requires liability of the insured within ten days.[548] If a claim is made against the insured, the insured must notify the insurer of such claim immediately.[549]

The insurer should respond to the notification of the policyholder within five days of receiving such notice.[550] In its response, the insurer informs the insured whether he or she undertakes to pursue all the necessary legal procedures in relation to a claim against the insured. If the insurer decides to provide legal assistance both the liability and necessary expenses shall be borne by the insurer.[551]

387. Alternatively, the insurer may not respond to the notification within five days or may not accept to undertake the procedure. In such a case, the insured pursues legal procedure.[552] The insurer must pay the compensation determined by the final judgment of the court. The dispute, however, between the insured and the claimant may be solved by the out-of-court settlement. If the dispute is solved by the settlement, consent of the insurer to such settlement is required. The insurer

544. Thus, all kinds of life and bodily injury insurance contracts are executed as insurance on amount. For further detail on insurance on amount *see* Can, (Mesleki Sorumluluk), p. 8; Kender, *Sigorta Hukuku*, p. 209.
545. The insurance on damage is the kind of insurance where the insurer compensates the concrete damage that is caused by the activity of the policyholder. For further detail on the insurance on damage *see* Can, (Mesleki Sorumluluk) p. 33; Çeker, pp. 138–139; Kender, *Sigorta Hukuku*, pp. 204–205.
546. Especially the liability insurance policy on professional activities may be cited as an example. For further detail *see* Can, (Mesleki Sorumluluk), p. 33.
547. The insurer should makeadvance payments in case the insured so demands. For further detail *see* Çeker, p. 260.
548. Article 1475 of the Turkish Commercial Code.
549. The term immediately should be understood as 'as soon as in the reasonable period of time' under the principle of bona fides. For further detail *see* Metezade & Güleli, pp. 179–180.
550. Article 1476 of the Turkish Commercial Code.
551. For further detail *see* Bozer, p. 137; Çeker, pp. 261–262; Metezade & Güleli, pp. 181–182.
552. Article 1476(4) of the Turkish Commercial Code.

must inform his or her decision on the consent within fifteen days of the notification. If the consent to settlement has not been given within fifteen days, such settlement is not binding upon the insurer, in other words, the settlement has no validity against the insurer. The insurer cannot, however, abstain from giving consent for unjust reasons.[553] The insurer is obliged to pay the compensation, after finishing the necessary investigation, but at the latest in forty-five days after the notification.[554] The insurer is not responsible for damage that is caused by the intentional act(s) of the policyholder or insured.[555]

§4. Direct Action and Set-Off

388. Former Turkish Commercial Code has only regulated the direct action of victims in liability insurance due to fire.[556] There was difficulty in the admissibility of claims of the injured third parties. Such a right of direct action has been recognized by the judgments of the Court of Appeals although such decisions were obviously contrary to law. The Turkish Commercial Code has overcome this problem. Accordingly, the victim can assert his or her claim directly against the insurer.[557] Such a claim must be asserted within the general prescription period.[558] As a counterbalance to the right of direct claim, the insurer can demand the necessary information, including documents from the victim regarding the determinant causes and the consequences of the damage.[559]

389. Set-off is the way to balance mutual debts between the creditor and the debtor. This concept has been regulated under the Law of Obligations. The insurer cannot set-off the compensation, payable to the victim, against any sum due under the contract of insurance.[560] In other words, the insurer cannot refuse to pay the indemnity or decrease the amount of it because of the premium debts of the policyholder.[561] The law protects the victims by forbidding the set-off.

§5. Subrogation

390. The right of subrogation[562] of the insurer under liability insurance contracts is a significant point for discussion because in the case of subrogation, the

553. Article 1476.
554. Articles 1427 and 1475(2) of the Turkish Commercial Code.
555. Article 1477.
556. Article 1310 of the Former Turkish Commercial Code. Act No. 6762 OG. No. 9353, 9.7.1956.
557. Article 1478 of the Turkish Commercial Code.
558. For further detail *see* Çeker, pp. 263–264; Metezade & Güleli, pp. 183–184.
559. Article 1479 of the Turkish Commercial Code. For further detail *see* Çeker, pp. 264–265; Metezade & Güleli, pp. 185. The content of this article is stipulated in detail under the general conditions and conditions of the different types of liability insurance contracts.
560. Article 1480 of the Turkish Commercial Code.
561. For further detail *see* Çeker, p. 265; Metezade & Güleli, pp. 185–186.
562. *See* paras 285 ff. above.

insurer can ask to be compensated by the policyholder, and this may not be appropriate with the concept of insurance. It is because in such a case both the insured and the party who is responsible for liability would be the same person. If both the insured and liable person are the same, then the insurer can subrogate to the insured to reimburse the compensation that he or she paid. Obviously, such a case does not make any sense, and in such a case there is no sense for the insured to pay a premium. However, there may be instances in liability insurance where the right of subrogation may arise.[563] The Turkish Commercial Code regulates this issue specifically under the liability insurance section and removes any uncertainty surrounding this issue. In case of *joint and several liabilities* between the persons liable for damage, the victim may recover his or her damage fully from one of the tortfeasors or from the insurer of the tortfeasor. Consequently, the insurer subrogates the right of his or her insured and can recourse to the other tortfeasor for the exceeding amount that he paid the insurer.[564]

§6. Time Limits

391. As distinct from the general provision in Article 1420 of the Turkish Commercial Code, stating the prescription is two years and six years respectively, the time limit under liability insurance is ten years from the date of occurrence of an event.[565]

§7. Professional Indemnity Insurance

392. There is a wide range of policies available to insure professionals against work-related liability, such as financial advisors, medical doctors,[566] lawyers, architects, engineers, travel agency operators, insurance agents and brokers against their potential liability in contract or tort.[567] Some professional activities are required by law to maintain liability insurance, such as medical doctors, insurance intermediaries and travel agents. Depending on the profession, there are specific clauses that must be inserted in the general conditions.

393. The insurance coverage is for all damage incurred from the liability of the insured. On this basis, there is no requirement for insurance indemnity if the insured is exonerated from liability.[568]

394. Professional indemnity insurance provides coverage for liability arising from incidents that take place during the insurance contract period and are claimed

563. M.K. Omağ, Türk Hukukunda Sigortacının Kanunu Halefiyeti, Vedat Kitapçılık, İstanbul 2011, sf. 97 ff.
564. Article 1481 of the Turkish Commercial Code.
565. Article 1482 of the Turkish Commercial Code.
566. S. Ünan, Zorunlu Hekim Sorumluluğu Sigortası, Sigorta Hukuku Türk Derneği, İstanbul, 2012.
567. K. Şenocak, Mesleki Sorumluluk Sigortaları Turhan Kitabevi Ankara 2000, pp. 116 ff.
568. Article A.1 of the General Conditions of the Professional Indemnity Insurance.

during the contract period or sometime after it (occurrence-based); or for claims that can be asserted solely during the insurance contract period arising from incidents that have occurred either before execution of the contract or during the contract period (claims-based).[569] It is also possible to have coverage for both types. However, such insurance does not provide indemnity for: (i) non-professional activities; (ii) damage that is caused intentionally; or (iii) incidents that are caused under the influence of alcohol, drugs or any narcotic substance.

Unless the parties agree otherwise, professional indemnity insurance does not cover the following:

- loss of any document or information that is under the supervision and control of the insured;
- any lawsuit that is commenced abroad or any arbitration;
- all types of unfair competition;
- infringement of any intellectual property rights;
- liability towards parents, siblings, spouse or children while fulfilling the professional activity;
- direct or indirect environmental liabilities;
- claims arising from nuclear fuel or waste, or radioactive, noxious, explosive materials;
- sickness including cancer caused by diethylstilboestrol, dioxin, urea formaldehyde, asbestos or claims arising from asbestos;
- claims exceeding the liability of the insured;
- emotional damages;
- fines and penalty clauses;
- damages due to the bankruptcy of the insured;
- expenses arising from criminal proceedings against the insured; or
- expenses in relation to indemnity exceeding the insured sum.[570]

395. Both the policyholder and the insured are under the burden of disclosure both at the time of execution of the contract and during the contract period.[571] For professionals such as lawyers, medical doctors, insurance agencies, accountants and chartered accountants, there are specific contractual clauses for professional indemnity insurance that must be inserted in the General Conditions.

569. Article A.1.
570. Article A.4.
571. Articles C.2 and C.3. *See* paras 226 ff. above.

Chapter 6. Legal Protection Insurance

Meltem Deniz Güner-Özbek

396. In Turkey, legal aid is available to some persons as a matter of right from the State, for both civil and criminal litigation.[572] However, all claims for legal aid are subject to an assessment of the applicant's level of income and the viability of the claim. As an alternative, this sort of financial insurance for legal services is generally available as part of the standard cover under liability insurance in accordance with Article 1474 of the Turkish Commercial Code. Insurance for legal services covers the cost of defending civil actions, criminal actions and recovery in respect of civil actions brought by the insured.[573] Accordingly, when a claim is asserted against the insured, reasonable expenses incurred in relation to the claim are borne by the insurer. This article provides unilateral protection, which cannot otherwise be agreed against the insured.[574] Expenses exceeding the insured sum are payable if the parties have agreed so.

397. Two issues are important for this type of insurance: the choice of lawyer to represent the insured and the resolution of different perspectives about the insured's chances of success. Furthermore, this insurance is also subject to the general principles described in detail above. With respect to the choice of lawyer, the general conditions for Legal Protection Insurance provide that the insured can engage any lawyer without any interference or recommendation by the insurer.[575] In relation to the other issue of a successful legal outcome, if the insurer considers that the insured does not have any chance of success, he can reject fulfilling his obligation. The insured must be informed of such rejection and its grounds in writing within the shortest possible time and without causing any loss of existing rights. In this case, the insured has the right to request that the legal dispute be referred to arbitration with an arbitrator appointed jointly. If the parties cannot agree on the arbitrator, the conflict is resolved by the arbitrator appointed by the commercial court where the insurance contract was executed.[576]

572. Article 334 of the Civil Procedural Law. (Law No. 6100 OG. No. 27836, Date: 4.2.2011); Arts 101 and 147 of the Criminal Procedural Law (Law No. 5271 OG. No. 25673, Date: 17.12.2004); Arts 176 ff. of the Attorneyship Act (Act No. 1136 OG. No. 13168, Date: 7.4.1969); The Union of Turkish Bar Association Legal Aid By-law (OG. No. 25418, Date: 30.3.2004).
573. K. Şenocak, Hukuki Himaye Sigortası, Dayınlarlı Yayınları, Ankara, 1993, pp. 93 ff.
574. Article 1486 of the Turkish Commercial Code.
575. Article B.4 of the General Conditions of the Legal Protection Insurance.
576. Article B.3 of the General Conditions of the Legal Protection Insurance.

Chapter 7. Aviation Insurance

Meltem Deniz Güner-Özbek & İlyas Gölcüklü

§1. Insurance Covering the Liability of the Air Carrier

398. Pursuant to Article 132 of the Turkish Civil Aviation Code[577] air carriers must hold liability insurances that cover liability arising from the contract of carriage. Such insurance should also cover damage resulting from the air carrier's servants or agents' actions. Any aircraft that is not covered by such liability insurance is banned from flying by the Ministry of Transport.[578]

399. In accordance with Article 132 of the Turkish Civil Aviation Code, By-law on Passenger, Baggage, Cargo and Postal Services Liability Insurance for the Aircrafts Operating in Turkey has been adopted.[579] The purpose of this By-law is to determine principles and procedures with respect to liability insurance covering the liability of the operators for damage to passengers, baggage and cargo.[580]

400. The Montreal Convention for the Unification of Certain Rules for International Carriage by Air dated 28 May 1999 ('Montreal Convention') became effective in Turkey on 26 March 2011. The Montreal Convention stipulates that State parties must mandate that their air carriers maintain adequate insurance covering their liability under the Convention.[581] It also gives a right to State parties to require liability insurance for carriers which operate to that State party. Warsaw Convention has no such provision requiring insurance. Turkish Law is in line with the Montreal Convention regarding liability insurance of carriers.

401. Under the Montreal Convention, an air carrier is liable for the death or bodily injury of the passenger due to an accident that takes place while embarking, disembarking or on-board[582] and for loss of or damage to baggage or cargo during the period when the carrier was in charge of the cargo or baggage.[583] The carrier is also liable for delay in the carriage of passengers, baggage and cargo.[584] Domestic carriage is regulated by the Turkish Civil Aviation Code. The provisions of the Turkish Civil Aviation Code on the carriage of passengers and cargo have been adopted by the Warsaw Convention as amended by the Hague Protocol. Turkey is a party to both Warsaw Convention and Hague Protocol.

577. Act No. 5290 OG. No. 18196, Date: 19.10.2983.
578. Article 132(4) of the Turkish Civil Aviation Code.
579. OG. No. 30136, Date: 27.7.2017. By-law repealed former By-law on Liability Insurance of Turkish and Foreign Civil Aircrafts which land or take-off within the Borders of Turkey.
580. Article 1 of the By-law.
581. Article 50 of the Montreal Convention.
582. Article 17 of the Montreal Convention.
583. Articles 17(2) and 18(3) of the Montreal Convention.
584. Article 19 of the Montreal Convention. *See also* Gölcüklü, *Hava Hukuku*, pp. 320–330.

402. Article 6(1) of the By-law states that for all types of damage provided for under Article 5(2), including guaranteed risks such as war, terrorism, hijacking, sabotage, out-law confiscation and public uprisings, an aircraft operator must maintain financial liability insurance. According to Article 6(2), an aircraft operator must be responsible for guaranteeing the validity of such insurance *for each flight* undertaken.[585]

403. Minimum cover is 250,000 Special Drawing Rights (SDR) for the death and bodily injury and SDR 5,346 for delay per passenger. For any flight undertaken by non-commercial aircraft and under the weight of 2,700 kilograms maximum take-off weight (MTW) the limit of coverage is minimum SDR 128,821, for death or injury.[586] Limit of coverage for baggage is SDR 1,288 per passenger and SDR 22 for cargo and post.[587] Except for SDR 250,000, all other limits are in conformity with the limits of the Montreal Convention as increased at the end of 2009. Limit of cover, insurance sum, is determined by the parties for cargo and postal carriages fulfilled by unmanned aircraft.

404. As mentioned above any aircraft which does not fulfil all of its liability insurance requirements under the relevant legislation is banned from taking-off and executing other flights.[588] These sanctions apply whether the aircraft is Turkish aircraft or foreign. Any such foreign aircraft that fail these fundamental requirements cannot use Turkish land or Turkish airspace, and Turkish aircraft will have their licences abrogated by the Turkish Ministry of Transport immediately in accordance with Article 10 of the By-law.

§2. Insurance Covering the Liability of the Operator

405. Article 138(1) of the Turkish Civil Aviation Code requires air operators flying aircrafts over the Turkish airspace to maintain liability insurance that covers damage to third parties.[589] Any aircraft which does not hold such liability insurance will be banned from flying by the Ministry of Transport as well. Accordingly, By-law on the Third Party Liability Insurance of the Civil Aircraft has been adopted.[590] Unmanned aircraft are also included in this new By-law.

585. 21st Circuit Court of Appeals, 15.3.2010, E. 2009/6138 K. 2010/2744 (Kazancı, accessed 5.4.2014).
586. Article 8 of the By-law. Limits of the By-law revised in accordance with the 3rd review of limits of the Montreal Convention in 2019.
587. *Ibid.*
588. 21st Circuit Court of Appeal, 15.3.2010, E. 2009/6138 K. 2010/2744 (Kazancı, accessed 5.4.2014); *see* Art. 132(4) of the Turkish Civil Aviation Code.
589. *See also* Art. 140 of the Turkish Civil Aviation Code.
590. OG. No. 30136, Date: 27.7.2017. This By-law repealed By-law on the Compulsory Third Party Liability Insurance of Turkish and Foreign Civil Aircrafts Executing Flights within Turkish Airspace.

406. 'Third party' is defined as anybody outside of the aircraft under the By-law.[591] It should rather mean anybody who has no contractual relation with the carrier. Civil aircrafts' third party financial liability insurance covers damages caused to third parties by the operated aircraft itself or by the detached particles of such operated aircraft.[592] According to Article 5(1), regardless of whether an aircraft is in the air or on land, or moving or not moving, an aircraft is considered in flight if it is directly going into operation for the purpose of operation of a flight.

407. Foreign aircraft operating in Turkish airspace are also subject to the third party liability insurance requirement. For instance, a foreign aircraft in Turkey is liable in circumstances where it drops an item that causes injury to a British tourist who is not a passenger and is just sightseeing in Istanbul. The importance of such compulsory insurance can be seen more clearly from this example as the tourist can claim compensation under such liability insurance.

Such insurance must also cover risks of war, terrorism, hijacking, sabotage, outlaw confiscation and public uprisings.[593] Aircraft operators must ensure the validity of such insurance for every single flight.[594]

408. The Aircraft Third Party Liability By-law sets out the minimum liability amounts according to the MTW of each aircraft, such as SDR 750,000 per incident for an aircraft holding an MTW of 499 kilograms; SDR 700,000,000 for an aircraft holding an MTW of 500,000 kilograms and above.[595] Not all damages caused to third parties are covered by such liability insurance. For instance, *loss of profits* or remote damages (indirect loses) are not directly covered by such insurance but parties can include such damages.[596] Article 8 provides some reductions for certain types of aircraft. For instance, aircraft used for agricultural protection or forest fighting purpose, used for educational purposes belonging to institutions that are not private companies, and used for non-commercial purposes are subject to a 20% reduction. Reduction is also available for unmanned aircraft depending on their category.

409. The sanction for not complying with compulsory third party liability insurance is just as strict as for third party liability passenger insurance discussed above. Similarly, any Turkish or foreign aircraft that does not fulfil all liability insurance requirements under the Third Party Liability Insurance By-law are banned from taking-off and executing other flights as well.[597] Such foreign aircraft cannot use Turkish land or Turkish airspace, and Turkish aircraft that *repeatedly* fail such insurance requirements will have their licences abrogated by the Ministry of Transport immediately in accordance with Article 9.

591. Article 4 of the By-law.
592. *Ibid.*
593. Article 6(1) of the By-law.
594. Article 6(3) of the By-law.
595. Article 8 of the By-law.
596. Article 6(2) of the By-law.
597. 21st Circuit Court of Appeal, 15.3.2010, E. 2009/6138 K. 2010/2744 dated (Kazancı, accessed 5.4.2014).

Chapter 8. Theft Insurance

Meltem Deniz Güner-Özbek & İlyas Gölcüklü

§1. GENERAL

410. Theft insurance generally covers all acts and risks related to stolen property. Burglary is defined to mean the unlawful taking of property within premises that have been closed and in which there have been visible marks evidencing forcible entry. Such a narrow definition is necessary to restrict burglary insurance coverage to a particular class of criminal act.[598] Under Turkish doctrine, theft is broadly understood as the loss of goods due to an act of stealing.[599] The definition of 'theft' under the *Theft Insurance General Conditions* highlights some basic features of theft insurance.[600] According to the general conditions, the unlawful taking of insured property, forcible entry into premises, loss of insured mercantile, damage to insured property due to theft incidents, etc., are common risks to be covered under the theft insurance policy.

411. Parties to the theft insurance contract are free to agree to include or exclude certain risks in accordance with the relevant legislation.[601] However, fire caused by thieves, war, insurrection, and theft by persons living with the insured are not subject to coverage under the theft insurance policy.[602] Damage caused to the insured property during the theft incident is also subject to such coverage.[603] Once a certain group of insured mercantile is covered in return for a certain premium amount, any property included in the same category later will also be subject to the same theft insurance policy. For example, all theft risks can be divided into different categories (such as safes, furniture, and white goods) and each category can be identified and covered under a theft insurance policy. In that case, if the insured person buys a new item falling under the category of furniture, then such item also becomes directly subject to that insured category in accordance with Article A(2) of the general conditions.

412. It is possible for the insurer to stipulate some provisions under the theft insurance policy requiring a certain way of protection for insured property. However, if this is ever contested by the insured in a dispute, the insurer has the burden of proving that the insured failed to maintain the correct protection for the insured property, contrary to the agreed provisions of the insurance policy. Otherwise, the

---

598. At https://www.britannica.com/topic/theft-insurance (Britannica Encyclopaedia, accessed 13.2.2022).
599. Can (Sigorta Hukuku), p. 182; Bozer, p. 111.
600. *See* A.1 of the General Conditions.
601. Article A(1) of the General Conditions of Theft Insurance.
602. Article A(2) of the General Conditions.
603. *Ibid.*

insurer will not be exonerated from liability to cover the damage arising from the theft incident. It is also possible to include various assets or items under theft insurance coverage by contractual agreement.

413. Determination of the type of risk is very crucial because some risks may be subject to a different insurance. In one case, the Court of Appeals held that motor vehicle theft is subject to *motor owner damage insurance*, not theft insurance.[604] Theft insurance may be issued for many kinds of risks. For example, business places may be insured against theft risks (burglary of fixtures, i.e.) as well as mercantile within domestic homes. Other different examples range from money being transferred over land and money safes, to the more abstract damage caused to the confidence of employees can also be insured against.

414. There are unlimited versions of theft insurance policies available; however, it is possible to categorize theft insurance contracts into two main groups according to the relation between the actual damage amount and the coverage amount under the agreement: *under insurance* and *over insurance*.

§2. Damage and Compensation

I. Duties of the Insured and Insurer upon Risk Occurrence

415. Except during emergencies, the insured should leave the damaged items and places of theft as they are in order to avoid any conflicts and suspicions. If there are any documents or data collected in relation to the theft incident, the insured must deliver those to the insurance company upon such request. Determination of the total damage is usually impossible at first, but the insured must provide an approximate amount of damage arising from the theft risk when required by the insurer.

416. In practice, it is possible to insure the same theft risk under different theft insurance policies and by various insurers as well. In such cases, the insured must notify the original insurer about the existence of such other insurers as well upon the occurrence of a theft incident. Expenses incurred for compulsory precautions by the insured as required by the insurance policy or in good faith are covered by the insurance, even if the insurer does not benefit from such precautions at all. If there is under-insurance, then such expenses are covered in accordance with the ratio between the insurance amount and the insured interest value in accordance with Article B(2) of the general conditions.

II. Determination of the Damage

417. Determination of the total damage incurred by the theft incident is made through a mutual agreement between the insured and the insurer. For example, if

604. 11th Circuit Court of Appeals, 25.1.1999, E. 1998/8318 K. 1999/71 (Kazancı, accessed 27.3.2014).

the insurance coverage is USD 100,000 for jewellery and two earrings have been stolen, then the insured and the insurer must try to negotiate and reach an agreement about the amount of damage caused by such loss. If both parties agree that the loss is USD 8,000 then only this amount is covered by the insurer. However, in many cases, the parties cannot reach such a mutual agreement, and arbitral experts need to be commissioned to calculate the damage in accordance with the principles set out in Article B(3) of the general conditions. Each party must pay for the expert that they appoint by themselves. However, if there is only one arbitrator or expert, then both the insured and insurer must share the expenses and payments equally.

III. Remuneration of the Determined Compensation

418. Upon receipt of the documents pertaining to the theft incident and insured risk, the insurer must pay the determined compensation within thirty days. Replacement in kind by the insurer is also possible for burglary of money or documents of title under theft insurance policies. If stolen items are subsequently found, either partially or completely, the insured must notify the insurer immediately. The insurer subrogates the rights of the insured as soon as the compensation is paid. The most important feature of such legal subrogation is that the insurer will then have all rights of the insured against thieves or other related third parties. In such a case, the insured has an obligation to provide all necessary documents and information with regard to the insured risk in order to facilitate these rights and procedures for the insurer. In cases of total loss, the contract terminates by law as the risk has been fully realized.[605]

605. Article B.5 of the General Conditions of Theft Insurance.

Chapter 9. Agricultural Insurance

Meltem Deniz Güner-Özbek & İlyas Gölcüklü

§1. General

419. Adverse weather conditions such as drought, excessive rains, storms and hurricanes cause heavy losses to farmers. Disasters can often not be prevented from happening, but they can be predicted, to some extent, and arrangements can be made to reduce their impact. However, in some cases, disasters cannot be predicted, and farmers will have to cope with major losses after the event occurs.[606] To cover such risks in favour of producers, an agricultural insurances pool has been constituted, and insurance companies have an obligation to transfer the premium collected from agricultural insurances to the pool.[607] Agricultural insurance, including livestock, fisheries and forestry, especially cover losses from such adverse weather and similar events beyond the control of farmers. Insurance spreads risk across the farming industry or the economy or, in the case of international reinsurance, to the international sphere.[608]

420. Under Turkish insurance law, agricultural insurance has a unique place because agriculture constitutes a significant source of State revenue.[609] Some agricultural insurance may therefore be state-sponsored and some may only be conventional agriculture.

§2. State-Sponsored Agriculture Insurances

421. In addition to its crucial role in the world population the agricultural sector is an extremely sensitive field of activity due to its structure and economic, social, political and technological nature and importance. In order to provide coverage for risks threatening the agricultural industry, an insurance mechanism was implemented by the Agricultural Insurance Act.[610]

422. In accordance with the Act an Insurance Pool[611] was established. The duties of the Pool are: introducing general conditions to provide coverage to the risk referred to under this Act; establishing the conditions for transferring risk under reasonable provisions; ensuring a centralized system of payment of indemnity upon the realization of risk; improving the system of agricultural insurance. All tasks of this Pool are carried out by the Agricultural Insurance Pool Management Company. This

606. Bahattin Çetin, 'Tarım Sigortaları' (Agricultural Insurances), Nobel Yayın Dağıtım Publication Ankara 2007, p. 6; Bozer, p. 127.
607. *See* Art. 4 of the Agriculture Insurance Act. Act No. 5363. OG. No. 25852, 14.6.2005.
608. Çetin, pp. 10–12.
609. *Ibid.*, 42–43, 67; Bozer, pp. 127–128.
610. Act No. 5363 OG.
611. www.tarsim.gov.tr.

company was established by the equal shares of the insurance companies participating[612] in the Pool. In this system insurance companies issue policies in their name; however, the risk and 100% of the premium must be transferred to the Agricultural Insurance Pool. The participating insurance companies may take a share from the Pool through retrocession. The State provides premium subsidies exclusively to insurance contracts executed in accordance with the Act.

Premium supports are determined by the President upon the proposal of the Ministry of Food, Agriculture and Livestock per year.[613] The main purpose of such support by the State is to encourage farmers in agriculture.

§3. Conventional Agriculture Insurances

423. Apart from State-sponsored insurance, many insurance institutions provide coverage for risks arising from drought, excessive rains, storms and hurricanes, greenhouse, hail, etc., under private insurance contracts. *Livestock raising* is explicitly accepted as an agricultural activity,[614] and a producer, for instance, apart from state-sponsored agriculture insurances, may want to cover risks of livestock raising (death of animals, sickness, etc.) under conventional agriculture insurance as well.

I. Hail Insurance

424. Under hail insurance policies for hail, the decrease in herbal product value caused by hail on lands registered with the *farmer registry system* is covered and insured. Optionally, farmers can also insure fruit and vegetables from hail and fire as well. As general conditions for hail insurance require, each product needs to be identified under the insurance policy. Damage caused to agricultural products needs to be determined very carefully by examinations undertaken by experts. In a recent case pertaining to hail insurance policy, the Court of Appeals held that it is the actual damage of the insured farmer, which must be determined by qualified experts before being compensated by the insurer.[615]

II. Frost Insurance

425. In certain cities of Turkey, such as Izmir, Manisa and Denizli, frost is a significant insurance risk, and frost insurance is often obtained in these cities. For

612. The list of participating insurance companies can be found at, http://www.tarsim.gov.tr/trsmWeb/subpageEng?_key_=6D7415BE31795E0576A7CE18FEDB4F2E1075802B4A34P5KD19YOGL60Z124062015.
613. *See* Art. 13 of the Agriculture Insurance Law.
614. Court of Appeals General Assembly of Civil Chambers, E. 2012/576 K. 2012/1368 dated 21.10.2009 (Kazancı, accessed 28.9.2014).
615. 11th Circuit of Court of Appeals, 6.2.2012, E. 2009/21-395 K. 2009/451 (Kazancı, accessed 27.9.2014).

example, a farmer with vineyards may require such frost insurance due to the possible decrease in temperature below 0°C, which can significantly harm the sprout and sucker of the plants.[616] Therefore it is usual for farmers to make sure that this risk is insured against. This coverage cannot be taken separately. There are no general conditions for frost insurance. General Conditions of Agricultural Insurance Products are used. Similar to circumstances of hail insurance, the Court of Appeals argued that any damage realized under frost insurance must also be determined by qualified experts before being compensated by the insurer. It is important to note that apart from conventional agriculture insurance, some national agricultural products significant for export are also insured against risks such as hail and frost. One common example recently identified by the Court of Appeals is the protection of peach products under the State-sponsored agriculture insurance policy.[617]

III. Greenhouse Insurance

426. Uncontrollable factors in the agriculture industry bring an element of uncertainty. The risks associated with such uncertainty carry a heavy responsibility, and insurance for greenhouses becomes an important consideration for many farmers trying to protect their products. According to general conditions, each product must be identified under the greenhouse insurance policy with its total field calculated in square metres (m^2). A greenhouse insurance policy basically covers risks causing damage to products grown in greenhouse structures built by technical equipment recognized in the industry. Optionally, farmers may also insure against storms, tornados, the weight of snow and hail, earthquakes, volcanic eruptions, landslides, vehicle crashes, collapse and floods as well under the single greenhouse insurance policy.

IV. Livestock Insurance

427. Various risks and diseases such as cattle plague, tuberculosis and mad cow disease of both bovine animals and small cattle are covered under livestock insurance policies. According to *general conditions*, venom or poison, natural disasters, compulsory slaughtering or death of the animals, sunstroke, etc., are also covered.[618] Upon the realization of the above-mentioned risks, the insurer undertakes to cover the actual direct damage to the livestock of the insured animal breeder. As with any kind of insurance, premiums vary based on the value of the animals insured. Further considerations, which may affect the pricing, terms and conditions of livestock insurance, are: husbandry standards, animal health status, availability and quality of veterinary facilities, local disease status, etc. In normal situations, standard livestock coverage basically includes death or humane destruction as a

616. Çetin, pp. 59–61.
617. 11th Circuit of Court of Appeals, 13.11.2013, E. 2013/4638 K. 2013/20326 (Kazancı, accessed 27.9.2014).
618. Article 1 of the General Conditions of Livestock Insurance.

result of an accident, sickness or disease. According to the general conditions, parties to the insurance contracts may exclude intentional and economic slaughter by breeder or slaughter by government order. An insurance company may also agree to cover losses arising from theft or disappearance risks of the insured animals as general conditions allow. Some diseases of animals, such as anthrax and rabies must be notified to governmental bodies.[619] The Turkish Ministry of Agriculture and Rural Affairs has the authority and duty to regulate such particular diseases and to provide effective solutions with regard to issues of damage control.

---

619. *See* Arts 4 and 5 of the Act on Veterinary Services, Plant Health, Feed and Food. Act No. 5996. OG. No. 27610, Date: 13.6.2010.

Chapter 10. Catastrophe Insurance

Meltem Deniz Güner-Özbek

§1. Compulsory Earthquake Insurance

428. This chapter briefly examines principles applicable to catastrophic risks such as earthquakes and nuclear contamination. Such risks are also called 'gross risks', which are not specifically regulated under Turkish Insurance Law, unlike jurisdictions such as Germany. On this basis, all general principles applicable to specific insurance contracts are equally applicable to catastrophic insurance or gross risks.

429. Due to high earthquake risk, compulsory earthquake insurance was introduced in Turkey after the earthquake disaster that took place on 11 August 1999 and caused the deaths of around 40,000 people. By the Decree on Compulsory Earthquake Insurance,[620] the Natural Disaster Insurance Institution was also established in 1999.[621] However, the Natural Disaster Insurance Act[622] later repealed this Decree when it was enacted in 2012. According to the Act, compulsory earthquake insurance is provided exclusively by this Institution, and it covers liability arising from fires, explosions, tsunamis and landslides caused by an earthquake.[623] If risk management necessitates, such coverage can be jointly provided by private insurance companies with the approval of the Minister of State, to which the Insurance and Private Pension Regulation and Supervision Agency is affiliated.[624] Accordingly, insurance provided under the Act is not a regular insurance scheme but represents a financial fund established under the Natural Disaster Insurance Institution. Compulsory earthquake insurance and other insurance policies provided by the Institution are offered by the Institution via direct sales or by insurance companies, which are authorized to conclude insurance contracts on behalf of the Institution, including these companies' agencies.[625]

430. The Natural Disaster Insurance Institution has divided Turkey into five regions defined by the level of risk of earthquakes. There are fifteen different premium tariffs calculated in accordance with these different earthquake regions and the type of the building, such as steel, reinforced concrete, stone and other buildings. The maximum insured sum is TRY 640,000 (approximately EUR 32,000.50) for all types of buildings as of November 2022.[626] In considering the high prices of

620. Decree No. 587 OG. No. 23919, Date: 27.12.1999.
621. At http://www.tcip.gov.tr/index.html.
622. Act No. 6305 OG. No. 28296, Date: 18.5.2012.
623. Article 7(1).
624. *Ibid.*
625. Article 23 of the By-law on the Operation Principles of the Natural Disaster Insurance Institution OG. No. 28385, Date: 15.8.2012.
626. Compulsory Earthquake Insurance Tariff and Directive OG. No. 32024, Date: 25.11.2022.

buildings, particularly in Istanbul and in other big cities, it is obvious that such an insurance amount is low. It is also important to note that the insured rate of buildings is only 39.30% throughout Turkey.[627] From these statistics, it is obvious that the compulsory earthquake insurance system is deficient and the reality is that prudent individuals require additional optional earthquake insurance in preparing for the tremendous potential for disaster from any earthquake.

§2. Insurance of Nuclear Risks

431. With respect to nuclear risks, it must first be noted that currently there is no nuclear power installation in Turkey. However, two ongoing projects require consideration for the future. On 12 May 2010, a cooperation agreement between Turkey and Russia was finalized for the establishment and operation of a nuclear power installation in Akkuyu in Turkey.[628] It was planned that construction would begin in early 2016, and the first plant would be operational in 2020. However, construction of the first unit started in 2018 and is expected to be operational in 2023.[629] Turkey signed another agreement with the Japanese government for the construction of another nuclear power plant in Sinop, Turkey, on 3 May 2013. This second plant was expected to be operational in 2023 but it was cancelled in 2019 due to an increase in the cost of construction. Now Turkey and Russia are discussing cooperation in the construction of nuclear power installation in Sinop.

432. Article 5.6 of the agreement between Russia and Turkey states that the Company operating the project must insure the entire project for both periods of investment and operation. Furthermore, Turkey is a party to both the Paris Convention on Nuclear Third Party Liability[630] and the Joint Protocol Relating to the Application of the Vienna Convention and the Paris Convention.[631] The first Act on nuclear energy in Turkey, the Nuclear Regulation Act came into force on 8 March 2022.[632] According to Article 14 of the Act, operators must have insurance or provide any other security. The liability of an operator is limited to EUR 700,000.000 for the nuclear reactors of which thermal power is over 10 megawatts, for nuclear facilities in accordance with the evaluation of the Nuclear Regulatory Authority and for the transit passage of nuclear materials within the borders of the Republic of Turkey for each distinct occasion. For other facilities and for the carriage of nuclear materials, liability is limited to EUR 80,000.000.

433. In order to ensure providing insurance for the liabilities of the operator under the Act an insurance pool is to be established. An operator may obtain insurance or any other security either from the national and international market or from

627. At http://www.dask.gov.tr/zorunlu-deprem-sigortasi-istatistikler.html.
628. OG. No.: 27721, Date: 6.10.2010.
629. At http://www.akkunpp.com/index.php.
630. At https://www.oecd-nea.org/law/paris-convention-ratification.html.
631. At http://www.iaea.org/Publications/Documents/Conventions/jointprot_status.pdf.
632. OG. No.: 31772, Date: 8.3.2022.

the pool. If an operator cannot obtain any or sufficient insurance or any other security in accordance with its liabilities under the Act, insufficiency is to be reimbursed in accordance with the rules set out by the President.

Chapter 11. Credit Insurance

Meltem Deniz Güner-Özbek & İlyas Gölcüklü

§1. Business Credit Insurance

434. Both natural persons and legal entities need various kinds of credit in order to make payments or purchase goods and services. By taking out such credit insurance, the aim is to secure and guarantee *deferred trade receivables* of the suppliers, while *enabling the buyer to get more* goods or services.[633] This type of insurance 'credit' means the credit provided by the supplier to the buyer and deferred payments are also credit provided in favour of the buyer in another sense. Credit is understood as 'trade receivables' according to Turkish legal doctrine as well.[634]

435. The Credit Insurance General Conditions ('General Conditions') were constituted in order to provide security and uniformity for credit insurance practices. According to the General Conditions, credit insurance covers risks pertaining to the buyer going bankrupt, judicial liquidation for failing to pay debts, any judicial decision binding the buyer and limiting its ability to pay the supplier, loan default or other documentation proving such failure, declaration of concordat, and the existence of a contract default debtor (buyer).[635] Across these different types of credit risks,[636] the contracting parties may choose to cover all or just a few of them.

436. Under some foreign legislation, credit insurance contracts are subject to provisions of contract law, especially for insurance that is understood to be 'high risk' ('gross risks'). However, Turkey is not very accustomed to such a term, and there is no reference to the 'high risks' element under Turkish Law when it comes to credit insurance contracts.[637] The practical result of this is that corporations are not subjected to any additional risk assessment, and they can obtain credit insurance protection the same as any natural person. The credit insurance model is threefold, and operates as follows.

633. Aynur Yongalık, 'Hukuki Açıdan Kredi Hayat Sigortası' (Credit Life Insurance from Legal Perspective), Banka ve Ticaret Hukuku Araştırma Enstitüsü Publication (Ankara), pp. 1–2.
634. Samim Ünan, 'Kredi (Ticari Alacak) Sigortası Genel Şartları Şerhi' (Credit Insurance General Conditions Annotation), (Kredi Sigortası) AIDA Turkey, (Özdil Basımevi Publication 2013), p. 9.
635. Credit Insurance General Conditions. Available at, http://www.tsb.org.tr/kredi-sigortasi-genel-sartlari.aspx?pageID=506 (accessed 27.9.2014).
636. These risks may be limited or extended upon mutual consent, *see* Ünan (Kredi Sigortası), p. 16.
637. Ünan, (Kredi Sigortası), p. 10.

Exhibit A Receivables Credit Insurance Scheme

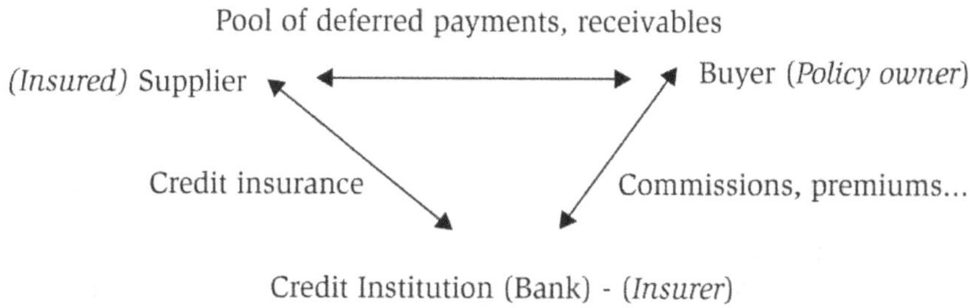

437. Instead of direct and advance payments for the purchase of goods or services, the buyer is inclined to make a purchase on deferred payment options, whereas the supplier desires to sell its products while trying to keep such a pool of deferred and unpaid payments within a reasonable amount. Usually in this threefold transaction as illustrated in Exhibit A, the supplier does not want to provide goods or services for deferred payment without holding security. Conversely, the buyer wants to get goods or services on the deferred payment system as much as possible. When the buyer applies to the credit institution to provide the supplier with a credit insurance policy securing deferred payments, the institution usually engages in a very detailed analysis of the credibility of such buyer before providing such a policy in return for payment of commissions, monthly premiums, profits, etc. If such an analysis of the credibility of the buyer indicates a very high-risk of future purchases, the credit institution provides a *credit insurance policy* in favour of the supplier. Such policy usually states that 'Provided that the buyer does not make its payments on the deferred date mutually agreed on, the institution will disburse 90% of the total deferred payments'. However, one should remember that if such non-payment occurs due to a breach of the sale contract by the supplier (defective goods, etc.), then the institution may reject such payment requests of the credit insurance policyholder. In addition, in the case of non-payment by the buyer, the policyholder may also have to wait for a reasonable time because such delay may be reasonable.[638]

438. As easily seen above, such credit undertakings are usually very risky for the credit institution. Therefore, the bank not only analyses the buyer's credibility about timely payments, financial situation, etc. for a certain period, but it always observes and carefully analyses the buyer's data collected during such enquiries in order to minimize the risk of non-payment by the buyer or to ensure that repayments will be duly made on the date(s) agreed to by the contracting parties. Some credit institutions provide credibility information about the buyer that the supplier can evaluate under the 'early warning' system. With the help of such services, the

638. Ünan (Kredi Sigortası) part I-1, 11.

supplier is able to decide whether to continue to provide services or cease to provide such services to the buyer. The goods or services are paid for by the buyer *within* the insurance liability period determined by the institution.[639]

439. In the event that the risks materialize and the insurer makes payment to the insured supplier, in accordance with *B.6-subrogation rule* of the General Conditions, the insurer assumes the legal position of the insured and obtains all rights of the insured to receive payment from the supplier.[640] The insured must then supply all required documents and beneficial data to the insurer upon such event. The rights of the insured can be transferred to a third party, without affecting the liabilities of the insurer, but only with the written approval of the insurer in accordance with Article *B.9* of the General Conditions.

§2. EXPORT CREDIT INSURANCE

440. Export credit insurance is similar to the credit insurance discussed above.[641] However, instead of regulating the supplier's receivables at a national level as general credit insurance does, export insurance creates a great opportunity for the supplier or exporter to secure the receivables from an importer in another country. Taking into account the international nature of the export credit insurance, it is possible to illustrate the transaction as follows.

Exhibit B Export Credit Insurance

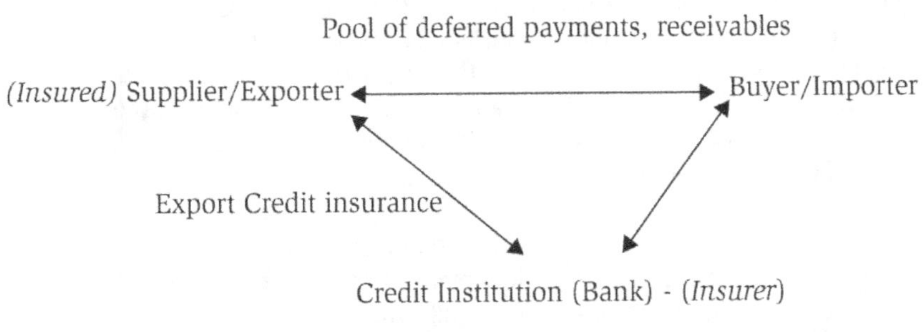

441. As demonstrated in Exhibit B, the main purpose of export credit insurance is to insure the receivables of exporters selling their products or services to other countries. The basic but most crucial feature of the export credit insurance is that it not only covers the commercial risks but also some political risks as well. According to Article A (7) of the general conditions of export credit insurance, the contracting parties may include war, insurrection, etc., as insured risks. The credit

639. Ünan, pp. 12–13.
640. *See* paras 285 ff. above.
641. *See* Exhibit A: Receivables Credit Insurance above.

institution assigns a certain limit provided through a delicate analysis of the importer's credibility. When the insured risk occurs and the damage is notified, the credit institution recovers all damages falling within the liability amount which is usually not the total amount of the receivables but a considerable amount, such as 90% of the receivables. In Turkey, in practice, it is possible to authorize the credit institution to collect money upon the occurrence of such risks.[642] This enables the allocation of risk and assists credit institutions to cover the risk easily.[643] Upon such authorization, the credit institution, since it has already paid a large amount of the receivables to the insured exporter, tries to collect all unpaid receivables from the importer. Once it has collected all of the receivables from the buyer, the credit institution usually pays the remaining part (10% of the receivables, i.e.) to the insured supplier as well.

442. Export credit insurance is mostly useful for suppliers or exporters of *cash against goods* because it is almost impossible for these exporters to pursue their receivables and assess the credibility of their buyers who are located in foreign countries. Since export credit insurance institutions usually work in cooperation with globally known debt-collecting companies such as *Coface*, such cooperation makes it easier to get receivables from recalcitrant importers because of the potential damage to their global credit reputation making further purchases from other countries very problematic.[644]

443. The export credit insurance system also enables the credit institution or insurer to notify its insured customer about any changes to the credibility of the importer. Such crucial information enables the exporter to effectively determine whether to continue exporting to a particular customer or to cease all exports. In return for the export credit insurance, the credit institution (for instance, a bank) receives the monthly premium payments for the period of its liability under the export credit insurance terms signed with the insured exporter.[645] Such premiums are determined in accordance with the volume of the goods or services provided.[646]

444. One should note that the basic difference between the export credit insurance system and factoring is that the counter party, or namely the importer, is not aware of the fact that there has been a credit limit assigned with regard to the sale of the purchased goods or services. In Turkey, the application of export credit insurance to exports made to a country is usually covered, but covering the exports made to only one importer is not very common and such a request is usually denied.[647]

642. Export Credit Insurance in Turkey, interview, Capital Magazine Online, 1 Feb. 2005, Available at, http://www.capital.com.tr/ihracat-sigortasi-nerede-ise-yariyor-haberler/16999.aspx (accessed at 10.9.2014).
643. Can, p. 14.
644. *See* Capital Magazine Online above.
645. Short-Term Export Credit Insurance Brochure, available at, http://www.eximbank.gov.tr/EN/belge/2-89/insurance.html (accessed at 10.9.2014).
646. *See* Capital Magazine Online above.
647. *Ibid.*

§3. Single Risk Insurance

445. Single risk insurance provides a potentially broader coverage than traditional credit insurance. The single risk covers a specific case.[648] In other words, the insurance policy is created specifically for that case and is therefore unique, i.e., single. The single risk insurance is irrevocable for the duration of the case.[649] The insurer may not withdraw any circumstances such as major political events and failure of the purchaser. Such an insurance contract may only be terminated if:

- the policyholder fails to fulfil his obligations; or
- the insured's right ceases to exist, or the activities of the insurer or the insured wholly or partly discontinue and/or the activities of the insurer and/or insured restructured or liquidated.

§4. Individual Credit Insurances

446. Individual or consumer credits are highly common in Turkey, and there are many types depending on the need such as housing and motor vehicles.[650] Consumer credit enables consumers to realize their current needs right away, for instance, allowing them to purchase a house with the assistance of the mortgage system.[651] Since consumers try to minimize the cost of the credit provided, research on consumer credit within Turkey shows that consumer demand for such credit is extremely influenced by the interest rates of the banks providing such credits.[652] Consumer credit or financial loans represent the expenditure of income before earning it, which fundamentally changes the timing of consumer purchasing.[653] For a consumer credit contract, the party with whom the credit institution executes an agreement must be a consumer.[654] Therefore, a credit contract between a creditor and a merchant will not constitute a consumer credit contract. Such differentiation is highly important since under Turkish law there are many regulations and restrictions in favour of consumers. Conversely, where the borrower is not a consumer, the credit institution can be exonerated from many restrictions.

447. For early payments of the instalments the consumer may benefit from many advantages.[655] The early payment amount should obviously exceed the minimum

648. Article A.1 of the General Conditions of Single Risk Insurance.
649. Article A.7 of the General Conditions of Single Risk Insurance.
650. *Ibid.*, 12.
651. *Ibid.*, 12–13.
652. M. İbicioğlu & M.B.Karan, 'Türkiye'de Faiz Oranlarının Tüketici Kredileri Üzerindeki Etkisi' (The Influence of Interest Rates on Consumer Credits in Turkey), Banking Regulation and Supervision Agency (BRSA) Banking and Financial Markets Volume: 3 No. 2, 2009, 11.
653. Ayfer Boylu Aydıner, Gülay Günay & Günsel Terzioğlu, 'Ailelerin Bankalarca Sağlanan Tüketici Kredilerini Kullanma Durumlarının İncelenmesi' (Analysis of Consumer Credit Usage by Families), Insurance Magazine Hacettepe University, p. 2.
654. According to Art. 3(1) (k) of the Turkish Consumer Protection Act, a consumer is 'real or legal person acting in a non-commercial and non-occupational manner'.
655. Articles 14 ff. of the Consumer Credits By-law OG. No. 29363, Date: 22.5.2015.

payment requirement for such an instalment. It is possible for the consumer to pay all of the remaining credit instalments as an early payment irrespective of the instalment amount or agreement type, and the paying consumer is entitled to benefit from the discount calculated by applying the formula promulgated in the relevant Regulation.[656]

448. However, measures undertaken by credit institutions to guarantee payments are even more crucial when it comes to consumer credit because consumers are more prone to fail to pay instalments when compared to investors. Therefore, credit institutions heavily rely on a detailed investigation of the consumer in order to minimize possible risks such as unemployment, death and temporary or permanent disability that may cause the consumer to be unable to pay instalments. Consumer credit insurance protects credit providers not only against the death of the insured but also against many common risks such as unemployment and unfitness for work due to accidents. Therefore, consumer credit insurance provides broad protection for institutions and consumers who are in a relatively weaker position compared to investors dealing with investment credit.

449. Such an insurance model is also three-fold in operation as best demonstrated in the model below.

Exhibit C Individual Credit Insurance Scheme

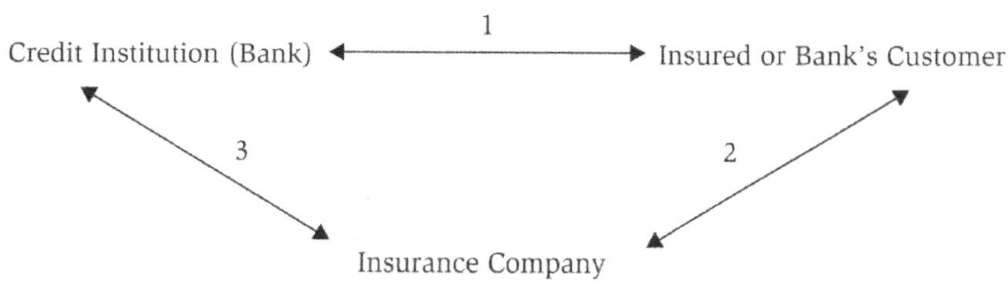

450. As illustrated in Exhibit C, the *first* step is for an applicant (usually an individual customer of the credit institution) to apply for an individual loan, such as a mortgage loan. Based on a detailed examination of the financial standing of the applicant, the bank decides whether or not to provide long-term individual credit. Such a decision is based on whether the applicant has the financial resources to repay this credit amount in monthly instalments (including interest repayments) until the total credit amount is fully repaid. The *second* step is for the *credit institution* to establish some type of guarantee for payment of all instalments. The applicant customer can obtain life insurance with an insurance company he desires by agreeing to pay a life insurance premium amount every month to the insurance company in addition to the credit repayments. By doing so, the insured ensures that if he or she dies within the period of the life insurance, the credit institution will be

656. *See also* Art. 27 of the Turkish Consumer Protection Act.

compensated by the insurance company as a *third step*. Taking out life insurance as security for credit is not compulsory. Normally the credit contract is made between the credit institution and the seller or supplier to insure payments by the buyer. However, credit life insurance is made between the customer of a credit institution and an insurance company to insure credit payments by the customer. These are two separate agreements.[657]

451. Article 29 of the Turkish Consumer Law regulates a different approach to consumer credit insurance conditions compared to other types of credit insurance, such as investment credit and export credit. According to Article 29, any insurance for consumer credit must not be made without the *explicit* request of the consumer in written form or by permanent data storage systems satisfying *written* requirements by the consumer (e-mail, internet, CD, disc, etc.). For such a request by a consumer, the credit institution must accept the insurance policy prepared by the other company which is selected by the consumer freely. In other words, the consumer cannot be forced to obtain credit insurance with the same credit insurance company providing consumer credit. Turkish Consumer Law also seeks to ensure that such consumer credit insurance is consistent with the subject of the credit and the remaining premium amount and debt due dates as well. The same principle is regulated under the By-law on the Application Principles of Insurances Related to Individual Credits.[658]

452. Decisions of the Court of Appeals are consistent with these protective provisions of the Turkish Consumer Law. Under Turkish law, any institution providing consumer credit may only request *necessary*, *justifiable* and *documented* expenditures from the consumer, but *not premiums* for securing the consumer credit instalments directly without request by the consumer in that regard.[659] The Court of Appeals accepts that the basic aim of credit institutions for providing life insurance for credit is to secure payments or instalments for the credit provided. However, since the court also accepts such insurance as an instrument in favour of the insured consumer as well, the court suggests a more delicate approach to such insurance rather than eliminating or invalidating it completely.[660] For instance, if the parties under a credit contract (mortgage, loan, etc.) do not agree on the amount of expenses to be used as filing fees, the Court of Appeals does not expect or approve such expenditures to be paid by the consumer credit customer because such costs are not justifiable and documented.[661] Survey fees, filing fees, bank charges, etc., are subject to strict analysis when it comes to consumer credit and consumer credit insurance.

---

657. *Ibid.*, 113.
658. Article 13, OG. No. 29294, Date: 13.3.2015.
659. 13th Circuit of Court of Appeals, 8.11.2012, E. 2012/23738 K. 2012/25211 (Kazancı, accessed 5.3.2014).
660. 13th Circuit of Court of Appeals, 26.2.2013, E. 2013/924 K. 2013/4474 (Kazancı, accessed 18.3.2014).
661. 13th Circuit of Court of Appeals, 10.2.2011, E. 2010/11726 K. 2011/1870 (Kazancı, accessed 18.3.2014).

453. The creditor must warn[662] the insured customer duly about the renewal of the insurance within the credit period, while the insured should also check whether such renewal has been completed or not by the insurance company.[663] In a case discussed by the Turkish Court of Appeal, the court also recognized a *tacit compliance of the credit institution*[664] since the institution reminded its customer of the renewal of mortgage credit insurance in two consecutive years 2006 and 2007 before the death of the insured in 2008. The court concluded that it is in favour of both the credit institution and the insured customer to renew such life insurance within the credit period, and there is 'concurrent negligence' of both parties where insurance is not renewed even in the case of death of the customer.[665]

454. Credit institutions usually stipulate a 'loss payee clause' in their individual credit contract so that in the event of non-renewal and the death of the credit customer, the credit institution is to be first compensated.

455. A credit card agreement is a *consumer* credit contract within the scope of the Turkish Consumer Act[666] when instalment payments for credit or interest are delayed for at least three months or more.[667] According to Article 22(3) of the Consumer Protection Act, all consumer credit card agreements must be executed in written form. Otherwise, they will be invalid and not enforceable against the consumer later.[668] In the event of a dispute, the credit institution is under the obligation to show that the consumer was provided with one copy of such written consumer credit card agreement. The *consumer* has the right to cancel the contract and may use such a right within fourteen days of signing the agreement without showing any grounds or paying any penalties in order to terminate such contract.[669]

456. A credit institution desires to ensure that payments made under a credit card provided to its customers are repaid fully by the agreed date. However, there are many risks regarding credit card payments. For instance, the customer may go bankrupt, lose his job permanently or temporarily, die or become disabled temporarily or permanently. Once these types of risks occur, it can become impossible for the credit card holder to make debt repayments, and the firms that provided services or

662. By –law on the Application Principles of Insurances related to Individual Credits. OG. No. 29294, Date: 13.3.2015.
663. 13th Circuit of Court of Appeals, 5.7.2011,, E. 2011/1729 K. 2011/11039 (Kazancı, accessed 5.3.2014).
664. *Ibid.*
665. The insurance period for individual credit insurance is available for persons between the ages of 27 and 70. When the insured person died within this liability period of the insurance company and the complainants or successors found out that the life insurance was not renewed in 2008 and demanded compensation, the Court of Appeals found both the credit customer and credit institution liable and decided that there is a concurrent negligence between both parties. *See* 13th Circuit of Court of Appeals, 5.7.2011, *E.* 2011/1729 K. 2011/11039 (Kazancı, accessed 5.3.2014).
666. Article 22(2).
667. Article 22(2) of the Consumer Protection Act.
668. 'Consumer Protection Act Guide for Lawyers', Ankara Bar Association Consumer Rights Committee, Anıl Publication Ankara 2012, 118.
669. *See* Art. 24(1) of the Consumer Protection Act.

goods for such payment will not be able to collect their receivables from the customer by the credit card statement date at the end of the month.

457. Credit card insurance is designed to cover such non-payment risks by requiring the insurer to pay the unpaid debts of the credit card holder on behalf of the insured customer. For instance, provided that the credit card holder of X Bank gets laid off and becomes unemployed, the insurer will make the payments under the credit card insurance policy. The 11th Circuit of the Court of Appeals also discussed the matter of remaining premiums under credit card insurance policy and the obligation of the insurer in the event of the death of the insured credit card holder.[670] According to the court, it is crucial to calculate the remaining premium debt of the insured while the insurer makes the credit card debt payments on behalf of the insured after death.

458. In Turkish legal practice, such insurance type is also called *credit card support insurance*. Under credit card insurance, the insurer undertakes to pay the statement debt of the insured upon the risk occurrence (unemployment, disability, etc.), including the remaining or future instalments up to the total amount stipulated under the insurance policy, which constitutes the liability limit of the insurer to make payments on behalf of the insurer. In practice, the premium for such insurance type is usually based on a percentage (usually 1%) of the account abstract and the total of the future instalments, provided that there is not any credit card debt for a month or any premium charged either.

459. There are many categories of such credit insurance depending on the type of risks and title of the insured: involuntary unemployment guarantee, temporary incapacity guarantee, life loss guarantee, and total disablement guarantee are common types under Turkish law.

670. 11th Circuit of Court of Appeals, 6.2.2006, E. 2005/1108 K. 2006/1012 (Kazancı, accessed 5.3.2014).

Chapter 12. Engineering Insurances

Meltem Deniz Güner-Özbek

460. In Turkish practice engineering insurances cover the contractors' all risk insurance, assembly work all risks insurance, machinery breakdown insurance and electronic device insurance. It is to be noted that the term 'all risk' is misleading since such insurances rarely include all risks in the conventional sense; there are many exclusions in such insurance contracts as well.

§1. Contractors' All Risks Insurance

461. Contractors' all risks insurance covers every stage during the construction activities from the time construction materials and supplies entered into the construction site until the construction is delivered to the employer. Contractors' all risks insurance covers any building projects such as a factory, hospital, school or any similar public buildings, highways, dams, airports, generating stations, bridges, tunnels, ports; and all types of modification work. As an all risks insurance, this insurance covers all the risks that are not excluded in the General Conditions. The main risks covered under such insurance are: earthquake, fire, lightning and explosion; theft; flood, rain, snow, avalanche, storm; landslip, aircraft collision and falling parts from an aircraft; electrical damages; damages caused by individuals; and other business accidents which are not excluded in the general conditions.[671] Moreover, temporary construction site facilities, third party liability, construction machines, debris removal costs, express transport, overtime, holiday wages and increments, strike, lockout, terror and sabotage, current buildings and facilities, and extended maintenance periods can also be included in the coverage if parties agree. Such an extension of the coverage is subject to the payment of an additional premium.[672]

§2. Erection All Risks Insurance

462. There are some risks in the erection and installation of machinery. Such risk can be very high resulting in heavy damage to property and contributing to huge financial losses to the principal or contractor. The Erection All Risks Insurance provides protection against the risks involved in the installation of machinery, plant and steel structures of any kind. As in Contractors' All Risks Insurance, the term 'all risks' is misleading. Erection All Risks Insurance covers the risks to which project work is exposed, starting right from the arrival of material at the site until successful testing and commissioning of the project. The coverage commences when the

671. Article A.2 of the General Conditions of the Contractors' All Risks Insurance.
672. Article A.3 of the General Conditions of the Contractors' All Risks Insurance.

erection materials arrive at the site and continue until the delivery of the tested machines upon the completion of the erection.[673]

463. Standard cover includes: earthquake, fire, lightning and explosion; theft; flood, rain, snow, avalanche, storm; landslip, aircraft collision and falling parts from an aircraft; accidents resulting from the onsite transport, and damages caused by individuals. Subject to the agreement of the parties and payment of the additional premium machines, equipment and temporary huts; third party liability, debris removal costs, additional transport and overtime costs due to covered risk, strike, lockout, experiment period exceeding four weeks, environmental damages, terrorist activities and sabotage caused by terrorist activities can also be covered.[674]

§3. Machinery Breakdown Insurance

464. Machinery breakdown insurance covers all sudden and unforeseen physical losses. The subject of insurance is individual machines or all plant machinery. Machinery breakdown insurance mainly covers material damage caused by the following reasons:[675]

- damage caused by the operation (breakage, excessive pressure, internal vacuum, overheating);
- damage caused by electric energy (short circuit, excess voltage or induction);
- damage caused by human element (faulty operation, lack of skill, negligence);
- damage caused by the manufacturer (faulty design, defects in material, faults at the workshop, faults in erection);
- damage caused by frost and drifting ice.

§4. Electronic Device Insurance

465. Electronic devices are indispensable parts of our daily life. When such a device is damaged or out-of-order, expenses and problems with a device that is not functioning can be frustrating. Devices in the offices are subject to many risks. A device can be damaged by carelessness or circuit disorder. Electronic Device Insurance provides coverage against sudden and unforeseen risks. Coverage of Electronic Device Insurance is similar to Machinery Breakdown Insurance.[676]

673. Article 1 of the General Conditions of the Erection All Risks Insurance.
674. Article 2 of the General Conditions of the Erection All Risks Insurance.
675. Article 1 of the General Conditions of the Machinery Breakdown Insurance.
676. Articles 1–3 of the General Conditions of Electronic Device Insurance.

Part IV. Motor Vehicle Liability Insurance

Meltem Deniz Güner-Özbek & İlyas Gölcüklü

§1. Compulsory Cover

466. Transportation by road can involve many risks that need to be insured against. One of the most common types of liability insurance is motor vehicle insurance.[677] According to Article 91 of the Highway Traffic Act,[678] *highway roads motor vehicles financial liability insurance* is compulsory in order to secure insurance payments for the liability of the operating company and registered owner of *the motor vehicle* who has damaged other vehicles or third parties in any accident that takes place on highways.[679] In order for a motor vehicle to operate on the road some documents and objects must be on-board. These are Document of Registry, Document of Traffic and licence plate. In order to obtain the necessary Document of Traffic proof of compulsory insurance liability is required as well.[680] Motor vehicles which are to be used temporarily on the highways and which are not registered must also have compulsory insurance coverage.[681] In accordance with Article 101 of the Highway Traffic Act, authorized insurers dealing with accident insurance are obliged to provide compulsory liability insurance.

§2. The Scope of Compulsory Cover

467. According to Article 85 of the Highway Traffic Act, both the vehicle operator and the owner of the company to which the operator is affiliated will be jointly and severally liable due to the motor vehicle's involvement in an accident that takes place on highways.[682] Both the operator and the affiliated owner shall be also held liable for the negligence of the drivers and others participating in the vehicle's usage

677. Ali Bozer, 'Sigorta Hukuku' (Insurance Law), Banka ve Ticaret Hukuku Araştırma Enstitüsü Publication Ankara 2007, 141; Yaşar Karayalçın. 'Sorumluluk Sigortaları' (Liability Insurances), Olgaç Publication Ankara 1984, 40.
678. The Highway Traffic Act. Act No. 2918. OG. No. 18195, Date: 18.10.1983.
679. 11th Circuit of Court of Appeals, 4.5.2010, E. 2008/9833 K. 2010/4912 (Kazancı, accessed 5.4.2014).
680. Article 25 of the Highway Traffic Act.
681. Article 26 of the Highway Traffic Act.
682. *See* Bozer, 148.

or operation. A motor vehicle should be in operation while causing an accident in order to hold the person or company operating the vehicle liable for such accidents.[683] Otherwise, the injured party has the burden of proving that such an accident occurred due to the negligence of the operator or other persons whom the operator can be held liable for or due to mechanical defaults of the motor vehicle.

468. In relation to the *active operation* of a motor vehicle involved in an accident on highways, there is no such burden of proof regarding negligence as a rule. However, Article 86(1) states that the operating person or its affiliated company can be excluded from liability if they can prove that the accident did not occur due to their negligence or from that of people whose actions are attributable to them *and* not due to mechanical defaults of the vehicle or the accident occurs due to force majeure or the accident is caused by the negligence of the injured or other third parties.[684] Article 85(4) states that *person(s) operating the vehicle* and/or *the owner of the operating company* can be held liable for damages caused to those persons trying to assist at the site of an accident caused by the operating person's negligence. For example, if someone tries to help injured third parties and this person causes additional damage, the owner and operator will also be liable for these actions.

469. Sometimes a person may be transported in a motor vehicle on a gratuitous carriage basis, meaning that the operator provides vehicle transportation for no fee or payment, service, etc. In these cases, if such a vehicle is involved in an accident, the liability of the operator and affiliated company is governed by general provisions such as Article 87 of the Highway Traffic Act and not by the specific provisions under the Highway Traffic Act. In other words, such gratuitous carriage service is not regulated by compulsory indemnity insurance.[685] This is a very crucial issue to note because, in contrast to general (namely *tort*) provisions of the Turkish Code of Obligations based on the claimant proving negligence, the Highway Traffic Act contains special provisions in favour of the injured as discussed above. The same legal principles also apply to the transportation of cargo, as opposed to *baggage or similar personal goods,* if it is done for free by operating a vehicle.[686] The party claiming that the vehicle involved in an accident was being operated for gratuitous carriage has the burden of proof.

470. For joint offenders in an accident, Articles 88 and 89 of the Highway Traffic Act state that each person's liability for the total loss is calculated in accordance with their degree of negligence as determined by the judge of a competent court by taking all evidence into account.

471. Article 99(1) states that the insurer must cover all damages (within the liability amount) within *eight working days* from the date that such report is sent to

683. *See* Bozer, 143–144, 153; Karayalçın, 43.
684. *See* Bozer, 155–156.
685. Court of Appeals General Assembly, 5.4.1995, E. 1994/11-689 K. 1995/274 (Kazancı, accessed 5.4.2014); *see also* Bozer, 150.
686. Bozer, p. 154; Karayalçın, p. 42.

the centre or agencies of the insurer. Upon such payment, the paying insurer can request from other *jointly and severally* liable insurers *in writing* to pay their share of the total damage according to their liability ratios for such an accident and any agreement among themselves. Third parties can also claim compensation from those liable in accordance with tort provisions under the Turkish Code of Obligation, provided that there are not any contractual relations between the liable person and the third party.[687] Compensations within the scope of compulsory financial liability insurance are subject to the methods and principals laid down in this Act.[688]

472. According to the Highway Traffic Act, the following are not *within the scope of the compulsory liability insurance:*[689]

- the operator's claims against people for whose acts he is liable to the third parties;
- the operator's claims arising from damage to his or her spouse's, lineal descendants' or adoptee's or cohabiting brothers' *properties*;
- damages done to something for which the operator cannot be held responsible within the scope of the Highway Traffic Act;
- motor vehicles' races which are done under liability insurance in accordance with the Article 105 of the Highway Traffic Act;
- immaterial damages; and
- damaged belongings transported in the motor vehicle.

§3. Sanctions for Failure to Insure

473. Under Turkish law, any vehicle that does not have compulsory liability insurance calculated in accordance with the acceptable limits of premiums is banned from traffic.[690] A vehicle holding a *foreign licence plate,* which does not have any valid compulsory liability insurance in Turkey, will acquire such insurance immediately when it is brought to Turkey's territorial boundaries.[691] According to the procedural rules provided by the ministry with which the Insurance and Private Pension Regulation and Supervision Agency is affiliated, Turkish customs must deal with the required procedures for such vehicles.

§4. Premium

474. In principle, insurance companies are free to determine the rate of premiums.[692] However, as already explained elsewhere in this book compulsory insurances are an exception to this principle. Tariffs and premium rates of compulsory

---

687. *See* Karayalçın, p. 41.
688. Article 90 of the Highway Traffic Act.
689. Article 92 of the Highway Traffic Act.
690. *See* Art. 91 of the Highway Traffic Act.
691. Article 91 of the Highway Traffic Act; Bozer, p. 153.
692. Article 12 of the Insurance Activities Act.

insurances are determined by the relevant Ministry.[693] As of 1 January 2014, insurance companies were free to determine the rate of premium for the highway motor vehicles' compulsory liability insurance.[694] In 2017, the price ceiling principle started to be applied to have control over the premiums. Premiums differed according to the traffic risk of each city, and maximum prices increased regularly every month. The rate of increase that was 1% became 1.5% as of February 2022 and an additional 20% increase also applied. The high inflation rate resulted in increasing the compulsory liability insurance cost. As of September 2022, the monthly increase rate is 4.75%.

§5. Third Parties' Rights under the Highway Traffic Act

475. Article 85(2) of the Highway Traffic Act states that if a motor vehicle within the meaning and scope of the Highway Traffic Act causes death or injury in an accident, public prosecutors can order the Traffic Registry Institution, where the damaging motor vehicle is registered, to record such an accident in the traffic registry in order to prevent the suspected offender from transferring any proprietary right or constituting any right in rem on the vehicle in order to avoid liability. If a court judgment is not obtained for the continuation of such restriction within one month of the date of such record, such annotation shall be null and void.

§6. Terms of the Coverage

476. Compulsory Liability Insurance for Motor Vehicles covers the liability under the Highway Traffic Act. The limit of the insurance is the limit provided in the Act. This liability insurance is only valid in Turkey. Drivers who are driving in a foreign country must take out Green Card Coverage under the Green Card System.[695]

477. It is quite common for motor vehicle insurance to also insure, including people other than the insured or policyholder who drive the vehicle in question. For instance, the spouse of the insured, particularly named driver or drivers who drive the vehicle on the insured's orders or with the insured's permission can be insured under this insurance. Such a person is named in the policy, and sometimes additional requirements such as having a licence for a certain period may also be necessary. On the contrary, sometimes insurance contracts have no such restriction regarding the driver of the vehicle in question; they cover everyone's liability who drives the car with the insured's permission. In Turkey generally, policies do not contain provisions regarding the condition of the insured vehicle, such as it must be roadworthy.

---

693. Article 12. Relevant ministry is the Ministry of Treasury and Finance.
694. Article 1 of the By-law on the Tariff Application Principles of Highway Motor Vehicles' Compulsory Liability Insurance.
695. At http://www.cobx.org/content/default.asp?PageID=1.

§7. Time Limit

478. Material damage claims arising from motor vehicle accidents are subject to the two-year and ten-year statute of limitations. For claimants, the two-year period starts from the date when they learned *both* the damage and the person liable for such an accident. In any case, such claims are time-barred after ten years starting from the date of the accident. For any accident that also involves some criminal element, the statute of limitation for civil law claims can be extended if such claims are brought before a criminal court and this criminal court sets a higher statute of limitation period. Recourse claims from various liable persons, including insurers of liable persons, is subject to a two-year statute of limitation starting from the date when the person liable fully compensate the damages and identifies other liable parties to whom he or she can have recourse. Any agreement limiting or abrogating the liabilities stipulated in the Highway Traffic Act is null and void.

§8. Assurance Account

479. An Assurance Account was set up under the Insurance Association of Turkey in accordance with Article 14 of the Insurance Activities Act to recover damages up to the determined limits under some circumstances in relation to compulsory insurances.[696] Application to the Assurance Account is possible in the following cases:

- for bodily injury if the insured cannot be determined;
- for bodily injury if the damage was caused by a person who did not have any or sufficient insurance coverage at the time of the accident;
- for both property damages and bodily injury if the licence of the insurance company in all branches of insurance has been revoked or the insurance company has bankrupted;
- for bodily injury caused by a stolen vehicle where the operator is not liable in accordance with the Highway Traffic Act;
- for payment done by the Turkish Motor Insurers' Bureau that operates Green Card Insurance.

480. Highways Motor Vehicles Compulsory Liability Insurance (Traffic Insurance) and Green Card Insurance are among the compulsory insurances covered by the Assurance Accounts.[697] Accordingly, persons suffering the above-mentioned damages have rights against the Assurance Account.

---

696. I. Ulaş, *Sigortacılıkta Güvence Hesabı (Güvence Hesabı),* 2009 Batider, Cilt: 25, Sayı:2.

697. Other compulsory insurances covered by the Assurance Account are: Compulsory Highway Transport Liability Insurance, Highway Passenger Transport Compulsory Individual Accident Insurance, Bottled-gas Compulsory Liability Insurance, Dangerous Goods and Dangerous Substances and Hazardous Waste Compulsory Liability Insurance.

§9. Direct Action

481. Victims have the right to direct claim[698] against the insurer in accordance with Articles 97 of the Highway Traffic Act and 1478 of the Turkish Commercial Code. The insurers are able to defend the claim on the basis that the driver was not in fact liable.[699]

§10. Turkish Motor Insurers' Bureau

482. Turkey is a party to the European Convention on Compulsory Insurance against Civil Liability in respect of Motor Vehicles.[700] The Turkish Motor Insurer's Bureau (TMIB) was set up in accordance with this Convention and Article 24 of the Insurance Activities Act.[701] Duties of the TMIB are:

- to form insurance or reinsurance pools with the participation of its members and to manage those pools;
- to be a guarantor for its members for the green card documents issued by its members;
- to prepare insurance tariffs which are to be implemented by its members;
- in order to reach its goals TMIB is authorized to make agreements and cooperate with any domestic or foreign institutions or insurance companies.[702]

483. Member of the TMIB refers to insurance companies that have a licence in the road vehicles liability insurance branch which has become the member of the TMIB.[703] TMIB bears the duty of insurer of the vehicles that have a foreign licence plate provided that foreign vehicles have a valid green card. Accordingly, claims arising from accidents that take place in Turkey in which vehicles having foreign licence plate is to be notified to the TMIB. TMIB evaluates the damage. If accepted, the damage is compensated under the liability insurance of the vehicle that has a foreign licence plate. As long as the TMIB bears the responsibilities of the third party liability insurer, a suit can be brought against the TMIB.

698. E. Yeşilova-Aras, Sorumluluk Sigortalarında Zarar Görenin Doğrudan Dava Hakkı, Yetkin, Ankara, 2013.
699. Serdar Acar, Sorumluluk Sigortacısının Doğrudan Davada Dayanabileceği Savunmalar, 2012 Marmara Üniversitesi Hukuk Araştırmaları Dergisi C.18 S.2. pp. 734 ff.
700. OG. No. 23873, Date: 11.11.1999.
701. By-law on the Working Procedures and Principles of Turkish Motor Insurers' Bureau OG. No. 26920, Date: 28.6.2008.
702. Article 5 of the By-law on the Working Procedures and Principles of Turkish Motor Insurers' Bureau.
703. Article 3 of the By-law on the Working Procedures and Principles of Turkish Motor Insurers' Bureau.

Part V. Insurance of Persons

Chapter 1. Workman's Compensation and Occupational Disease

Meltem Deniz Güner-Özbek

484. Under the social security regime, an employee injured at work has the right to claim compensation from the State under the social security legislation regardless of fault. Moreover, if the employer, or someone for whom he is responsible, is at fault, then the injured employee has also the right to claim under the general law of obligations. However, unlike some other countries,[704] Employers' Liability Insurance is not compulsory insurance in Turkey.

§1. Employers' Liability Insurance

I. Scope of Insurance

485. Employers' Liability Insurance covers compensation claims of employees arising from occupational accidents in the workplace. Employees have rights under private contracts of employment as well as the Social Security Institution (*'Sosyal Güvenlik Kurumu'*). The compensation payable under this Employers' Liability Insurance is compensation that exceeds the public benefits that are not provided by the Social Security Institution for employees. This insurance also covers any recourse claims that the Social Security Institution has against the employer.[705]

II. Exclusions

486. Employers' Liability Insurance does not cover the following claims unless the parties agreed otherwise:[706]

- accidents that occur at the time of commuting with other personnel to/from the workplace in a vehicle provided by the employer;

704. For instance, the United Kingdom.
705. Article 1 of the General Conditions of the Employers' Liability Insurance.
706. Article 2.

- accidents that occur at a time when the employee is not performing his or her principal job because he or she is being transferred to another site location by the employer for other duties;
- accidents that occur outside Turkey;
- claims arising from occupational diseases; or
- claims for mental anguish.

487. In addition to these general exclusions, the deliberate acts of the insured employee or damage caused by war or terrorism or by nuclear materials, claims arising from a special contract or fulfilment of a contract that exceeds the legal liability of the employer are also not covered, and parties cannot agree otherwise.[707]

707. Article 3.

Chapter 2. Personal Accident and Bodily Injury

Meltem Deniz Güner-Özbek

§1. General

488. Personal accident insurance provides benefits in the event of personal injury or death arising from an accident. Sometimes such coverage is added to motor vehicle insurance. *Accident* is defined by Article 2 of the General Conditions of the Personal Accident Insurance as 'death or injury of the insured as a result of a sudden and external event'. The following are also considered accidents within the meaning of the law: death or injury due to respiration of gases that spread suddenly and unexpectedly, burns and trauma, nerve damage, poisoning from snake or insect bites, and hydrophobia arising from bites.[708]

489. However, death or injury arising from all types of illnesses and the consequences thereof do not come within the meaning of *accident*, including overheating, freezing, sunstroke and congestive, unless such medical conditions can be considered within the meaning of accident under the insurance. Other examples that come outside the meaning of *accident* include committing suicide or attempting to commit suicide, intoxication or drug consumption, surgery and radiography unless it is required as a result of the accident covered by the insurance.[709]

§2. Exceptions

490. Other occurrences that are not covered by Personal Accident Insurance include war or activities similar to war, strikes, civil commotion, committing crime or murder or attempting to commit such crimes, terrorist activities and biological pollution, contamination or poisoning due to the interference by public authorities in order to prevent or diminish such terrorist activities and nuclear risk.[710] Most importantly, any intentional or wilful exposure to a high degree of danger is also excluded, except in an attempt to save human life or properties in danger.[711]

708. Article 3 of the General Conditions of the Personal Accident Insurance.
709. Article 4.
710. Article 5 (a)–(c), and (e).
711. Article 5(d).

Chapter 3. Private Healthcare Insurance

Meltem Deniz Güner-Özbek & İlyas Gölcüklü

§1. Scope of Private Health Insurance

491. Turkish Law differentiates between health insurance and sickness insurance. Accordingly, health insurance compensates the cost of treatment while sickness insurance provides the payment of the sum stipulated in the policy.[712] Both insurances can be executed in favour of third parties. Private health sector in Turkey is growing rapidly with many Turkish citizens and also expatriates choosing to obtain private cover, as waiting lists for treatments are shorter, and the standard of healthcare in private hospitals is generally higher than in public hospitals. The maximum age at which a person can enter the private health sector in Turkey is 65. If one of the parents holds private health insurance, infants also become a party to their general health insurance after birth unless otherwise agreed in the policy.[713] Most insurers provide various pensions and health insurance packages. Insurance companies provide a list of hospitals and doctors where people insured with them are covered for treatment.

492. Insured persons are usually provided with a 'private insurance card' which is valid for a certain period of time, and the insured can also use his or her citizenship number to prove insurance coverage. However, it is important to note that not all medical treatments are covered under private health insurance, and each health insurance policy clearly determines the types of treatments that are subject to coverage. Private health insurance basically covers the sickness or medical treatment risks of insured persons. Covered risks are determined under the specific policy, and the insurance may cover both outpatient treatment and inpatient treatment.[714]

493. Private health insurance is different from social security services. The insured can receive treatment in both a private hospital and a public hospital if the said treatment is covered under the health insurance policy. However, a person holding general public health insurance may only be entitled to a partial discount for the treatments in a private hospital if the hospital has an agreement with the Social Security Institution. If there is no such agreement between the private hospital and the Social Security Institution, the person must pay the full cost of treatment at the private hospital.

494. Private health insurance premiums may vary according to the type of coverage. Since inpatient treatment for surgery, birth or critical care, etc., requires more

712. *See* Art. 1511 of the Turkish Commercial Code.
713. *See* Art. 1517 of the Turkish Commercial Code.
714. *See* Art. 1513 of the Turkish Commercial Code; *see also* Art. 1 of Health Insurance General Conditions; Court of Appeals General Assembly of Civil Chambers, E. 2009/10-573 K. 2009/605 dated 30.12.2009 (Kazancı, accessed at 10.9.2014).

effort and care, premiums for such coverage are usually higher than that of coverage for outpatient treatment. Other factors affecting the amount of premium payable for private health insurance coverage relate to personal individual matters, such as the policyholder's medical background, age, and gender, which are very crucial for determining the premium amounts and coverage type as well. According to decisions of the Turkish Court of Appeal, an employer, or policyholder cannot deduct premiums paid for employees from their wages.[715] The same argument is also valid for the enforcement of premium receivables; the insurance company must have recourse against the employer and not the insured employee.[716]

§2. Exclusions

495. According to 'the Health Insurance General Conditions' there are some risks which cannot be covered under health insurance policies.[717] These risks include being involved in war, committing a crime, putting oneself into a dangerous situation on purpose, using drugs, being involved in nuclear risks, terrorist attacks and sabotage, suicide attempts by the insured and other circumstances excluded by mutual agreement under the *private conditions* of the insurance policy. Furthermore, natural disasters such as earthquake, flood, and landslide are not normally covered by private health insurance, but the parties may agree to otherwise include them under the coverage. In other words, if the parties have not agreed upon such natural disaster risks and the insured needs treatment in such circumstances, the insurer is not liable for such treatment. Even though insurers may apply additional individual conditions under private health insurance policies, these conditions must not contradict or conflict with other applicable laws such as the Turkish Commercial Code, the Turkish Code of Obligation and the general conditions of insurance.

496. It is important to note that the use of private health insurance constitutes a significant part of 'working conditions' within the scope of the Turkish Employment Act as well.[718] Therefore, any amendment or changes made to employee insurance policy can also attract other legal liabilities for the employer under Turkish employment law. According to Article 14 of the general conditions all notifications to the insurer, intermediaries and agencies must be in writing or sent by the notary.

497. The Insurance and Private Pension Regulation and Supervision Agency (formerly it was Undersecretariat of Treasury) also promulgated the Private Health Insurance By-law.[719] The main purpose of this by-law is to regulate procedures and

715. Court of Appeals Assembly of Civil Chambers, E. 2009/10-573 K. 2009/605 dated 30.12.2009 (Kazancı, accessed at 10.9.2014).
716. Act No. 4857 OG. No. 25134, Date: 10.6.2003. 10th Circuit of Court of Appeals, 26.1.2009, E. 2007/21097 K. 2009/443 (Kazancı, accessed 10.4.2014); *see also* 21st Circuit of Court of Appeals, 25.5.2010, E. 2009/14845 K. 2010/5953 (Kazancı, accessed 10.9.2014).
717. *See* Art. 2 of the General Conditions.
718. 9th Circuit of Court of Appeals, 15.12.2008, E. 2008/6311 K. 2008/33680 (Kazancı, accessed 10.9.2014).
719. OG. No. 28800, Date: 23.10.2013.

rules with regard to private health insurance transactions in Turkey. Travel health insurance is excluded from the content of this by-law. Article 2 regulates matters such as the lifetime replacement guarantee, different types of agreements, tariffs, the obligation to employ a health expert and working conditions under private health insurance. According to Article 6, private health insurance is categorized as *individual/group insurance* or *lifetime replacement guaranteed/lifetime replacement non-guaranteed insurance.*

§3. Lifetime Renewal Guarantee

498. The insurer can provide a lifetime replacement guarantee in the insurance policy as private condition. The insurer can also stipulate the scope and conditions of such a guarantee under disclosure form, policy or private conditions. According to Article 7(1) of the Private Health Insurance By-law, the lifetime replacement guarantee basically means the lifetime renewal of the same health insurance policy, which cannot be amended against the interests of the insured.

499. Such a prohibition on unilateral amendment is very crucial because even during times of sicknesses or treatment for the insured, the insurer is prevented from imposing an *extra sickness premium* on the insured. The insurer is required to provide electronic or written notification about the status of such lifetime replacement guarantee every year. If the insured cancels the private health insurance contract within the first thirty days of the execution, the paid premiums must be refunded to the insured if no compensation has been paid. Such refund must be received within five business days of termination as a gross payment.

500. According to Article 11 of the By-law, if the health insurance policy agreement expires and another contract is not executed between the parties, the insurer remains liable for previously covered inpatient treatment for at least ten days. The insurance company must employ at least one physician or medical specialist or health occupation member in order to receive assistance in providing health insurance.

Chapter 4. Life Insurance

Meltem Deniz Güner-Özbek

§1. Regulatory Framework

501. As explained earlier, companies wishing to conduct life insurance business in Turkey must obtain authorization from the Insurance and Private Pension Regulation and Supervision Agency.[720] Life insurance is sold by direct selling, business arrangements or intermediaries.

§2. Categories of Life Insurance

502. The insured event under life insurance is the death of an individual or reaching a stated age,[721] and there are individual policies and mixed life insurance policies that cover both death and a stated age. Uncertainty in life insurance relates to whether death occurs or not during a certain period. If the insured dies or reaches the stated age, then the risk is realized, and the insurer must pay the insured sum. However, the obligation of the insurer to pay the insured sum may not always arise. For example, when only death is covered under the policy but the insured does not die during the contract period, the insurer has no duty to pay the insured sum. Likewise, when the stated age is covered, but the insured dies before that age, the obligation of the insurer to pay the insured sum does not arise either.[722] Under a life insurance contract, the insured sum may be a fixed amount of money or depends upon the performance of investment funds.[723] The parties can agree on the payment of a fixed sum or periodical payments for the agreed sum.[724] There are also life insurance policies that cover weddings, births and similar other significant events in the individual's life.[725] It should be noted that unit-linked life insurance is currently not available in Turkey.[726] It is believed that implementation of such insurance would benefit to increase short- and medium-term investments.[727]

720. Article 5 of the Insurance Activities Act.
721. Article 1487 of the Turkish Commercial Code.
722. Ünan, Hayat Sigortası Sözleşmesi, p. 2.
723. Article 7 of the Life Insurances By-law OG. No. 28437, Date: 10.10.2012.
724. Article 16 of the Life Insurances By-law.
725. Article 5 of the Life Insurances By-law.
726. Uzun Vadeli Hayat Sigortaları Ürünlerinin Geliştirilmesi', http://www.tsb.org.tr/Document/Yonetmelikler/10.%20kalkinma%20plani_Hayat%20komitesi%20g%C3%B6rs%C3%BC.pdf, 1–3; Türkiye'de Satılabilecek Alternatif Hayat Sigortası Ürünleri at https://sigortastrateji.com/inceleme/alternatif-hayat-sigortasi-urunleri/ accessed on 14.2.2023.
727. *Ibid.*

§3. Formalities and Cancellation Rights

503. Life insurance policies are, generally, long-term contracts. An associated concern is that individuals may enter into a life insurance contract that is not entirely suitable for them due to the powers of persuasion of the insurance salesman. Therefore, the law provides a cooling-off period for such persons. Accordingly, the insured can rescind the contract within fifteen days of the notification of this right of rescission.[728] The burden of proof is on the insurer that such notification has been duly made. If such notification has not been made, the right of rescission extends until one month after the payment of the first premium.

504. Regarding pre-contractual disclosure requirements, there are no specific rules for long-term insurance policies in Turkey. Nevertheless, as expressed earlier, the Insurance Activities Act briefly mentions the issue of disclosure by the insurer in Article 11(3). The Turkish Commercial Code – which came into force five years later regulates pre-contractual disclosure in its Article 1423 and provides that the form and content of such disclosure notification are determined by the Insurance and Private Pension Regulation and Supervision Agency by taking into account regulations of different countries, particularly in the EU. The By-law on the Duty of Information under Insurance Contracts came into force on 14 February 2020 and repealed the former By-law. The Circular on the Application of the By-law on the Duty of Information in the Insurance Contracts prepared by the Insurance and Private Pension Regulation and Supervision Agency came into force on 1 July 2022 and repealed the former Circular numbered 2008/7.[729] Attached to this Circular, there is a general sample framework for insurance disclosure forms. The sample framework for the form prepared by the Insurance and Private Pension Regulation and Supervision Agency contains information on the insurer, type of the insurance its agency, coverage of the insurance, the insured sum, exceptions and exemptions, multiple insurance, limits and clauses, geographical area, duties during the contract period, general information on the compensation, premium and date and form of the payment of the premium, duration and termination ways of the contract, and whether the insurance company member of the special insurance arbitration system. Although there are no special rules for long-term life insurance pre-contractual disclosure some insurance companies have disclosure forms titled 'long-term life insurance disclosure form'.[730]

§4. Assignment of Life Insurance Contracts

505. Life insurance contracts are valuable pieces of property. The assignment of a contract means assignment of all rights and obligations under the contract. As stated earlier, insurance law is regulated under the Sixth Book of the Turkish Commercial Code. Under the section titled 'Life Insurance', Article 1490 requires that

728. Article 1489 of the Turkish Commercial Code.
729. Circular No. 2008/7.
730. For instance Agesa: www.agesa.com.tr.

the policyholder or beneficiary must have an insurable interest on the continuance of the life of the person whose life is going to be insured. This interest must exist at all times from the execution of the contract for the duration of the contract period. If the interest ceases to exist during the contract period, the contract becomes null and void. When considering these two provisions, it is questionable if life insurance contracts are actually assignable. It is to be noted that the assignment of the entire contract is different to assignment of claims or obligations under a contract.[731] Except for Article 1490, there are no other provisions in the Sixth Book regulating assignment. However, Article 1454 does state that if there are no provisions in this Book applicable to insurance contracts in relation to any specific issue, provisions of the Turkish Code of Obligations apply. As an alternative, the General Conditions of Life Insurance state that rights or obligations under insurance contracts can be assigned, which supports the interpretation that the General Conditions allow the assignment of rights or obligations separately.[732] The assignment of *rights or obligations* is regulated by Articles 183–204 of the Turkish Code of Obligations. Moreover, the new Turkish Code of Obligations regulates assignment of contracts, which was formerly not regulated under repealed Turkish Law of Obligations.[733]

506. As noted above, it is questionable if a life insurance contract can be assigned because interest is a fundamental element which must exist both at the time of execution and during the contract period. Thus, if the interest ceases to exist during the contract period and the contract becomes null and void, there will be no right or obligation to assign. Even if assignment of a contract were possible, due to the interest requirement at all times, the interest of the assignee would be necessary at the time of assignment.

507. Apart from the assignment of a life insurance contract, assignment of a life insurance claim is also possible. This is done in accordance with the Turkish Code of Obligations,[734] which states that the contract assigning the claim must be in writing and the consent of the insurer is not required.[735]

§5. Group Insurance

508. If there is a group of at least ten persons, group life insurance is a possible option.[736] Employers or members of any institution or society and their families can be insured under the same collective policy. This type of group life insurance contract is usually operational for one year and covers the death or disability of the insured.

731. *See* paras 492 ff. above.
732. Article C.8.
733. Article 205 of the Turkish Code of Obligations.
734. Articles 183–194 of the Turkish Code of Obligations.
735. Article 183.
736. Article 1496 of the Turkish Commercial Code.

Chapter 5. Pensions

Meltem Deniz Güner-Özbek

§1. General

509. The modern historical use of the social security system began in 1945 in Turkey. This relatively young system was administered under three different institutions until 2006, which were then collectively reformed into the Social Security Institution. As such, the social security system in Turkey is still developing to overcome perceived deficiencies. One main perception is that the extent of social security is insufficient in Turkey, as is the case in many other countries. The social reality is that many individuals receiving some type of assistance under the governmental system feel that they need to take benefits from additional arrangements as well. Taking into consideration the documented insufficiency of the social security system in Turkey, the Individual Pension System was created by the Individual Pension Saving and Investment System Act in 2001.[737] This system was drafted as a complementary service for the social security system, but it is not compulsory and individuals are free to be involved in it or not. By directing an individual's pension savings into investment, individuals can derive extra revenue, and this positively affects the level of their wealth. Furthermore, such a pension system creates long-term resources for the Turkish economy and promotes employment and economic development. Although the relatively low levels of income in Turkey have created some difficulties for the system, it has improved with the involvement of more people over the years.

510. As the Individual Pension System has been quite successful, the government has decided to expand its application. The Act was amended effective from 1 January 2017. The amendment provides an alternative participation for employees. This alternative system is based on automatic participation of the workers in the individual pensions system.

§2. Operation of the Individual Pension System

511. All individuals with legal capacity can be involved in the Individual Pension System. In order for an individual to qualify for retirement under the system, he or she must remain involved for at least ten years in the system and must be at least 56 years old. It is to be stressed that these two conditions must exist together. When an individual qualifies for retirement, he or she has three options: collective payment, payment in accordance with a payment plan determined by individual preferences or payment in accordance with an annuity.[738]

737. No. 4632 Date: 28.3.2001 (OG. No. 24366, Date: 7.4.2001).
738. Article 6 of the Individual Pension Saving and Investment System Act.

512. Most insurance companies providing pension insurance services also provide life insurance, i.e., they are both life and pension insurance companies. Pension insurance companies are regular insurance companies, and they are subject to auditing in accordance with the Insurance Activities Act discussed earlier.[739] Furthermore, the normal business activities of the insurance companies in the system are monitored by the Pension Monitoring Centre in an electronic environment.[740] The Pension Monitoring Centre has been established to ensure that the Individual Pension System operates safely and efficiently and that the rights and interests of participants are protected. As a control mechanism, the following are some of the tasks that the Pension Monitoring Centre performs in addition to tasks determined by the Insurance and Private Pension Regulation and Supervision Agency that are related to life insurance and the other branches of insurance:[741]

- electronic monitoring and surveillance of the business activities of pension companies and e-reporting to public authorities on a daily basis;
- consolidation of data, based on the daily transactions of pension companies;
- providing information to the public and participants;
- generating information based on statistics and actuarial;
- providing analysis and reports;
- implementing the licensing exam of Intermediaries and keeping track of the electronic registries of results;
- meeting the demand for joint presentations, training activities, software and relevant subjects;
- analytically querying the system;
- organizing data for timely intervention in possible problems;
- managing complaints from individual participants;
- coordinating projects with international associations to enhance the system;
- giving support to pension companies;
- calculating State contributions based on data provided by pension companies;
- allocating subsidies paid by the Undersecretariat among pension companies to individual pension accounts; and
- storing standardized data for all individual accounts.

513. In order to ensure the transparency of the system, individual participants have access to daily information about their pension account created by the company on its website. One of the most notable peculiarities of the system is State contribution. As of 1 January 2013, the Turkish government contributes 25% of the contribution paid by individual participants.[742] Formerly, there was a tax benefit for the participants. However, in order to improve the Individual Pension System, this was replaced by State contribution, which has helped increase the number of individual participants. As of December 2014, Turkey's population is approximately 78

739. *See* paras 95 ff. above.
740. Article 20/A of the Individual Pension Saving and Investment System Act.
741. Pension Monitoring Centre Working Principle By-law OG. No. 31269, Date: 9.10.2020.
742. Article Ek 1 of the Individual Pension Saving and Investment System Act.

million[743] and the number of participants is approximately 5,308,246.[744] Nevertheless, both the number of participants and their percentage of the total population are still low in comparison with developed countries. And it is uncertain whether State contribution will continue or not; there are already discussions that the percentage of the contribution will be decreased incrementally and eventually, it will either be removed completely from the system or will be reduced to 3%–5%.

514. The savings of participants are managed under pension investment funds by professional managers.[745] Intermediaries are also available to assist participants with their pension plans in terms of expectations for retirement, income rate and age.[746] Fund allocation is determined in accordance with the participant's preference. If the participant does not prefer fund allocation, savings are transferred to standard investment funds determined by the Undersecretariat of Treasury.[747] Under the framework for pension plans, participants are free to buy any fund that they wish to invest in and choose any level of risk. Moreover, participants are allowed to make alterations in the fund distribution of their savings in the pension account and investment contribution six times a year.[748] Likewise, alteration of the pension plan can be made four times a year.[749] In the case of unexpected developments in the financial situation of a participant, he or she can suspend the payment of contribution.[750] It is also possible to change the individual pension company. However, new participants must be contracted to the same pension company for at least two years before they can transfer the contract to a new company and other participants who have previously changed pension companies must remain contracted to the new company for at least one year before transferring to another company again.[751]

515. It is possible for employers to provide the Individual Pension System as a benefit to their employees. In other words, employers can pay pension contributions on behalf of their employees as part of the remuneration package they provide. Contributions paid for the employees can then be deducted as an expenditure from their income entitlements. Such a deduction provides tax benefits.[752] Employers can determine the entitlement period between one and seven years.[753]

516. In the first year of the Turkish Republic, financial initiatives establishing private funds resembling social insurance were highly restricted in terms of the persons covered and the type of risks. The first specific Social Insurance Act[754]

743. As of 27 Mar. 2015. For regularly updated statistics on the Individual System *see,* http://www.egm.org.tr/weblink/BESgostergeler.asp.
744. *See,* www.tuik.gov.tr and http://www.egm.org.tr/weblink/BESgostergeler.asp.
745. Article 18.
746. Article 11.
747. Article 5 of the By-law on the Individual Pension System OG. No. 28462, Date: 9.11.2012.
748. Article 10 of the By-law on the Individual Pension System.
749. Article 11 of the By-law on the Individual Pension System.
750. Article 14.
751. Article 12.
752. Article 40 of the Income Tax Act No. 193 OG. No. 10700, Date: 6.1.1961.
753. Article 18.
754. Article Ek 36 Act No. 506 OG. No. 11766–11779, Dates: 29–31.7.1964, 1.8.1964.

continued to allow the operation of such funds. Accordingly, banks, insurance companies, chambers of commerce, chambers of industry, stock exchanges and other companies established such funds to provide assistance in the case of disability, retirement or death of their employees. The current Social Insurance and General Health Insurance Act[755] has repealed the previous Social Insurance Act and merged the three existing social security services under a single institution. Likewise, the provisional Article 20 of the Act enforced the transfer of private funds to the Social Security Institution to initially be completed within five years. However, this period has been extended twice until the final date of 8 May 2015. An Act that entered into force on 23 April 2015 amending the Occupational Safety and Security Act and some other acts and decree-laws gave the Council of Ministers the right to determine the date of transfer of private funds to the Social Security Institution. With the transfer of some powers to the President under the new political system this right has been given to the President. So far President has not determined any date for the transfer or the private funds. Therefore, the transfer time is still uncertain. One main reason for this delay is the financial burden on the State's economy. However, archive systems of private funds have become electronic and merged with the information system of Social Security Institutions. Members of such private funds are able to follow the services of such private funds at www.turkiye.gov.tr.

§3. Automatic Participation in the Individual Pension System

517. Turkish citizens and persons having *blue cards*[756] who are private or public employees[757] and under the age of 45 automatically participate in the system. Employees participate in an individual pension plan via their employers. In other words the employer contracts with the insurer on behalf of employees. While choosing an insurer, the employer takes into account quality of services, deductibles, etc. Employees have the right to choose funds with or without interest at the time of participation. If an employee has not had any preference, the employer determines his or her fund. Employee contribution is 3% of the tax base of salary. Under the framework of automatic participation system the employee himself or herself pays his or her contribution via his or her employer. An employer cannot pay contribution as a benefit for his or her employee. An employer may offer such benefits under the group retirement insurance. An employee may voluntarily pay contribution above the legally determined amount. Contribution is paid by the employer on behalf of the employee on the next day of the payment of the salary. If the employer does not pay the contribution timely or at all, he will be responsible for the economic damages an employee suffers. Additionally, the employer will be fined by the Ministry of Labour and Social Security for each violation.

---

755. Act No. 5510 OG. No. 26200, Date: 16.6.2006.
756. In accordance with the Turkish Citizenship Act (Act No. 5901 OG. No. 27256, Date: 12.6.2009) Art. 28 persons who have renounced birthright Turkish citizenship to have a citizenship of another country which does not allow dual citizenship are given blue card to use their birthright citizenship's rights.
757. Social Insurances and General Health Insurance Act Art. 4.a,c Act No. 5510 OG. No. 26200, Date: 16.6.2006.

518. An employee participates in this system even if he or she has an individual pension plan mentioned above in paragraphs 502 ff. Companies or public bodies having over 1,000 employees started to apply for automatic participation on 1 January 2017. Participation has been taking place gradually based on the number of employees and will be completed by 2 January 2019.

519. The employee may terminate his or her contract within two months after he or she is informed of such a contract. If the employee does not terminate the contract within two months, he or she receives a one-time State contribution in the amount of TRY 1,000 (approx. EUR 200). Additionally, the participant, i.e., an employee, is entitled to a 25% State contribution calculated based on his or her contribution. However, there are time limits for entitlement to 25% State contribution. In order to be entitled to State contribution, the contributor must stay at least three years in the system. A minimum of ten years in the system is required for full entitlement to 25% State contribution.

Part VI. Private Insurance as a Social Security or As a Complementary of Social Security

Meltem Deniz Güner-Özbek

520. Under the Social Insurance and General Health Insurance Act, individuals covered by the Act are entitled to receive permanent disability income from the State. However, this social security may not provide adequate protection against the loss of earning power. Therefore, individuals may also take out one or more insurance options available to compensate for long-term disability. This section of the book does not examine the social security system but rather outlines the options available in the private insurance market to complement the social security system.

§1. Permanent Health Insurance or Disability Insurance

521. Permanent health insurance as referred to in the UK[758] or *disability insurance* as referred to in the USA provides some part of the insured's income for an extended period when he or she cannot work at all or can work only part-time due to disability. However, this type of insurance is not available in the Turkish insurance market, at least for the present time.

§2. Critical Illness Insurance

522. Critical illness insurance is an insurance that provides a lump sum payment in the event that the insured has suffered a specific medical condition as defined in the policy. Even though there is no agreed list of medical conditions covered at present, medical conditions that are normally covered include – *inter alia* – cancer, hemiplegia, myocardial infarction, coronary artery disease, heart valve disease, multiple sclerosis, and renal failure whose treatment may take longer and be expensive. Some insurers stipulate an age limit for the policyholders, such as between 18 and 50, 18–55 with an upper age limit of 65 for the maximum duration of coverage. Benefits are usually financed between approximately EUR 4,000 and EUR 100,000.

758. Birds, 213.

§3. Personal Accident and Sickness Insurance

523. The principal issues concerning personal accident and sickness insurance were considered earlier.[759] It is noted here that there is also an alternative form of private social security. Considering that permanent health insurance or disability insurance is not currently offered in Turkey, the importance of *personal accident and sickness* insurance becomes even more significant. Both insurances provide coverage for daily compensation, i.e., loss due to being unable to work, if parties agree so, in addition to any lump sum payable.[760]

§4. Complementary Health Insurance

524. Some of the private medical institutions in Turkey have contractual agreements with the Social Security Institution. Under such agreements, individuals are able to receive medical services from private health institutions. Depending on the costs determined by the private institution for such services, individuals must pay the difference between the basic cost of the services normally provided by the Social Security Institutions and the cost of the services provided by the specific private medical institution, if there is any. In addition to such expenses, complementary or supporting health insurance covers expenses that exceed the coverage of the Social Security Institution and expenses not covered by the Social Security Institution.[761]

525. Although the Social Insurance and General Health Insurance Act has been instituted to represent the interests of all of Turkish society, it faces some financial problems as in many other countries. The main reason for such financial problems is the increase in healthcare expenditure. As a result, the complementary or supporting private health insurance options discussed in this section have become very significant alternatives for Turkish citizens.[762]

759. *See* paras 474 ff. above.
760. Article 8 of the General Conditions of Individual Accident Insurance; Arts 1 and 10 of the General Conditions of Health Insurance.
761. Article 98/3 of the Social Insurances and General Health Insurance Act; Art. 18 of the Private Health Insurances By-law OG. No. 28800, 23.10.2013.
762. Türkiye İçin Tamamlayıcı ve Destekleyici Sağlık Sigortası Modeli, www.tsb.org.tr/Document/Yonetmelikler/TSS_Rapor_16.05.14.docx (visited 24.1.2015).

Part VII. Insurance Intermediaries

Meltem Deniz Güner-Özbek & İlyas Gölcüklü

526. Insurance is a broad and complex concept. Therefore insurance needs to be distributed in a number of different ways. The most common way is through insurance intermediaries as regulated under the Insurance Activities Act.[763] Under Turkish law, insurance intermediaries as *agents* or *brokers* are also significantly regulated under the Turkish Commercial Code.[764] Insurance intermediaries serve as the 'critical link between insurance companies seeking to place insurance policies and consumers seeking to procure insurance coverage'.[765] Insurance intermediaries which are traditionally called '*brokers*' or '*agents*' or '*producers*' or '*insurance experts*' or '*individual pension intermediaries*' generally offer consultation, information and other services in connection with the 'solicitation, negotiation and sale' of insurance.[766] However, due to uncertainty about the true nature of producers, *brokers* and *agents* are the most widely accepted types of insurance intermediaries under Turkish Law.[767] The basic function of insurance intermediaries is to facilitate the placement and purchase of insurance and to provide services to insurance companies and consumers that 'complement the insurance placement process'.[768]

§1. Insurance Brokers

527. Insurance brokers typically work for the policyholder during the insurance process and act *independently* in relation to insurers. Insurance brokers assist clients in the choice of their insurance by presenting them with alternatives with regard

763. *See* Arts 21–23 of the Insurance Activities Act.
764. *See* Arts 102–123 of the Turkish Commercial Code.
765. *See* Kender, *Sigorta Hukuku*, p. 118; Kubilay, p. 239; E. Yazıcıoğlu, 'Sigorta Aracıları Hukuku I' (Law of Insurance Intermediaries), XII Levha Publication (Istanbul 2010), pp. 2–3; *see also* the Council of Insurance Agents and Brokers publication, 'The Role of Insurance Intermediaries', 2 available at, https://www.ciab.com/wp-content/uploads/2017/04/RoleOfInsInt.pdf (accessed at 13.02.2023).
766. M. Özdamar, 'Sigorta Brokeri ve Hukuki Niteliği' (Insurance Broker and Its Legal Aspects), AÜHFD Law Faculty Magazine 2008, pp. 527–529.
767. Kender, *Sigorta Hukuku*, pp. 118–119; *see also* Art. 2 of the Insurance Activities Act.
768. 'The Role of Insurance Intermediaries', pp. 2–3; Özdamar, p. 530.

to both insurers and products. The main purpose of the broker is to make sure the insurance contract is executed in accordance with the needs of the insured.[769]

528. Acting as the 'agent' for insurance buyers, brokers usually work with multiple companies to place coverage for their clients. Brokers obtain quotes from various insurers and guide clients in determining the adequate policy from a range of products.[770] However, the wording of 'acting' as an agent in the Insurance Activities Act has been criticized by Turkish doctrine[771] for the reason that the broker does not actually represent any client. Brokers are subject to the rules and provisions of the Insurance and Reinsurance Brokers By-law (Brokers By-law).[772] As the title states, the Brokers By-law deals with both insurance and/or reinsurance. Reinsurance brokers solicit, negotiate and sell reinsurance cessions and retrocession on behalf of ceding insurers seeking coverage with reinsurers. Reinsurance brokers can also be involved in the retrocession of certain risks on behalf of reinsurers. However, in all circumstances, a broker must act objectively in avoiding any biased treatment for a particular insurance company among others.[773]

529. The difference between the meaning of an agent and a broker is not an easy distinction to make. An intermediary's status is determined by *the totality of the facts regarding the specific transaction* at issue. An intermediary might be called a 'broker', but actually represent the insurance company as an 'agent' in a particular transaction.[774] In such situations where there is an obvious representation of the insurance company, the broker is actually and legally considered as the company's agent, and not a broker for the customer.[775] Therefore an activity-based analytical approach should be used in order to determine whether the intermediary is an agent or a broker in any given situation.

I. Conditions for Broker's Incorporation

530. According to Article 4 of the by-law, there are some crucial criteria for both real[776] and legal persons.[777] For periods of time during which brokers are active,

769. Özdamar, p. 532; Kender, *Sigorta Hukuku*, pp. 130–131; Kubilay, p. 257; Yazıcıoğlu, pp. 78–79.
770. The Role of Insurance Intermediaries, pp. 3–5, Kubilay, pp. 257–258.
771. Kender, *Sigorta Hukuku*, p. 130, *see* Art. 2 of the Insurance Activities Act for the wording.
772. OG. No. 29368, Date: 27.5.2015.
773. Özdamar, pp. 533–535; Kubilay, p. 258.
774. Kender, *Sigorta Hukuku*, p. 131; The Role of Insurance Intermediaries, p. 7; Yazıcıoğlu, pp. 105–106.
775. Özdamar, p. 546.
776. Article 4(1), any natural person who desires to be a broker must:

- be resident in Turkey;
- have *disposal capacity* in accordance with the Turkish Civil Code;
- not be or have been subject to imprisonment or any other sentence under Art. 3 of the Insurance Code;
- be a graduate with at least a four-year university degree;
- have a minimum of ten years of work experience in a related field;

they are also considered 'merchants' within the scope of the Turkish Commercial Code.[778] The minimum paid capital for a legal person broker company is TRY 250,000. For each branch of an insurance brokerage licence, an additional TRY 50,000 is required. Real-person brokers must have assets in the same amount. For legal person brokers, equity capital cannot fall below 10% of the annual transaction earnings. In case of incompleteness, the remaining equity capital shall be completed by the end of the year, at the latest.[779]

II. Brokerage Licence and Professional Indemnity Insurance

531. Once the applicant has completed all of the requirements pursuant to the Brokers By-law and the company is registered in the Trade Registry Gazette, the applicant can obtain the brokerage licence by applying to the Insurance and Private Pension Regulation and Supervision Agency. Brokerage licences are issued for one or more of the fields of life insurance, non-life insurance or reinsurance. All approved applicants are required to have professional indemnity insurance before being registered officially in the Trade Registry Gazette. Licensed brokers can also then advertise their services on the internet website. As protection against possible damage or loss caused to the insured, broker companies must have professional indemnity insurance coverage of at least TRY 200,000 for each liability. In addition, the broker companies must have a minimum of TRY 1,000,000 coverage for all liabilities in a year. Professional indemnity insurance is very crucial, and without such insurance, a broker cannot participate in brokerage transactions.[780] If a licensed brokerage company suspends its operations for more than one year or acts in contravention of any provisions of applicable insurance legislation, the broker must first be warned by written notification.[781] If such contravention or irregularity is not remedied within three months from such notice, the Secretariat can then abrogate the brokerage company's licence.

III. Brokers Established Abroad (Foreign Brokers)

532. According to Article 7(1), any foreign real person and legal person desiring to conduct brokerage business in Turkey must adhere to the conditions discussed above. Brokers originally established abroad can only participate in the brokerage sector in Turkey by establishing a branch in Turkey. Liaison offices or

- meet the minimum capital requirements; and
- fulfil the physical, technical and administrative requirements.

777. Article 4(2).
778. Özdamar, p. 545.
779. Article 11(4) of the Insurance and Reinsurance Brokers By-law.
780. Özdamar, pp. 540–541; Kubilay, p. 264; Yazıcıoğlu, pp. 84–85.
781. *See* Art. 21 of the Insurance and Reinsurance Brokers By-law.

branch offices other than the main office are not permitted under Turkish law. Any documents obtained from a foreign country for submission by an application must be *legalized* by the authorized institutions of the relevant country or by the Turkish Embassy or General Consulate of Turkey in the relevant country or should comply with the requirements of the *Convention* Abolishing the Requirement of Legalisation for Foreign Public Documents.

IV. Obligations and Restrictions

533. Brokerage authorization may be given by a written document, by e-mail or orally. The coverage, limits and duration of the authorization are determined in the authorization document. The brokerage authorization shall not be transferred to any other broker or any person. Authorized brokers obtain offers by representing the authorization and informing the customer of the offers and comparative prices. Brokers shall not engage in any other business than brokerage; they can only receive brokerage commission, consultancy and risk management fees.[782] Furthermore, brokers cannot issue an insurance policy or any other relevant documents. They cannot make insurance payments either.

534. The coverage and limits of the authorization to be given by insurance companies are determined by a protocol between the parties. In principle, premiums are collected by the insurance companies. However, a broker may be authorized by the insurance company for this purpose. In that case, payment made to the broker is deemed to be made to the insurance company. This is particularly important for the commencement of insurance cover.[783]

§2. Insurance Agents

535. Insurance Activities Act defines[784] agent similar to the Turkish Commercial Code and also sets out that provisions of the Turkish Commercial Code in relation to agents are applicable to insurance agents as well. Articles 102–123 of the Turkish Commercial Code regulate the crucial role of agents as intermediaries in general. There is also Insurance Agents By-law.[785] It is to be noted that some institutions, such as branches of banks, can also operate as insurance agents in accordance with special acts.[786]

782. Article 17(3) of the Insurance and Reinsurance Brokers By-law.
783. Articles 16 and 17 of the Insurance and Reinsurance Brokers By-law.
784. Article 2(1) m.
785. OG. No. 28980, Date: 22.4.2014.
786. For instance Art. 4(u) of the Banking Activities Act. Act No. 5411 OG. No. 25983, Date: 1.11.2005.

I. Conditions for Agent Incorporation

536. There are some crucial criteria for both real and legal persons. Any natural person seeking to be an agent in Turkey must:[787]

- be a resident of Turkey;
- carry the title of *technical* personnel;
- not be or have been subjected to imprisonment or sentences of more than five years for intentional crimes and other miscellaneous crimes such as embezzlement, fraud, and financing terrorism;
- fulfil the minimum capital requirements under Article 9;
- have appropriate physical, technical, administrative requirements and human resources to conduct agency transactions; and
- fulfil the educational requirements and complete occupational training as required.

537. On the contrary, any legal entity who desires to be a broker must:[788]

- establish its business in Turkey;
- incorporate as a joint stock company or limited company;
- not be or have been subjected to bankruptcy and concordat;
- meet the minimum capital requirements;
- ensure that any shareholders of the joint stock company or limited company be free from bankruptcy and concordat as well; and
- ensure that all executives (other than the most senior executive in the broker company) have at least five years of work experience in a related field.

538. The most senior executive is subject to additional conditions apart from the other executives in that he or she must be a graduate with at least a four-year university degree in the same field as the broker company and must have a minimum of ten years of work experience as required for a natural person incorporating a broker company.

539. Agents can operate branch offices but such branches must be given the title 'branch', and they must operate under the same business title as the agent.[789] The minimum paid capital for legal persons operating as agent companies, save the minimum amount required by the Ministry of, and total assets to be declared by natural person agents must not be less than TRY 25,000. A minimum of 50% of such assets or minimum paid capital can consist of investment tools such as cash, bank deposits, and domestic government bonds, which can be easily converted into cash.[790] An agent is liable for probable damage arising from its agent transactions. Therefore, the Insurance and Private Pension Supervision and Regulation Agency

787. Article 4(1) of the Insurance Agents By-law.
788. Article 4(2).
789. Article 8 of the Insurance Agents By-law.
790. Article 9.

has the discretion to require professional indemnity insurance or similar collateral to provide security to insurance customers.[791] If a licensed agent decides to terminate any agent transactions, such termination must be notified to the Turkish Union of Chambers and Commodity Exchanges within five days of the date of such termination.[792] If an agent fails to pay premiums required by the judicial authority, its licence will be temporarily suspended by the Insurance and Private Pension Supervision and Regulation Agency until such payments are made.[793]

II. Foreign Insurance Agents

540. Any foreign natural person or legal entity wishing to operate as an agent in Turkey is subject to the same conditions as agents operating in Turkey.[794] Natural persons must be residing in Turkey, and legal entities must set up a branch in order to operate as an agent. Foreign agents operating in Turkey shall only act on behalf and account of the insurance companies which are operating in Turkey. That is to say; foreign agents cannot act on behalf and account of insurance companies located abroad.

III. Legal Relations Between the Agent and the Principal

541. Article 102(1) of the Turkish Commercial Code states that contrary to employees of a business organization, an agent works independently in accordance with the terms of an agreement mutually agreed to by the principal and the agent. An agent can act as an insurance intermediary in two different roles. The agent can either be involved in the preparation of insurance contracts relating to the business organization of the principal or be directly responsible for executing such agreements on behalf of the principal as a profession. Article 15 of the Agents By-law provides detailed information on what matters should be included in an agency contract executed by the insurance company and the agent, such as duration and termination conditions. The agent must protect the interest of the insurer. The insurer is responsible for the acts and omissions of the agent who causes damage to the policyholder or the insured negligently in performing duties at the time of the execution of or during the contract.[795] Negligent acts of the agent often arise at the time of the preparatory stage of the contract. The persons willing to take out insurance are falsely directed by the agents generally in answering the questions in the proposal form. Correct answers to such questions are important for the determination of the risk. The insurer becomes liable for such negligent acts of the agent in *culpa in contrahendo.*

791. Article 11.
792. Article 23.
793. Article 23(4).
794. Council of Ministers' Decision on the International Activities in the Insurance Sector. Decision No. 2007/12467 OG. No. 26602, Date: 3.8.2007.
795. Kender, *Sigorta Hukuku*, p. 123.

IV. Exclusivity

542. Under Turkish insurance law, exclusivity provides an important protection in favour of insurance agents. The main purpose of such exclusivity provision is to prevent the principal from appointing another agent for the same territorial area already assigned to the previous agent. Exclusivity also protects the principal by forbidding the agent to engage in activities with other business organizations that are competitors of the principal.[796] According to Article 104 of the Turkish Commercial Code, unless otherwise agreed in writing by the principal and the agent, the principal will not appoint another agent dealing with the same branch of business for the same duration and within the same territorial area or place. Similarly, once appointed by the principal as its exclusive agent within a specific area of business, the agent must not undertake any work on behalf of other business organizations in competition with the principal. However, the agent can work for other insurers in different insurance branches, and the principal may appoint new agents for different branches of insurance.

V. Authorization of the Agent

543. As an intermediary or actor on behalf of the principal, an agent has the authority to give and accept notices, announcements and disputes on behalf of the principal regarding agreements executed with third parties. The scope of this authorization is very crucial because in daily life most clients have little understanding of this relation between the insurance company principal and its agent.[797]

544. In relation to disputes that arise from insurance contracts executed by the agent and third parties, the agent has the authority to file a lawsuit against the contracting party on behalf of its principal. Conversely, the agent may also be subjected to a lawsuit initiated by third parties in relation to the same dispute. Under Article 105(2) of the Turkish Commercial Code, any provision stating that an agent shall not be subjected to such a lawsuit under an agreement between a Turkish agent and a foreign principal is null and void. There is further protection for agents when it comes to litigation. According to Article 105(3), any court decision made against a principal in Turkey cannot be enforced against the agent who acted on their behalf.[798] However, it is important to note that although an agent is not an employee of the principal, it does not act entirely independently either. In some cases, written and private authorization or proxy of the principal is required for the agent to make some specific transactions.[799] Furthermore, Article 107 of the Turkish Commercial

796. Yazıcıoğlu, p. 202; Kubilay, p. 242; Kender, *Sigorta Hukuku,* pp. 125–126.
797. Yazıcıoğlu, p. 130; Kender, *Sigorta Hukuku*, pp. 121–124; Kubilay, p. 239.
798. *See* Art. 105(3) of the Turkish Commercial Code.
799. For example according to Art. 106 of the Turkish Commercial Code, an agent needs written and private authorization or proxy of the principal in order to accept the payment of goods that it did not deliver in person and to accept the delivery of goods for which it did not pay. This is important when the principal operates in the goods sector and requires his agent to help with deliveries as well.

Code states that in order to execute contractual agreements on behalf of the principal, written and specific authorization by the principal is mandatory. The agent is also obliged to register and announce such authorization documents to the public. Such authorizations are important in insurance law because they determine the scope of the agent's authority and liability.

VI. Authorization Exceeding (*Ultra Vires*)

545. Where an agent acts without the required authorizations or exceeds its authorization defined by its agreement with the principal, there is *ultra vires* and the possible liability of the agent to third parties and the principal. In the event that the agent executes an agreement without such authorization or exceeds the authorization, the principal may nevertheless consent to such transaction, i.e., agree to be bound by it.[800] If not, then the agent is liable for the contractual obligations.[801]

VII. Rights and Liabilities in Agency Relationship

546. The agent must protect the interests of its principal in the appointed area of business and must report any changes to the appointed area of business to the principal immediately. The agent is also liable for keeping the goods or property for the principal's account and liable for any damage to the good during such keeping period unless the agent proves that it does not have *negligence* for such damage. The agent must also be contracted to the principal during the agency period in order to receive remuneration.[802] The agent is entitled to postpone a transaction in the absence of clear instructions from the principal until it receives such a response. The agent is obliged to transfer money collected for the principal via the means agreed by the parties at the agreed time under the contract. Otherwise, the agent must pay any interest accrued since that date and may also have to pay compensation when necessary.

547. The insurance agent is entitled to claim the amounts agreed by the parties for the agency period. The agent may also ask for higher amounts where it enhances the client portfolio by including new clients. Even after the agency period expires, the agent may be entitled to remuneration if it can be shown that the agent assisted in the negotiation of a new transaction during the agency period, which was subsequently executed after his or her agreement with the principal expired. The agent is entitled to remuneration payment when the transaction is finalized.[803] For any forthcoming transactions with third parties, if it is clear that such a transaction will not be executed for whatever reason, the agent loses its right to remuneration and all pre-paid remuneration need to be refunded by the agent. According to Article

800. Article 108 of the Turkish Commercial Code.
801. Yazıcıoğlu, p. 140.
802. *Ibid.*, p. 203.
803. *Ibid.*, pp. 207–209.

116(1), the agent must be paid within three months of the date of remuneration and in all circumstances upon termination of the agency agreement. The agent also has the right to ask for the extraordinary expenses it incurred in the fulfilment of its duties under the agency agreement.[804] The agent has the right of lien over moveable property belonging to the principal in the event that the principal does not pay receivables that are due. Such a right may be used for any kind of receivables of the agent from the insurance company, such as remuneration, or compensation.[805]

VIII. Termination of the Agency Agreement

548. An agency agreement executed for an indefinite period can be terminated by either party giving three months prior notice in writing. Agency agreements with fixed or definite duration periods can be terminated at any time or immediately for *just causes.*[806] An agency contract creates a permanent liability relation between the parties.[807]

However, if the parties continue to enforce an agency agreement beyond a definite period, such an agreement becomes indefinite as well. Bankruptcy, death or disability of the agent or the principal is another reason under the Turkish Commercial Code to terminate agency contracts. After termination, one of the most crucial rights of the agent is the right to be remunerated for lost commissions expected from the constituted client portfolio for a certain and equitable time period in the future as well.[808] Any party terminating the agency contract without complying with the *just cause* or termination notice requirements must compensate the other party. Termination must be communicated via a notary, return receipt request or by telegraph.[809]

549. Moreover, a competition restriction agreement can be agreed between the agent and its principal after termination. However, such a competition agreement must be made in writing, signed by both parties, and a copy must be given to the agent. Such agreements can be made for a maximum of two years as of the termination date with respect to the appointed area of the particular type of business during the agency period. These provisions are generally designed to protect agents, and therefore any agreements providing provisions in favour of agents are valid. Conversely, those provisions not in favour of agents and contrary to the Turkish Commercial Code will be unenforceable.

804. *Ibid.*, p. 215.
805. *Ibid.*, pp. 216–217.
806. *Ibid.*, p. 222; Özge Ayan, 'Acentenin Denkleştirme Talep Hakkı' (Agent's Right to Equalization Payment), Seçkin Publications (Ankara 2008), p. 48.
807. Ayan, p. 2.
808. Yazıcıoğlu, pp. 234–242.
809. Ayan, p. 51, Art. 20/3 of the Turkish Commercial Code.

Part VIII. Reinsurance

Meltem Deniz Güner-Özbek

§1. General

550. According to Article 1403, the insurer can reinsure the interests that he already covered. The Insurance Association of Turkey defines reinsurance as 'insuring an already insured risk partially or completely again'. Reinsurance basically means 'insuring again' as the words suggest.[810] Insurers are inclined to insure the risk again mainly when the particular risk can cause devastating effects beyond their ability to cover, leading to bankruptcy or insolvency. With the help of the reinsurance system, the insurer can have the opportunity to cover much higher risks with higher premiums payable in return.

551. Under the reinsurance system, the risk is allocated among various insurers. Depending on the type of the reinsurance contract, the reinsurer gets a percentage of the premiums collected or direct payments from the insurance company ceding to the reinsurer. In essence, reinsurance is insurance for insurance companies.[811] Reinsurance is a 'contractual arrangement under which an insurer secures coverage from a reinsurer for a potential loss to which it is exposed under insurance policies issued to original insured. The risk indemnified against is the risk that the insurer will have to pay on the underlying insured risk'.[812]

552. As explained at the beginning of this book, insurance companies and *reinsurance companies* operating in Turkey must be established as a joint stock company or a cooperative.[813] Accordingly, just as for insurance companies, reinsurance companies must not be engaged in any other businesses except for insurance transactions and businesses that are directly related to insurance operations. As of 2022, there are four active reinsurance companies in Turkey, Milli Reasürans, Türk

810. *See* The Insurance Association of Turkey official web site: http://www.tsb.org.tr/reasurans.aspx?pageID=440 (accessed at 16.3.2014); Can, 324; Kubilay, p. 168, *see also* Merkin, Robert, *A Guide to Reinsurance Law* 4 (Informa Publication 2007).

811. Kubilay, pp. 167–168.

812. David M. Raim & Joy L. Langford, *Understanding Reinsurance New Appleman Insurance Practice Guide* 40–45 (LexisNexis Group 2015).

813. *See* Art. 3 of the Insurance Activities Act.

Reasürans A.Ş., Türk Katılım Reasürans and VHV Reasürans A.Ş.[814] Milli Reasürans meets the demands of the Turkish market at the rate of 25%.[815] Türk Reasürans A.Ş. began its operations in 2019 in accordance with the amendment of the Insurance Activities Act in the same year. Its capital belongs to the Ministry of Treasury and Finance. The main purpose of founding such a company was to both increase the national reinsurance capacity and to provide insurance and reinsurance coverage for the risks which are difficult to insure or reinsure across the country.[816] Whereas, VHV Reasürans A.Ş. is a 100% German investment. Its share belongs to the VHV Allgemeine Versicherung AG Germany. Türk Katılım Reaürans started its operations in September 2021. Its main shareholder is the Türk Reasürans AŞ.

§2. METHODS OF REINSURANCE

553. Principally, there are two types of reinsurance arrangements: Facultative Reinsurance and Treaty Reinsurance. Furthermore, facultative and treaty reinsurances can both be defined as proportional or non-proportional. There is also further sub-classification for these proportional and non-proportional reinsurance arrangements.

I. Facultative Reinsurance

554. Facultative reinsurance is a reinsurance arrangement where both the insurer (cedent or ceding company) and the reinsurer have the option, i.e., *faculty* to cede and accept the risk.[817] Accordingly, the term facultative means optional. In this type of reinsurance arrangement, the ceding company has the option to offer an individual risk to the reinsurer. Likewise, the reinsurer has the option to accept or reject the risk. The ceding company submits a precisely defined offer to the reinsurer, including all information on the risk offered. The reinsurer examines the offer and decides whether to accept the risk or not. Facultative reinsurance is the oldest type of reinsurance arrangement.[818]

II. Facultative Obligatory Reinsurance

555. Under the facultative obligatory reinsurance a category or a sub-category of risks are covered.[819] When the insurer has a claim falling under the treaty, he decides to cede or not to cede it to the reinsurer. In this sense, such a treaty is optional for the insurer. On the contrary, the reinsurer is obliged to accept the sessions decided by the ceding company.

814. At https://www.seddk.gov.tr/tr/kuruluslar/sigorta-reasurans-ve-bes-sirketleri.
815. At http://www.millire.com/KurumsalProfil.html.
816. Insurance Activities Act Annex Art. 4.
817. Merkin, p. 10; Carter p. 229.
818. Griselda Deelstra & Guillaume Plantin, *Risk Theory and Reinsurance* 48 (Springer 2015).
819. Deelstra & Plantin, p. 48.

III. Treaty Reinsurance

556. Treaty reinsurance is the most common type of reinsurance arrangement and usually creates a long-lasting relationship between the cedent and the reinsurer.[820] Under Treaty reinsurance arrangements, the reinsurer accepts a specific group of risks from the ceding company. Contrary to facultative reinsurance, the characteristic feature of treaty reinsurance is the *obligatory nature* of such an arrangement. The ceding company cedes, and the reinsurer is required to accept all the risks within the terms of the reinsurance contracts. All the risks insured in a specific portfolio that is specified in the treaty are covered by this type of arrangement. Treaty reinsurance provides a good opportunity to develop commercial relations because the ceding company avoids the risk and significant task of seeking reinsurance for every accepted risk. However, a new process of acceptance is not necessary for each business as it has already been covered under the treaty provisions. Each risk is covered without requiring the express declaration of the reinsurer.

IV. Proportional or Non-proportional Reinsurance

557. Facultative or treaty reinsurance can be either proportional or non-proportional.[821] Under proportional reinsurance, the reinsurer shares the same proportion of the premium and the losses of the ceding company. By placing its risk on the reinsurer, the ceding company proportionally *follows the same fortunes* as the reinsurer in accordance with the terms and conditions of the reinsurance contracts. Under non-proportional reinsurance, however, the reinsurer indemnifies a ceding company against the amount of loss that exceeds the ceding company's retention. In other words, the reinsurer becomes liable to indemnify the ceding company when the claim exceeds the retention.

§3. Common Forms of Treaty Reinsurance

I. Proportional Treaty Reinsurance

558. Under proportional treaties, the reinsurer participates in a predetermined proportion of the risk ceded to it and the cost of the premium.[822] In the case of property damage insurance, participation of the reinsurance company is based on the insured sum stated in the policy whereas in other types of insurance such as life, personal accident or liability, participation of the reinsurance company is based on the limit of indemnity stated in the policy. The share of the reinsurance company is the same as the liability accepted by the insurer under the original policy. In other

820. Dan Gerber & Jeff Kingsley, *Introduction and General Principles of Insurance Law* s. 71.03[1][a] (LexisNexis 2014).
821. Christoph Bugmann, *Proportional and Non-proportional Reinsurances*, Swiss Reinsurance Company, 1997, p. 7; Merkin, 14; *see also* Lyde & Gilbert Barlow, *Reinsurance, Practice and The Law* part 4.25–4.38 (Informa 2010).
822. Carter, p. 245.

words, the insurance company cedes the risk at the original conditions agreed between him and the policyholders. The liability of the reinsurer begins simultaneously with that of the ceding company. Proportional treaty reinsurance provides the ceding company with automatic reinsurance coverage on every risk within the framework of the reinsurance contract. As a result, the ceding company's capacity for accepting greater limits increases. Common types of proportional treaties include quota share and surplus.

A. *Quota Share Treaty Reinsurance*

559. Under the quota share treaty, the reinsurer indemnifies the ceding company for a fixed percentage of loss for each risk covered by the treaty.[823] For instance, when the reinsurer and the ceding company agree on a quota share treaty that establishes a 60% quota share for the ceding company, 40% of the losses and premiums are retained by the ceding company, and 60% of the losses and premiums are ceded to the reinsurer. In the event that the reinsured risk occurs, liability for any damage is based on the same quota proportion.[824] Quota share treaties are relatively simple in terms of administrative matters.

B. *Surplus Treaty Reinsurance*

560. Under surplus treaty reinsurance, the insurer retains some share of the insured sum and cedes to the reinsurer the share of the sum exceeding its own retention.[825] This retention is referred to as the *line*. Any risk that falls within this line or retention is the responsibility of the ceding company. When the ceding company insures a risk that is larger than its retention, the amount exceeding its retention is ceded to the reinsurer.[826] The degree of participation by the ceding company and the reinsurer in the premiums and claims is equivalent to the percentage retained and accepted by the parties respectively. For instance, if the surplus treaty reinsurance is an eleven-line treaty, the reinsurance company is transferred an insurance capacity that is eleven times the amount retained by the ceding company.[827]

561. One of the advantages of the surplus treaty is that the ceding company has discretionary power over which risks it will not require the involvement of the reinsurer. The ceding company applies high retention for risks with low exposure and low retention for risks with high exposure. Consequently, the ceding company obtains a uniform portfolio for its own liability, which is homogenous in quantity

823. Merkin, Guide to Reinsurance Law, p. 15.
824. Merkin, p. 15; Barlow, part 4.29.
825. Merkin, p. 36.
826. Bugmann, pp. 8–9; Merkin, pp. 36–38.
827. Bugmann, pp. 10–11; Merkin, p. 38; Barlow, paras 4.39–4.53.

and quality.[828] However, the main disadvantage of such a treaty is the high administrative costs involved with the insured applying the appropriate line of retention, deciding on the percentage of the cession to the reinsurer and calculating the distribution of claims that have arisen.

II. Non-proportional Treaty Reinsurances

562. Under non-proportional treaties, premiums and related risks are not shared between the ceding insurance company and the reinsurance company.[829] Thus, the operative word here is *retention.* The parties agree on a limit of loss or retention, and the ceding company retains losses that are less than this predetermined limit. The reinsurer then becomes liable for damage exceeding the predetermined limit of loss or detention.[830] Unlike proportional reinsurance, which is based on the original liability and proportional cession, non-proportional reinsurance limits the amount of loss and cover without setting any proportionality. Furthermore, non-proportional reinsurance cover is separate from the original portfolio and therefore separate from the terms of the original policies and premiums.[831] In such treaties, premiums have no proportional relationship with the premiums collected by the ceding company from its insured clients, and premiums are therefore subject to analysis and negotiation. As such, the prior loss experience of the ceding company, its loss potential, geographic area for business and desired retention levels have a significant influence on the determination of premium.

563. For example, assume that an insurer needs a capacity of USD 500,000 to write a casualty business. It determines that it can retain the first USD 150,000 of any risk. The insurer needs reinsurance for the part of any loss that exceeds the retained limit of USD 150,000. On this basis, the insurer pays the first USD 150,000 of *all losses*, and the reinsurer pays *any excess amount up to a maximum of USD 50,000.*

A. *Per-Risk Excess of Loss*

564. In Per-Risk Excess of Loss treaties, the reinsurer indemnifies the ceding company for any loss in excess of the specified retention on each risk.[832]

828. *An Introduction to Reinsurance*, Institute of Insurance Sciences 61–62 (Mapfre Foundation 2013) (http://www.mapfre.com/documentacion/publico/i18n/catalogo_imagenes/grupo.cmd?path=1074274).
829. Merkin, pp. 41–42; Carter, p. 287.
830. Merkin, pp. 63–64.
831. Bugmann, p. 20; for other types *see* Merkin, pp. 41–42.
832. *Reinsurance, A Basic Guide to Facultative and Treaty Reinsurance* 22 (Münich Re), https://www.munichre.com/us/property-casualty/publications-expertise/knowledge-publications/reinsurance-basic-guide/index.html.

B. Catastrophe Excess of Loss

565. Catastrophe Excess of Loss treaty protects the insurance company against adverse losses resulting from the accumulation of losses arising from a single major disaster such as an earthquake or hurricane. Claims arising from the same disaster or event are added, and retention is applied to the total claims.[833]

C. Stop Loss

566. This reinsurance treaty is designed to cover amounts paid for damage by the ceding insurer during the treaty term, which is usually one year. The reinsurer does not cover excess damage arising from one particular risk but compensates damage that exceeds a previously agreed ratio of *whole risks* in favour of the ceding insurance company.[834] After exceeding such an agreed limit, the reinsurer compensates for the exceeding damage within its liability amount, which is also based on a certain percentage of total damage. For instance, by making a stop-loss reinsurance treaty, the parties may agree that if the total damage exceeds 90% of the risk portfolio, the reinsurer will be liable for cover from this percentage up to 120%. In other words, any damage in excess of 90% of the total coverage of the insurer will be compensated by the reinsurer up to 120%. Stop-loss reinsurance can be a beneficial solution where the insurer is looking for protection against a real threat to its operational existence as a result of an accumulation of negative influences in the same year.[835]

III. Common Forms of Facultative Reinsurance

567. Facultative reinsurance usually uses proportional or non-proportional methods.

A. Proportional Facultative Reinsurance

568. With respect to proportional facultative reinsurance, the ceding company and reinsurer agree to share a percentage of both the original premiums and any claims.[836] For instance, if the ceding company retains 25% and allocates 75% to the reinsurer, participation of the reinsurer is also expressed as 75%. The premium then due to the reinsurer is 75% of the original premium that the ceding company has received minus the ceding commission payable to the ceding company.

833. *An Introduction to Reinsurance*, p. 49.
834. Merkin, p. 63; *An Introduction to Reinsurance*, p. 49.
835. Bugmann, p. 26.
836. *An Introduction to Reinsurance*, p. 57; Gerber & Kingsley, s. 71.03[2][a]; *Reinsurance, A Basic Guide to Facultative and Treaty Reinsurance* 8.

B. Non-proportional Facultative Reinsurance

569. In the case of non-proportional or excess of claims facultative reinsurance, the reinsurer pays the share of accepted risks that exceed the ceding company's retention or the capacity provided by the establishment of the stipulated *line*.[837] This type of reinsurance requires analysis of the potential severity of losses. The ceding company determines a level of loss that is compatible with net and treaty guidelines. This is used as the measure of retention, and the reinsurer provides coverage in excess of this retention.

837. *Reinsurance, A Basic Guide to Facultative and Treaty Reinsurance*, p. 10; *An Introduction to Reinsurance*, pp. 10 and 32.

Part IX. Taxation of Insurance

Meltem Deniz Güner-Özbek

570. As in many countries, the taxation system in Turkey is highly complex and can be classified under three main headings: (i) income tax, such as Individual Income Tax and Corporate Income Tax; (ii) taxes on expenditure such as Value Added Tax (VAT) or Banking and Insurance Transaction Tax or Stamp Tax; and (iii) taxes on wealth, such as Property Tax or Inheritance and Gift Tax.

§1. Income Tax

571. Article 63(3) of the Income Tax Act[838] regulates taxation of income-earning workers, and Article 89(1) applies to taxpayers who submit annual tax returns. Both of these provisions state that any premiums payable under an insurance contract executed with an insurance company based in Turkey for personal insurance policies for the benefit of any person, his or her spouse or children under the age of 18, such as life, death, accident, illness, disability, maternity, birth and retirement may be deducted from the person's income tax base. However, there are some conditions attached to these entitlements, including the requirement that all premiums must be documented with an invoice or receipt. Furthermore, the total deductible amount cannot exceed 15% of any month's income or exceed the total gross minimum wage of any year.[839] In calculating the deductible, the total amount of premiums, dues and contributions (payments to more than one insurance company and/or the premiums of unemployed, dependent family members that the taxpayer has provided for) are taken into consideration.

572. As explained earlier in relation to Individual Retirement Insurance, policyholders are required to make a 25% State contribution in addition to contributions made to the Individual Retirement Insurance since January 2013. Formerly, there was a tax benefit of 10% similar to entitlements for life, accident and health insurance discussed above. However, statistics have shown that only 35% of the participants have received the tax benefit with the remaining 65% receiving no entitlements. This disparity shows that the potential for participants to benefit under the

838. Act No. 193 OG. No. 10700, Date: 6.1.1961.
839. In 2015 minimum wage is TRY 1603.12 *see,* https://www.csgb.gov.tr/home/Contents/Istatistikler/AsgariUcret.

system was relatively weak. By considering these matters, the tax benefit system was revised to the current 25% State contribution, which has increased the number of participants by 50% since it was introduced on 1 January 2013.[840]

§2. Capital Gains Tax

573. Capital gains on movable assets are defined as dividends, interest, rent and similar assets on movables.[841] In addition, included within the meaning of capital gains are the various payments made to pension funds, relief funds and retirement and insurance companies that have legal personality.[842] However, any income derived from pension funds and the like is excluded from the taxation of capital gains.[843]

§3. Inheritance Tax

574. Payment of inheritance tax depends on the type of life insurance. For example, compensation for death under non-cumulative life insurance is subject to inheritance tax.[844] However, compensation payable in the event of the death of the insured under personal accident insurance is not subject to inheritance tax. There are also exceptions for the type of beneficiary, such as where the insured sum is payable to a third party rather than the heir or heirs of the deceased, then such personal accident insured is subject to inheritance tax. In relation to cumulative insurance, the amount of accumulation payable to legitimate heirs is subject to inheritance tax. If the beneficiary is a third party who is not the heir, then inheritance tax is also payable. If there is a mixed insurance policy, the cumulative and non-cumulative payments are distinguished and made in accordance with the rules explained above.

§4. Insurance Premium Tax

I. Banking and Insurance Transaction Tax

575. Article 33 of the Expense Taxes Act[845] provides that the Banking and Insurance Transaction Tax levies 5% of all insurance transactions. Banking and

---

840. At http://web2.egm.org.tr/webegm2/chart/besgosterge/wg_sirketview_tablolu.asp?raportar1=19.03.2010&raportar2=13.03.2015&sirketlist=100&raportip=10&yayin=W.
841. Article 75 of the Income Tax Act. All articles of this Act except the one regarding Banking and Insurance Transactions Tax were repealed by Art. 61/a of the Act No. 3065 Date: 25.10.1984.
842. Paragraphs 15 and 16 of Art. 75 of the Income Tax Act.
843. Article 86 of the Tax Income Act.
844. Circular on the state of the payments done to the legitimate heirs and beneficiaries in case of the death of the insured in cumulative, noncumulative, and mix insurance contracts over against inheritance tax. ('Birikimli, birikimsiz ve karma sigorta poliçelerinde sigortalının vefatı üzerine kanuni mirasçılara ve lehdarlara yapılacak ödemeler ile sigorta tazminatlarının veraset ve intikal vergisi karşısındaki durumu'). Date: 31.8.2007 Inheritance and Estate Tax ('Veraset ve İntikal Vergisi Kanunu') 3/2007-1. Inheritance and Estate Tax Act No. 7338 OG. No. 10231, Date: 15.6.1959.
845. Act No. 6802 OG. No. 9362, Date: 23.7.1956.

Transaction Tax is an intermediate obligation, which is charged to the person taking out insurance. In this sense, the insurance company is the taxpayer.[846] It is important to note the following exceptions to this tax:[847]

- monies received pursuant to the contract and policy for a private pension, life insurance (including life insurance contracts under which personal accident, disability due to disease and critical diseases coverage is provided as additional coverage), health insurance and marine insurance for exported goods;
- premiums, commissions and other charges received on account of double insurance transactions and retrocession transactions;
- monies received on account of agricultural insurance taken out for any crop which has not yet been harvested or collected and for agricultural livestock;
- monies received on account of insurance taken out against nuclear risks;
- monies received on account of any transactions executed by mortgage financing institutions, home financing institutions and home financing funds regarding home financing as defined in the first paragraph of Article 38(A) of the Capital Markets Law No. 2499.

576. In the event of cancellation of the insurance contract, insurance companies are allowed to deduct the portion of tax pertaining to the period after the date of cancellation and until the agreed expiry of the contract. Accordingly, the cancelled Banking and Insurance Transaction Taxes are deductible in the next periods. Likewise, any tax not deducted in the next period can be deducted in the tax returns for subsequent periods.

II. Fire Insurance Tax

577. Article 40(5) of the Revenues of Municipalities Act[848] states that premiums received for fire insurance taken out for movable and immovable properties within municipal boundaries and adjacent areas are subject to Fire Insurance Tax. The taxpayer in this instance is also the insurance company,[849] which must pay 10% of the total premiums received on account of the fire insurance transactions as Fire Insurance Tax.[850]

III. Security (Assurance) Account

578. The Insurance Activities Act requires the establishment of a *Security Account* in respect of the compulsory liability insurance imposed by Article 13 of

846. Expense Taxes Act General Declaration Serial Number: 86 OG. No. 26948, Date: 26.7.2008.
847. Article 29 paras i, j, k, l and u of the Expenses Act.
848. 'Belediye Gelirleri Kanunu' Act No. 2464 OG. No. 17354, Date: 29.5.1981.
849. Article 41 of the Act on the Revenues of the Municipalities.
850. Articles 42 and 43 of the same Act.

these individual codes: the Road Traffic Law No. 2918 and dated 13 October 1983; the Road Transportation Law No. 4925 and dated 21 December 1959 and compulsory insurance imposed by the Insurance Supervision Law No. 7397 and dated 21 December 1959 which has been abolished by the Insurance Activities Act. Furthermore, an Assurance Account is established under the auspices of the Association of the Insurance, Reinsurance and Pension Companies of Turkey to cover losses under certain conditions up to the relevant insured sum. Application to the Security Account is possible under the following cases:[851]

- personal injuries to a person where the insured cannot be identified;
- personal injuries caused by parties who do not have compulsory insurance coverage at the date the risk occurs;
- indemnities for personal injuries represent the difference between the coverage limits of compulsory insurance and the coverage limits set forth in the insurance policy;
- personal injuries and damage to property for which the insurer is obliged to pay due to the withdrawal of his or her licences in all branches permanently or due to bankruptcy;
- personal injuries for which the operator of the vehicle is not held responsible in accordance with the Road Traffic Law No. 2918 in an accident where the vehicle involved is stolen or seized by violence;
- the payments made by the Turkish Motor Insurers' Bureau in relation to Green Card Insurance applications.

579. The Security Account is funded by a variety of financial contributions, including from all insurance companies operating in Turkey, which are required to pay 1% of the total net premiums collected for compulsory insurances each year. Other contributions are made by persons purchasing compulsory insurance, who must pay 2% of the net premium in addition to the payments made to the insurance company.

IV. VAT and Stamp Duty

580. It is worth noting that all kinds of insurance transactions are exempted from VAT and Stamp Duty.

§5. Tax Obligation of Insurance Companies

581. According to Corporation Tax Law,[852] capital companies, cooperatives, economic public enterprises, economic enterprises belonging to societies or foundations and business partnerships are defined as taxpayers. As explained earlier in

851. Article 14/2 of the Insurance Activities Act.
852. Act No. 5520 OG. No. 26205, Date: 21.6.2006.

this book, insurance companies are founded either as a joint stock company or as a cooperative, thus incomes earned by the insurance companies over an accounting period are subject to corporation tax.

Selected Bibliography

Acar, Serdar. Sorumluluk Sigortacısının Doğrudan Davada Dayanabileceği Savunmalar, 2012 Marmara Üniversitesi Hukuk Araştırmaları Dergisi C.18 S.2., 734–748.

Amasya, Serap. *Abonman Sigortaları*, Yeni Türk Ticaret Kanununda Deniz Sigortaları, Deniz Hukuku Derneği & Sigorta Hukuku Derneği, 2012, 132–176.

Ansay, Tuğrul. 'Law of Obligations'. In *Introduction to Turkish Law*, edited by Tuğrul Ansay & Don Wallace Jr. The Hague: Kluwer Law International, 2005.

Antalya, Gökhan. Borçlar Hukuku Genel Hükümler, Beta Yayınevi, İstanbul, 2012.

Aral, İrem. Hayat Dışı Sigorta Şirketlerinin Denetimi, XII Levha Yayınları, Şubat, 2010.

Atmeh, Sharo Michael. 'Regulation Not Prohibition: The Comparative Case Against the Insurable Interest Doctrine'. North-western Journal of International Law & Business 32, no. 1 (2011): 92–140.

Atamer, Kerim, et al. Free Translation of the Provisions of the Turkish Commercial Code Regarding Insurance Contracts, Sigorta Hukuku Türk Derneği (AIDA Turkey), İstanbul, 2012.

Atamer, Kerim. *Yeni Türk Ticaret Kanunu Uyarınca Zarar Sigortaları'na Giriş Batider* Cilt:27, Sayı:1, 2011.

Atamer, Yeşim M. *Yeni Türk Borçlar Kanunu Hükümleri Uyarınca Genel İşlem Koşulları- nın Denetlenmesi – TKHK m. 6 ve TTK m. 55, f. 1, (F) İle Karşılaştırmalı Olarak, Türk Hukukunda Genel İşlem Şartları Sempozyumu,* Ankara, 8 Nisan, 2011.

'*Avukatlar İçin Tüketici Hukuku*', Ankara Bar Association Consumer Rights Committee, Anıl Matbaası, Ankara, 2012.

Ayan, Özge. Acentenin Denkleştirme Talep Hakkı, Seçkin, Ankara, 2008.

Bahtiyar, Mehmet. Ortaklıklar Hukuku, Beta Yayınevi, 7. Baskı, 2012.

Barlow Lyde & Gilbert. *Reinsurance, Practice and the Law*. Informa, London, 2010.

Bilgili, Fatih & Demirkapı, Ertan. Şirketler Hukuku Dersleri, 9. Baskı, Dora Yayınevi, Şubat 2013 (Bilgili/Demirkapı, Dersler).

Boylu Aydıner, Ayfer, Günay, Gülay & Terzioğlu, Günsel. *Ailelerin Bankalarca Sağlanan Tüketici Kredilerini Kullanma Durumlarının İncelenmesi*, Hacettepe Üniversitesi Sosyolojik Araştırmalar e-dergi. 15 Ağustos 2007, ISSN 1304-2823. http://www.sdergi.hacettepe.edu.tr/makaleler/aabgggt.pdf.

Bozer, Ali. Sigorta Hukuku, Banka ve Ticaret Hukuku Araştırma Enstitüsü, Ankara, 2009.

Selected Bibliography

Bozer, Ali. *Zorunlu Deprem Sigortası Batider*, Cilt:21, Sayı:1, 2001.

Budak, Ali Cem. *Yeni Hukuk Muhakemeleri Kanunu'nun Tahkim Hükümleri, Uluslararası Ticaret ve Tahkim Hukuku Dergisi*, V.1. No. 1 31–60, 2012.

Budak Ali Cem. *Sigortacılık Kanununda Tahkim: Sigortacılık Kanunu'nun 20. Maddesi, HMK'nun Yürürlüğe Girmesi ve 6327 Sayılı Kanun ile Değişikliğinden sonra Nasıl Yorumlanmalıdır?(Sigortacılık Kanununda Tahkim)*, C.2 S.2 Uluslararası Tahkim ve Ticaret Hukuku Dergisi, 53–69, 2013.

Bugmann, Christoph. *Proportional and Non-proportional Reinsurances*. Swiss Reinsurance Company, 1997.

Can, Mertol. Birden Çok Sigorta, İmaj Yayınevi, Ankara, 2004.

Can, Mertol. Mesleki Sorumluluk Sigortası Genel Şartlarına Genel Bir Bakış (Mesleki Sorumluluk), Banka ve Ticaret Hukuku Araştırma Enstitüsü, Yayın No. 431.

Can, Mertol. Türk Özel Sigorta Hukuku, İmaj Yayınevi, 3. Baskı, Ankara, 2009 (Sigorta Hukuku).

Çapa, Sadık. *Geçmişe Etkili Sigorta*, Gazi Üniversitesi Hukuk Fakültesi Dergisi, C.XVIII S.3-4, 405–426, 2014.

Çeker, Mustafa. Sigorta Hukuku, 9. Baskı, Karahan Kitabevi, Adana, 2014.

Çetin, Bahattin. Tarım Sigortaları, Nobel Yayın Dağıtım, Ankara, 2007.

Demir, Şamil. Hukuki Koruma Sigortası, Adalet Yayınevi, Ankara, 2013.

Doğrusöz Koşut, Hanife. *6102 Sayılı Ticaret Kanunu'na göre hayat sigortalarında sigorta ettirenin sözleşmenin yapılması anındaki beyan yükümlülüğünü ihlal etmesinin müeyyidesi*, Batider Cilt:29, Sayı:3 (Doç.Dr. Nurkut İnan'a Armağan Sayısı), 2013.

'Dünyada ve Türkiye'de Zorunlu Sigortalar, Türkiye Uygulamaları, Sorunlar ve Çözüm Önerileri', İktisadi Araştırmalar Vakfı, Ankara, 2012.

Güvel Enver Alper & Güvel Öndaş Afitap. Sigortacılık, Seçkin Yayınevi, 6. Baskı, Ankara 2012.

Hatemi & Gökyayla. Borçlar Hukuku Genel Bölüm, Vedat Kitapçılık, İstanbul, 2011.

İbicioğlu, Mustafa & Karan, Mehmet Baha. 'Türkiye'de Faiz Oranlarının Tüketici Kredileri Üzerindeki Etkisi'. Banking Regulation and Supervision Agency (BDDK) Banking and Financial Markets Volume: 3 No. 2, 2009.

Karayalçın, Yaşar. Sorumluluk Sigortaları, Olgaç, Ankara, 1984.

Kaya, Ferudun. Sigortacılık, Beta Yayınevi, 3. Baskı, İstanbul, 2013.

Kayıhan, Şaban. Sigorta Sözleşmesinde Prim Ödeme Borcu, Seçkin Yayınevi, Ankara, 2004.

Kender, Rayegan. Türkiye'de Hususi Sigorta Hukuku (Sigorta Hukuku) 13. Baskı, XII Levha Yayınları, İstanbul, 2014.

Kender, Rayegan. *Mesuliyet Sigortasının Mahiyeti ve Türleri* (Mesuliyet Sigortası), Zorunlu Sigortalar Paneli, Sigorta Hukuku Türk Derneği, 19.11.1993 (Paper presented during the panel organized by the Association of Turkish Insurance Law).

Kender, Rayegan. *Sigorta Hukukunda Tüketicinin Korunması (Tüketicinin Korunması)*, Erhan Adal'a Armağan Yeditepe Üniversitesi Hukuk Fakültesi Dergisi, C.8 S.2., 1–27, 2011.

Korkmaz, Sibel. Sigorta Sözleşmelerinde İspat Sorunları, Güncel Yayınevi, İzmir, 2004.

Kubilay, Huriye. Yeni Değer Sigortası, Dokuz Eylül Üniversitesi Hukuk Fakültesi Döner Sermaye İşletmesi Yayınları No. 51, Ankara, 1994.

Kubilay, Huriye. Özel Sigorta Hukuku, İzmir, 1999.

Kubilay, Huriye. *Sigorta acenteleri zorunlu mesleki sorumluluk sigortası hakkında bir değerlendirme Batider* Cilt:25, Sayı:4 (Reha Poroy anısına armağan), 2009.

Kubilay, Huriye. Uygulamalı Özel Sigorta Hukuku, Barış Yayınları, İzmir, 2003.

Kılıçoğlu, M. Ahmet. Borçlar Hukuku Genel Hükümler, Turhan Kitabevi, 16. Baskı, Ankara, 2012.

Memiş, Tekin. Yangın Sigortasında Riziko, Seçkin Yayınları, Ankara, 2001.

Meriç, Özge. Sigorta Şirketlerinin Kuruluşu ve Faaliyete Geçmesine İlişkin Esaslar, Adalet Yayınevi, 2013.

Merkin, Robert. A Guide to Reinsurance Law, Informa, London, 2007.

Oğuzman, Kemal. Öz Turgut, Borçlar Hukuku Genel Hükümler, Vedat Kitapçılık, İstanbul, 2014.

Omağ, Merih Kemal. *Türk Hukukunda Mecburi Sigortalara ve Sorunlarına Genel Bakış,* Zorunlu Sigortalar Paneli, Sigorta Hukuku Türk Derneği, 19.11.1993 (Paper presented during the panel organized by the Association of Turkish Insurance Law).

Özdamar, Mehmet. *Sigorta Brokeri ve Hukuki Niteliği (Broker)*, AÜHFD Law Faculty Journal, 525–559, 2008.

Özdamar, Mehmet. *Alman Hukukunda Sigorta Ombudsmanlığı (Ombudsmanlık), Batider,* Cilt:24 Sayı:3, BATİDER, 309 ff, 2008.

Özdamar, Mehmet. Sigortacının Sözleşme Öncesi Aydınlatma Yükümlülüğü (Aydınlatma Yükümlülüğü), Yetkin Yayınları, Ankara, 2009.

Özdamar, Mehmet, *Sigorta Hukukunda Uyuşmazlıkların Çözümünde Tahkim Sistemi (Tahkim Sistemi)*, Gazi Üniversitesi Hukuk Fakültesi Dergisi, C.17 S.1-2, 831–855, 2013.

Poroy, Reha, Tekinalp, Ünal & Çamoğlu, Ersin. Ortaklıklar ve Kooperatifler Hukuku, Vedat Kitapçılık, 11. Baskı, 2009.

Pulaşlı, Hasan. Şirketler Hukuku Genel Esaslar, Adalet Yayınevi, 2. Baskı, Ankara, 2013.

Raim, David M. & Langford, Joy L. *Understanding Reinsurance, New Appleman Insurance Practice Guide*, LexisNexis Group, http://www.chadbourne.com/files/Publication/b3b45e9d-566d-4433-8198-68078ae54acf/Presentation/PublicationAttachment/441ebf2d-7946-4a56-958a-5d6ab2da6c9d/013-60099_60099-ch0040.pdf (last visited 14 March 2015).

Reisoğlu. Türk Borçlar Hukuku Genel Hükümler, Beta Yayınevi, 23. Baskı, İstanbul, 2012.

Sergici, Erdoğan. 'Mesuliyet Sigortası Türleri', Teori ve Uygulama Açısından Mesuliyet Sigortaları, III. Sigorta Semineri İstanbul 4–7 Nisan 1977, Sigorta Hukuku Türk Derneği.

Somer, Mehmet. 'Türk Hukukunda Başkası Hesabına Sigorta', İstanbul 2000, Yayınlanmamış Doçentlik Tezi.

Sirmen, Sedat. *Türk Kanunlar İhtilafı Hukukunda Zarar Sigortaları Kapsamına Giren Milletlerarası Unsurlu Sigorta Akitlerine Uygulanacak Hukuk,* 2010 *Batider* Cilt:26, Sayı:3.

Şeker, Zehra. Deniz Yoluyla Yük Taşımasında Sigorta Himayesinin Kapsamı, Beta,

İstanbul 2001.
Şenocak, Kemal. *Hayatı Sigorta Edilecek Kişi (Riziko Şahsı)* (TTK m. 1490), 2012 *Batider* Cilt:28, Sayı:4.
Şenocak, Kemal. *Geçici Sigorta Himayesi (Geçici Güvence),* 2003 Batider, Cilt:22, Sayı:1.
Şenocak, Kemal. *Takseli Sigorta*, 2009 Batider Cilt:25, Sayı:2.
Şenocak, Kemal. Mesleki Sorumluluk Sigortaları (Mesleki Sorumluluk), Turhan Kitabevi Ankara, 2000.
Şenocak, Kemal. Üçüncü Şahıs Lehine Hayat Sigortası Sözleşmesi (Hayat Sigortası Sözleşmesi), Turhan Kitabevi, Ankara, 2009.
Şenocak, Kemal. Hukuki Himaye Sigortası (Hukuki Himaye), Dayılarlı Yayınları, Ankara, 1993.
Topaloğlu, Mustafa. Konut finansman sisteminde Mortgage sigortası *Batider*, Cilt:24 Sayı:1, 2007.
Ulaş, Işıl. *Sigortacılıkta Güvence Hesabı (Güvence Hesabı),* 2009 Batider, Cilt:25, Sayı:2.
Ulaş, Işıl. *Sigortacılıkta Tahkim*, 2007 BATİDER, Cilt:24, Sayı:2 (Seza Reisoğlu'na Armağan Sayısı).
Ulaş, Işıl. *Rehin ve Sigorta İlişkisi (Rehin)*, (2008) *BATİDER* Cilt:24, Sayı:4.
Ulaş, Işıl. Can Sigortası Hukuku: Hayat ve Kişisel Kaza Sigortaları (Can Sigortaları), Turhan Kitabevi, Ankara, 2002.
Ulaş, Işıl. Uygulamalı Zarar Sigortaları Hukuku (Zarar Sigortaları), Turhan Kitabevi, 8. Bası, Ankara, 2012.
Uluğ, İlknur. *Sigorta Hukukunda Riziko Kavramı ve Bu Kavramdaki Değişiklikler,* Türkiye'de Sigorta Hukukunun Sorunları ve Geleceği Sempozyum, Türkiye Barolar Birliği, 19–20 Kasım 2004.
Ünan, Samim. Kredi (Ticari Alacak) Sigortası Genel Şartları Şerhi (Ticari Alacak Sigortası), AIDA Turkey, Özdil Basımevi 2013.
Ünan, Samim. İsteğe Bağlı Genel Sorumluluk Sigortasında Riziko (Riziko), Beta Yayınevi, İstanbul, 1998.
Ünan, Samim A. & Karayazgan, Ahmet. Bireysel Emeklilik Hukuku, Sakala Yayıncılık, İstanbul, 2009.
Ünan, Samim. Türk Ticaret Kanunu Taslağının Sigorta Hukuku Başlıklı Altıncı Kitabı Hakkına Düşünceler (Türk Ticaret Kanunu Taslağı), (2005) Sigorta Hukuku Dergisi, Özal Sayı:1, 109–196.
Ünan, Samim. Hayat Sigortası Sözleşmesi, Beta, İstanbul, 1998.
Ünan, Samim. Zorunlu Hekim Sorumluluğu Sigortası, Sigorta Hukuku Türk Derneği, İstanbul, 2012.
Ünan, Samim. Some Aspects of the New Turkish Legislative Work (Legislative Work), in Kompatibilitaet des türkische und europaeischen Wirtschaftsrechts / Der neue türkische HGB-Entwurf und benachbarte Rechtsgebiete, eds. Atamer, Yeşim M. & Hopt J. Klaus, Mohr Siebeck 2009.
Yazıcıoğlu, Emine. Sigorta Aracıları Hukuku I, XII Levha, Istanbul, 2010.
Yazıcıoğlu, Emine. Tekne Sigortası Sözleşmesi, Beta İstanbul, 2003.
Yongalık, Aynur. 'Hukuki Açıdan Kredi Hayat Sigortası' Banka ve Ticaret Hukuku Araştırma Enstitüsü, Ankara, 2002.
Yongalık, Aynur. *Zorunlu Deprem Sigortası Batider*, Cilt:21, Sayı:2.

Index

The numbers here refer to the paragraph numbers.

Index

Index

www.ingramcontent.com/pod-product-compliance
Lightning Source LLC
Chambersburg PA
CBHW071438230926
51846CB00001B/273